Divorce

in

New Hampshire

*The Legal Process,
Your Rights, and What to Expect*

Jessica L. Ecker, Esq.
Dana E. Prescott, J.D., M.S.W., Ph.D.

Addicus Books
Omaha, Nebraska

An Addicus Nonfiction Book

ISBN 978-1-950091-43-0

Typography Jack Kusler

This book is not intended to serve as a substitute for an attorney. Nor is it the authors' intent to give legal advice contrary to that of an attorney.

Library of Congress Cataloging-in-Publication Data

Names: Ecker, Jessica L., 1980—author. | Prescott, Dana E., 1958—author.

Title: Divorce in New Hampshire : the legal process, your rights, and what to expect / Jessica L. Ecker, Esq.; Dana E. Prescott, , J.D., M.S.W., Ph.D.

Description: Omaha, Nebraska : Addicus Books, Inc., 2021. | Includes index.

Identifiers: LCCN 2021028781 | ISBN 9781950091430 (trade paperback)

Subjects: LCSH: Divorce—Law and legislation—New Hampshire. | Divorce suits—New Hampshire. | Divorce—Psychological aspects. | Domestic relations courts—New Hampshire—Rules and practice.

Addicus Books, Inc.
P.O. Box 45327
Omaha, Nebraska 68145
www.AddicusBooks.com
Printed in the United States of America
10 9 8 7 6 5 4 3 2 1

*To professionals
and clients who share the belief that knowledge
about the law and the courts helps families maintain
their dignity and personal autonomy*

Contents

Acknowledgments

I would like to thank my law partner Kimberly Weibrecht, who supported me while I took time to work on this book. I would also like to thank my associate Melissa Fay and all of our staff, who supported me along this journey. Thanks to my husband and children for helping me find the time to dedicate to this labor of love.

Each time I represent a client going through what is often the most difficult time in his or her life, I learn something that helps me become a better attorney. To my clients: Thank you.

Jessica L. Ecker, Esq.

I am grateful to Rod Colvin and his colleagues at Addicus Books for encouraging us to write this book. To our readers, we hope we have organized the ideas and details about New Hampshire family law practice in a way that is more easily accessible to the reader than trying to read statutes and case law.

I have had the benefit of reflecting upon our experiences with our clients both in our offices and in the courts. I would like to express my appreciation for our clients, without whom we could not have accomplished the task of writing this book. I also wish to thank our partners and our assistants for their help and dedication.

This book is not intended to substitute for professional advice, but we hope this book will help you better understand the language and policies of divorce law in New Hampshire;

with this information, you will be better prepared to ask questions that will help you navigate the divorce process.

I would also like to express my appreciation for my assistant, Tami Yee, for her patience with editing and tracking drafts. I am grateful, too, for my granddaughter Charlotte, now age six; she reminds me of the joy and hope that children possess and that there is much to be said for unicorns and rainbows.

I am grateful, too, to the extraordinary group of judges, lawyers, and other professionals in New Hampshire who help families and children through the process of separation and divorce in a way that encourages reconciliation and reduces conflict.

Dana E. Prescott, J.D., L.M.S.W., Ph.D.

Introduction

As attorneys, we meet with people every day who are struggling as they move through the divorce process. If you are going through a divorce, whether you initiated it or are responding to it, you are facing major changes in your life. No area remains untouched from a divorce—parenting, family relationships, finances, social networks, your residence—all may be affected in divorce.

Our purpose in writing *Divorce in New Hampshire* is to help you navigate through an uncertain journey while keeping sight of your values, your dignity, and your money.

We know from experience in counseling hundreds of clients over the years that in order to reach a place of growth and healing, it requires a tremendous amount of support throughout the journey. We hope this book helps you move through this time of transition with more clarity and ease. Our book is not intended to be a substitute for advice from a lawyer. Rather, it is intended to assist you in partnering with your lawyer to reach your goals.

The more control and clarity you feel throughout the process, the better you will be able to make sound decisions throughout the journey upon which you now embark. During your divorce, you may experience grief while coming to grips with the end of a relationship; and, you will face uncertainty at times, but you will get through it. In the end, may you find relief in letting go of the past as you re-create yourself and contemplate new possibilities for yourself.

1

Understanding the Divorce Process

At a time when your life can feel like it is in utter chaos, sometimes the smallest bit of predictability can bring a sense of comfort. The outcome of your divorce may be unknown, therefore increasing your fear and anxiety. But there is one part of your divorce that does have some measure of predictability, and that is the divorce process itself.

Most divorces proceed in a step-by-step manner. Despite the unique aspects of your divorce, you can generally count on one phase of your divorce following the next. Sometimes just realizing you are completing each stage in the legal process can reassure you that it will not go on forever.

Therefore, it is critical that you acquire a basic understanding of the divorce process. This will lower your anxiety when your attorney starts talking about *discovery* or *going to trial* and you feel your breathing accelerate and your heart start pounding as frustration and costs mount. Most importantly, understanding the divorce process in the environment of the court will make your experience easier to organize and manage. We frequently hear the complaint that "no one told me what would happen." You have the right to know the "whats" and "whens" of the process so you can make informed and intelligent decisions about your life.

1.1   What is my first step in the divorce process?

We assume that you have tried to work through the issues that are creating stress in your marriage. Divorce has serious and lifelong consequences, so, as attorneys, we want to help

1

you make sure that your decision is carefully thought through and that you've considered the consequences of divorce, financially and personally. In some marriages the decision to divorce is a joint one, and in other cases one person has made the decision and wants the other person to accept that decision even if he or she disagrees.

We do encourage people considering divorce to make sure they have first explored the decision with a qualified therapist, mediator, or pastor because once this process starts it does not usually result in a do-over between spouses. So be sure this is a decision you are making with as much rationality, clarity, and independence as you can muster in the moment. If you are the one triggering the divorce, your very first step is to reflect backward in time and make very sure your decision to divorce is one you wish to live with for the rest of your life.

1.2   Do I need a lawyer, or can I represent myself?

The New Hampshire Supreme Court has written many decisions over many years telling litigants that they have every right to represent themselves in court without a lawyer. The term for doing so is *pro se,* which in Latin means "on one's own behalf." In other words, the person seeking a divorce represents himself or herself in court. We believe it's a person's right to represent him- or herself. Our experience is that some individuals find the cost of a family lawyer unaffordable. And in fact, litigation between private parties, whether in family law or in any other civil lawsuit, can be expensive, emotionally and financially. If you do choose to represent yourself, we advise you to at least get some legal advice; you want to avoid making legal errors that could be costly down the road. The courts are like any government institution with complicated rules and very serious consequences.

New Hampshire courts say that if you represent yourself, you will be held to the same rules of practice and evidence that apply to a client with a lawyer. Fair or not, those are the rules of divorce hearings or trials in New Hampshire for all judges, lawyers, and those seeking divorce. Organizing and conducting a trial, when a settlement is not possible for whatever reason, is not simple. Many of the rules of evidence that apply to all civil cases, including divorce, have evolved over centuries. For example, some of the special rules or exceptions are a function of legislative policies concerning domestic violence or child abuse.

If you read this book and still decide to represent yourself, you should find a lawyer who handles divorce as a regular part of his or her law practice, so you can consult with them during your case. This is sometimes called *coaching* or *limited representation* and can be helpful to those who are representing themselves. Knowing what documents to prepare is essential to your success in court. Also knowing what court deadlines mean and how to follow procedures is important to protecting yourself. For example, you may frequently hear terms like *hearsay* or *objection* in courtrooms on television shows, but understanding what those terms mean and how they are applied to your evidence at trial can be challenging. Whatever you do, you should not wait until the last minute to get advice, but make sure that your consulting arrangement is comfortable for you and in place before you face a trial.

1.3   How do I find a lawyer?

The best recommendations for a lawyer come from people who have knowledge of a lawyer's experience and reputation. Word of mouth can be helpful—perhaps you know someone who has been divorced and is satisfied with the legal service they received. You can use the Internet to search for fellows of the American Academy of Matrimonial Lawyers, members of the Family Law Section of the New Hampshire Bar Association, and the New Hampshire Lawyer Referral Service. You may also wish to ask therapists, accountants, domestic violence agencies, or other professional organizations that work with family law lawyers. We have listed Resources at the end of this book.

Be careful with online reviews or one person's opinion. A lawyer may have handled hundreds of cases over many years ethically and professionally, but then have an outcome that angers one person who may have written a negative review online.

At a minimum, you should have an initial consultation with an attorney to discuss your rights and duties under New Hampshire law, including creative solutions and referrals to other professionals you may not have considered or even known could help, such as a forensic psychologist or accountant.

Even if you are not ready to file for divorce yourself, your spouse might be, so call to schedule an appointment to obtain information in order to protect yourself. Make sure the lawyer you contact conducts a conflict check to make sure your spouse has not already made an appointment. This frequently happens in small towns. Unless the lawyer is working for you both as a mediator, the lawyer you hire cannot represent both you and your spouse (note that a mediator does not *represent* either party, but does work with both of you).

Ask what documents you should bring to your initial consultation. Make a list of your questions for your first meeting. You may be quite nervous, so write everything down and take notes. Any competent lawyer will respect and encourage you to do so.

Although you need to start making plans for how you will pay your attorney to begin work on your case, slow down and reflect on what you hear from any lawyer you meet. Ask yourself: Does this advice fit my values or rubber stamp my feelings of hurt or anger? Is the advice objective about the outcome of the case or does it feel like a sales pitch? Will this lawyer be able to help protect me from unfair use of the judicial system? Will this lawyer encourage my spouse and me to treat each other respectfully, to tell the truth, to be transparent about finances, and to protect our children from conflict? Am I hearing advice that I would not want my children or family members to hear because it sounds like a plan for an expensive and unforgivable solution for my family rather than an intelligent and ethical approach?

1.4   What general steps are taken during the divorce process?

The divorce process typically involves the following listed steps. We will provide more details and definitions later in the book, but this is the basic list to have in mind as you read. This is not a short list because it is intended as a road map that you can save or print. Refer to it when you need to know where you are on the map. Ask questions when you feel lost or when a pathway seems missing or obscured from view.

Understanding the Divorce Process

- Client obtains a referral for a lawyer or several lawyers to interview.
- Client schedules an appointment with an attorney.
- Client prepares questions and gathers needed documents for initial consultation.
- Client meets for initial consultation with attorney.
- Client pays retainer to attorney and signs a written retainer or fee agreement.
- Client provides requested information and documents to their attorney.
- Client takes other prefiling actions as advised by attorney, such as opening or closing financial accounts or obtaining records before those records disappear.
- If needed, client creates a safety plan and gets a referral to their local domestic violence agency.
- Attorney and client counsel whether they will file based on irreconcilable differences (no fault) or fault grounds.
- Attorney prepares petition for divorce and affidavits for temporary matters for client's review and signature.
- Attorney files a petition with the relevant court and requests hearing dates for temporary hearing, if appropriate.
- The clerk's office may send spouse a letter to advise them to pick up the petition with the court.
- If the spouse does not pick up the petition, orders of notice will be issued to the attorney to serve to the spouse.
- Spouse is served papers by sheriff, or, better yet, spouse or spouse's attorney voluntarily accepts service.
- Client and attorney or paralegal work on collecting financial documentations for the mandatory disclosure under the rules. These documents *must* be exchanged prior to the first hearing or mediation. You can find court-sponsored information and forms at www. courts.state.nh.us/fdpp/divorce_parenting.htm and www.courts.state.nh.us/fdpp/forms/alphaforms.htm.

- Negotiations may begin regarding terms of temporary order on matters such as parenting, support, and temporary possession of the family home.
- If minor children are involved, a first appearance will be held as the first event in the case, but if no minor children are involved, the court may schedule a scheduling conference to help determine next steps.
- Mediation or case manager conference is mandatory before any substantive hearing occurs in cases with minor children.
- If mediation fails and temporary issues remain, a temporary hearing is held.
- If there are minor children involved, parties must attend a parent education class called the *Child Impact Seminar* (*See* Resources at the end of this book for contact information).
- If minor children are involved, client's lawyer may recommend the appointment of a *guardian ad litem* to investigate and make recommendations concerning the best interest of the children or to help the court make better decisions if the case does not settle.
- Both sides conduct *discovery* to obtain information regarding relevant facts.
- Client obtains valuations of assets, including expert opinions if needed, because although some property or income can be understood by anyone, some opinions require special accounting or forensic (court) skills, like the valuation of a business or commercial real estate, economic misconduct, pensions, or tax consequences.
- Attorney provides a litigation budget to help client anticipate and prepare for the overall cost of litigation and understand why one expert or person is needed more than another, because client may need to prioritize.
- Client confers with attorney to review facts, identify issues, assess strengths and weaknesses of case,

review strategy, and develop proposals for settlement as early in the case as feasible.

- Spouses, with support of attorneys, attempt to reach agreement through written proposals, mediation, settlement conferences, neutral case evaluation, or other forms of negotiation.

- Parties reach agreement on all issues so that a written agreement is reached before any trial, and early in the case, if possible.

- Attorney prepares divorce decree, parenting plan, support orders, and court orders for the division of retirement plans, assets and debts, spousal support, or other matters specific to your case, such as a name change, for approval by spouses and attorneys.

- If your entire case settles, the documents are sent to the judge, who reviews them, and if he or she believes they comport with the law, they will be signed off on and returned to attorneys by mail. The case is then done. Typically, you will receive a copy of the signed orders within a few weeks.

- If your case has not settled previously, a pretrial conference is held so your case will be prepared to be scheduled for trial. Attorneys must exchange final proposed documents and updated financial affidavits at pretrial.

- Following the pretrial hearing, you should receive your trial date or dates.

- Parties prepare for trial on unresolved issues, including updated financial affidavits, organization of exhibits to be exchanged with counsel and submitted to the judge, and arrangements for experts and other witnesses to come to court to testify.

- Trial preparations proceed, including legal research on contested issues, pretrial motions, proposed findings and rulings, proposed divorce decree, parenting plan and other documents, preparation of direct and cross-examination of witnesses, and subpoenas of witnesses.

- Client meets with attorney for final trial preparation. This may involve several hours of work, depending on the length of trial and the issues.

- Following the trial, the judge makes a decision in writing, usually four to twelve weeks after the trial. The clerk mails the decision to counsel for clients to read.

- One or both parties, if they wish, within ten days of the clerk's notice ask the judge to clarify or to reconsider the decision.

- Judge grants or denies the motion(s), and then either party has thirty days to file a notice of appeal to the New Hampshire Supreme Court.

- If there is no appeal, then the decree becomes final and the parties must complete all the transfers of property by deed or title, pay all debts or support, implement the parenting plan in good faith, and complete any other parts of the agreement.

1.5   Is New Hampshire a *no-fault* state, or must I have *grounds* for divorce?

We get this question a lot. New Hampshire, like most states today, is mostly a no-fault divorce state, which means that most divorces are granted on the grounds of *irreconcilable marital differences.* This means that unless one spouse raises a *fault* claim, such as adultery, cruelty, abandonment, being a habitual drunkard, treatment of the other spouse so as to endanger his or her reason, or cruel and inhuman treatment, neither you nor your spouse is required to prove that the other is *at fault* in order to be granted a divorce.

The fault grounds in New Hampshire date back to before there was no-fault divorce. To prove fault, you must also prove that the fault was the cause of the breakdown of the marriage. Cases that involve fault grounds can be stressful as well as expensive to litigate.

Economic misconduct, such as spending marital funds on another person for travel or gifts or hiding assets or income, which is then connected to a fault ground, may lead to the ability to recoup the damage to the marital estate. A claim of fault by itself, however, may make one party feel better given the hurt and pain at the moment, but it usually only increases the cost of the divorce without adding anything significant to the end result. Having seen many fault-based divorces litigate from start to finish, we have seen many clients believe they will feel better when they are *heard* by the judge, but they often learn that judges wish to reduce conflict between spouses. Accordingly, unless your facts to support fault grounds are easily provable and shock the conscience of the court, fault grounds are often a losing proposition.

1.6   Must I get divorced in the same state in which I got married?

No. Regardless of where you were married, you may seek a divorce in New Hampshire if the *jurisdictional requirements of residency* are met. In all states, the court in which the divorce is filed must have subject matter and personal jurisdiction. *Subject matter jurisdiction* means that the court has authority to grant the divorce to you. This is very rarely a problem, but it can happen. In most cases, the question is whether the New Hampshire divorce court has personal jurisdiction over one or both parties, a point discussed in the next question.

1.7   How long must I have lived in New Hampshire to get a divorce here?

You must have been a resident of New Hampshire for at least one year to meet the residency requirement for a divorce.

If legal residence is an issue or neither party meets the residency requirement, talk to your attorney about other options.

1.8   What New Hampshire court has jurisdiction to grant a divorce?

In New Hampshire, only the family courts in each county have jurisdiction to grant a divorce and decide all the issues in your case. In New Hampshire, a judge or referee hears your divorce case as a *bench trial* or *final hearing*. This means only a single judge or referee (previously called a *marital master*) assigned to your case that day may hear the evidence or your arguments. There is no right in New Hampshire to a jury trial in a divorce.

The family court also hears domestic violence petitions and child abuse and neglect cases brought by the Division of Children, Youth and Families.

Just to be clear: You may hear people talk about other New Hampshire courts. The Superior Court is the court in every county that conducts jury trials in criminal cases or civil cases like personal injury suits or contracts in which a party asks for a jury trial. The Superior Court no longer has authority to decide divorces or other family law matters.

The New Hampshire Supreme Court is a court of appeals only and does not hear the actual trials of the facts. The court is made up of a chief justice and four associate justices. This means that if you appeal your case after a final divorce decree to the Supreme Court, it will receive the transcripts, copies of the exhibits admitted at trial, and the arguments of the parties in the form of a brief, which is only in writing. Some cases may get brief oral arguments that will only be based upon the legal arguments in the case. The Supreme Court rarely vacates a decision of a lower court after a trial unless there is an error of law or a clear abuse of discretion (which does not mean a different judge may have decided the case differently or that you disagree with the outcome of your case).

The other court is New Hampshire's probate court, which is a court of very limited jurisdiction over estates, guardianships, wills, and trusts. The probate court cannot hear divorces. There are some instances where a person may be able to choose between the probate and family court, such as in the guardianship over a minor case.

1.9   What is the difference between a *judge* and a *referee* or *marital master* in New Hampshire?

A family or district court judge is an appointed judge nominated by the New Hampshire Judicial Selection Committee, chosen by the governor, and approved by the New Hampshire Executive Council. Judges serve until age seventy. Judges hear many different kinds of civil and criminal cases, and they have the power to put people in jail if convicted of certain crimes or for contempt of court.

There are other types of quasi-judicial persons in New Hampshire who you may run into during the process of divorce.

First, as of this writing, there remain two marital masters in New Hampshire. *Marital masters* are triers of fact who were appointed for terms and who heard only family matters on a daily basis.

Several years ago, the New Hampshire Legislature, after some angry litigants complained, thought it wise to end the marital master program, thinking it would resolve the problems in the process that some folks complained about. However, most marital masters simply were appointed as family court judges as their terms ended. Marital masters' orders must be reviewed and approved by a judge (cosigned). They also do not have the power to hear a *show cause hearing* (a hearing where a party in contempt must show cause as to whether they should be incarcerated for contempt).

A second type of hearing officer is a referee. A *referee,* also known as a *hearings officer,* is a lawyer appointed by the family division administrative judge. Referees are much like marital masters and can cover the same hearings they can, and need their orders cosigned. *Child support referees* are a specific type of referee who only conduct hearings and submit recommendations for orders on issues of paternity establishment, child support, medical support, and tax exemptions as well as registrations of court orders from other states.

1.10   Where can I file my divorce, and what is *venue?*

You may file your divorce in the family division court with jurisdiction over the town or city where you live. If your spouse resides in the same county in New Hampshire, you can file in either the family division court for your town or city or the family division court in your spouse's town or city, if different. If your spouse resides outside your county or out of state, you must file in your family division court (unless you file a joint petition, in which case you can file it in either spouse's county court). The city in which the case is filed is called the *venue.* Sometimes the court or the parties may change venue for the privacy of the family or because a judge in one county cannot hear the case, making it necessary to move it to another court.

1.11   What is a *divorce petition?*

A *divorce petition* is an official document signed by the person filing for divorce under oath and then served on the other spouse and filed with the clerk of the court to initiate the divorce process. The petition sets out in very general terms what the petitioner is asking the court to order (on occasion more specifics may be included). These forms are available in a packet directly from the court or online from the court website. A sample petition form may be found in the Appendix or on the website listed in the Resources at the back of this book.

1.12   What does it mean to *file for divorce?*

When lawyers use the term *filing,* they are ordinarily referring to filing a legal document at the courthouse, such as delivering a petition for divorce to the clerk of the court. Sometimes a person who has hired a lawyer to begin a divorce action uses the phrase "I've filed for divorce," although no papers have yet been taken to the courthouse to start the legal process.

In New Hampshire, you file the petition first with the clerk of the court, who then processes the *orders of notice* with the petition and then returns it to you or your attorney to serve your spouse (either by sheriff or by certified mail). An official filing means that the clerk has *docketed,* or stamped and accepted, your paperwork. The petition is recorded by the clerk in the computer, and you are then assigned a docket number. You will use that docket number for your case on all correspondence and filings for the divorce, as well as any other motions to modify, to enforce, or for contempt that may be filed in the future by you or your spouse.

1.13   Does it matter who files for divorce first? What happens after the filing?

Yes and no. The person who files a divorce is the *petitioner* and the person who is served with the divorce is the *respondent.* The respondent often files an *answer* or *counterclaim* for divorce, which usually repeats the same allegations as a divorce petition. This is not mandatory but is a recommended practice so that both parties will have equal standing in court. The court, as a neutral decision maker, will not give preference to either party. Both parties will be given adequate notice, and each will have a chance to be heard and present their arguments.

Sometimes, however, a spouse who feels hurt or abandoned by the other spouse leaving the marriage does not want to file first because they did not *cause* the divorce. This is a legitimate feeling that deserves respect, but from the legal perspective of a judge it does not matter.

New Hampshire divorce law does not give any *legal* disadvantage for filing a petition first, but you should discuss with your attorney whether there are any advantages to you for doing so. Your attorney may advise you to file first or to wait until your spouse files, depending upon the strategy for your case and your personal and economic circumstances.

For example, if there is a concern that your spouse will begin transferring assets upon learning about your plans for divorce, your attorney might advise you to file sooner so that you can get the orders in place that make transferring certain assets a violation of the orders. However, if you are separated from your spouse but have a beneficial temporary arrangement, such as health insurance under your spouse's plan, your attorney may counsel you to wait to file a petition. This allows you to have the insurance benefits for a longer period of time. The decision on when to file (or wait) depends on the circumstances of your case.

There may be strategic reasons that it's better for one or the other party to file first, having to do with fault grounds. Filing first really does matter if there is a dispute about the "home state" of children if you recently moved from a different state or country, were in the military, or came to New Hampshire for your safety, for example. There are federal and state laws that give an advantage to the person who files first, so if this applies to you it is very important that you immediately consult with a lawyer who understands interstate or international child custody law and can help you. Waiting could otherwise hurt your case.

You can also file a joint petition if both parties agree, which simply means that both of you want the divorce. Most often, joint petitions are used when both parties agree to all the terms and have mediated their case or have resolved all differences. On occasion, people file a joint petition but have not agreed to all the terms being discussed, in which case the divorce will proceed as it would any other case.

If the case goes to trial, the person who files the petition, the petitioner, typically testifies first along with any witnesses. All these persons are then subject to cross-examination by the other spouse's attorney.

When the petitioner has no more evidence to offer the judge, the petitioner tells the judge this and *rests*. Then, the respondent offers all his or her evidence.

1.14 Can I get a divorce even if my spouse objects or refuses to cooperate?

Yes. New Hampshire does not require that your spouse agrees to a divorce. The New Hampshire law considers *irreconcilable differences* have occurred when one party believes the marriage has irretrievably broken down, regardless of whether the other spouse agrees. If your spouse threatens not to *give* you a divorce, this may prolong the case and make it more expensive, but eventually the case will proceed to trial and the court will grant the divorce. This is sometimes hard to explain to spouses who, for personal or religious reasons, object to the divorce. Usually the passage of time or counseling can help, but divorce is often a difficult emotional issue.

1.15 Can I divorce my spouse in New Hampshire if he or she lives in another state?

Provided you have met the residency requirements for living in New Hampshire for one year or more, you can file for divorce here even if your spouse lives or resides in another state. Discuss with your attorney the facts that need to be proven and the steps necessary to give your spouse proper notice. Your attorney can counsel you on whether it is possible to proceed with filing for divorce in New Hampshire.

Be careful, however. Sometimes there may be advantages and disadvantages to filing for divorce in New Hampshire compared to a different state. For example, New Hampshire law may require shorter periods of child support than other states.

Here's another consideration. New Hampshire may treat an asset, such as an inheritance, as marital property that may be divided between the spouses, but another state may treat the asset as nonmarital property not subject to division. Yet another state may have no spousal support calculation, but New Hampshire does, making spousal support much more predictable here. Child support amounts and calculations can also vary widely from state to state. Each state is different, so if any of these situations apply to you, get clear legal advice before proceeding to file.

1.16 Can I get a divorce even if I do not know my spouse's address?

You can, but New Hampshire law requires that you make a good-faith and diligent effort to find your spouse. All civil suits—and divorce is a civil suit—require that a party be *served* with process, which means giving notice that someone is asking a court to take action, like award support, divide property, or allocate parental rights and responsibilities. This is not just applicable to divorce law, but it is an important constitutional right called *due process*. Due process means that every person has the right to notice of a lawsuit and a chance to appear for a hearing before his or her rights to children or assets are decided by a judge.

Only after you have contacted family members, friends, former coworkers, or anyone else who might know your spouse's whereabouts, can you ask the court to allow you to proceed. After your attorney attempts to give notice to your spouse without success, it is possible to ask the court to proceed with the divorce by giving notice through publication in a newspaper, or more-modern options may allow service on social media platforms such as Facebook or by e-mail.

1.17 I just immigrated to New Hampshire. Will my immigration status prevent a divorce?

If you meet the residency requirements for divorce in New Hampshire, you may get a divorce in New Hampshire even if your immigration status is unclear or under review by federal immigration authorities. Talk to your immigration lawyer about the likelihood of a divorce leading to immigration challenges, however. Immigration is subject to federal law, not state law, so you want to make sure that a divorce will not hurt your status in the United States.

If you are a victim of domestic violence, tell your divorce lawyer at the earliest opportunity. You may be eligible for a change in your immigration status under the federal *Violence Against Women Act,* but immigration law is a specialty practice so you should consult immediately with a legal expert in that area of law.

1.18   I want to get divorced in my Indian tribal court, so what do I need to know?

Each tribal court may have its own laws governing divorce. Requirements for residency, grounds for divorce, and the laws regarding property, spousal support, and custody of children vary substantially from state law. Some tribes have very different laws governing the grounds for your divorce, removal of children from the home, and cohabitation, for example. Contact an attorney who is knowledgeable about the law in your tribal court or about the requirements for recording a divorce obtained in state court with the clerk of the tribal court. Do not assume that the laws are the same in all tribal courts or that state law will recognize all aspects of a tribal court decision in a divorce.

1.19   Is there a waiting period for a divorce in New Hampshire?

No. In New Hampshire, as soon as your divorce paperwork is filed, if you agree on all issues, you can be divorced within a matter of weeks. The emphasis on "all" issues is important to reflect upon. Some people agree on parental rights and responsibilities early on or even before filing but cannot agree on financial issues like the value of a house or business, or the amount of support. In New Hampshire, to have a *final* divorce you must settle all the issues or have a judge resolve the ones you do not settle. You cannot have a final divorce until everything is done but we certainly encourage and support spouses resolving as much as they can privately and without court.

1.20 Can I stop the newspaper from publishing notice of my divorce?

Documents filed with the court, such as a divorce petition, court orders, pleadings, or a final decree, are matters of public record. Newspapers have a right to access this information, and many newspapers publish this information if your case has some aspect of public interest. In very rare cases, a divorce file may be kept private, referred to as being *sealed* or *under seal,* if the court orders it. By law, it is typically difficult to get the case sealed.

1.21 Is there a way to avoid embarrassing my spouse and not have the sheriff serve the divorce papers at their workplace?

Talk to your lawyer about the option of having your spouse sign a document known as an *acceptance of service.* Filing of this document with the court can eliminate the need to have your spouse served by the sheriff. Samples of acceptance of service documents may be found in the Appendix. As mentioned earlier, serving by certified mail is another option.

Service by a sheriff at a former spouse's workplace should rarely be done and only if there is a legitimate emergency. You want to avoid embarrassing your spouse because that may make your case unnecessarily more difficult to settle.

Having your former spouse served with divorce papers is not appropriate for all cases, so discuss with your attorney the better choice for your case.

1.22 Should I sign an *acceptance of service* even if I do not agree with what my spouse has written in the divorce petition?

An acceptance of service is just your acknowledgment that you received the paperwork without having to be served by the sheriff. Signing it does not mean that you agree with anything your spouse has stated in the divorce petition or anything that your spouse is asking for in the divorce. Signing the acceptance of service simply prevents the sheriff from personally handing you the documents. You do not waive the right to object to anything your spouse has stated in the petition for divorce.

Follow your attorney's advice on whether and when to sign an acceptance of service.

1.23 Why should I contact an attorney right away when I receive divorce papers?

If your spouse has filed for divorce, it is important that you obtain legal advice as soon as possible. Even if you and your spouse are getting along, having independent legal counsel can help you make decisions now that could affect your divorce later.

After your acceptance of service has been filed with the court or you have been served by the sheriff, an *entry of appearance* must be filed within fifteen days of the date you were served. And, a *written answer* and/or *cross-petition* for divorce, responding to your spouse's divorce petition, must be filed with the court within thirty days of the date you were served. Although this time frame can be flexible, you risk a *default judgment* by a judge against you if you do not respond to the court. Whether you hire a lawyer or not, you should always go to the courthouse and fill out an answer and entry of appearance. Do not ignore the petition. Serious ramifications may occur if you do.

After your spouse has filed for divorce, if there are minor children, typically a *first appearance* is scheduled, at which time the court will ensure that your case will be scheduled for mediation as a next step and that the parties have signed up for the child impact seminar. Thereafter, if mediation is unsuccessful, a scheduling conference and temporary hearing can be scheduled at any time by the clerk. In New Hampshire, lawyers may request a temporary hearing, but lawyers cannot pick the date and time for that hearing.

A *temporary hearing* is a very limited trial that may last thirty minutes or up to a couple of hours. The hearing usually concerns immediate, temporary issues, such as who may live in the home or apartment, the amount of temporary child or spousal support, who may be responsible for paying which bills, or a temporary parenting plan if the parents cannot agree on time with each parent or school placement, for example. The temporary orders typically remain in effect until a final order is agreed upon or issued.

Although temporary orders in your case are not supposed to impact what happens at a final hearing, often a judge will strive to keep things *as close to normal* as possible, especially where parenting matters are concerned. However, things can change as more information is brought to a judge's attention. This may include such things as actual income and appraisals, which may impact how the judge decides on a final basis.

It is possible that you will receive only a few weeks' notice of a temporary hearing. You may be better prepared for a temporary hearing if you have already retained an attorney in advance.

1.24   What is a *non-hypothecation order* in a New Hampshire divorce, and when is it effective?

This order is important to understand. New Hampshire law automatically enters a court order that is legally effective against the parties once the divorce petition is served and filed with the court. A *non-hypothecation order* prevents either party from hiding or wasting assets, incurring debt (unless in the ordinary and usual course of paying bills or running a business), canceling health insurance, or impairing or interfering with the ability of the judge to distribute assets. The non-hypothecation order, unless modified by court order, reads as follows:

- Any time after the filing of a parenting or divorce petition, a parent shall not relocate the residence of a child without a court order unless:

  - relocation results in the residence being closer to the other parent, or

  - relocation is to any location within the child's current school district, or

  - relocation is necessary to protect the safety of the parent or child, or both, as later determined by the court.

- Until further order of the court, each party is restrained from selling, transferring, encumbering, hypothecating, concealing, or in any manner whatsoever disposing of any property, real or personal, belonging to either or both spouses except:

- by written agreement of both parties, or
- for reasonable and necessary living expenses, or
- in the ordinary and usual course of business.

• You are required to comply with Family Division Rule 1.25-A. This manditory disclosure rule requires parties to disclose to each other numerous financial and other documents. A website link about Rule 1.25-A is available in the Resources section along with other public information.

If a spouse violates these orders, that spouse can be held in *contempt* by a judge and made to pay attorney fees, costs of the other party, or other equitable relief. If you and your spouse cannot agree or you have any doubt about whether you may violate the court orders, your lawyer may file a motion asking the judge to give you permission to modify or alter the non-hypothecation orders.

For example, perhaps you own a car in your name only that requires replacement, but your spouse refuses to cooperate and threatens you with contempt if you sell it. You may be able to sell the car without a risk of contempt if you are acting in good faith and really need the new car, but it may be safer to file the motion.

What will not work is to *pay* debts to your father or mother or sibling that were unpaid for ten years until after the divorce was filed, or to transfer a snowmobile to a friend for less than fair market value or cash. New Hampshire courts may treat these types of violations seriously, and these actions can influence your entire case in ways you may not like.

1.25   What is a *scheduling conference,* and must I go?

Yes, you must attend the scheduling conference. The primary purpose of a *scheduling conference* is to identify the issues on which you and your spouse agree or those temporary issues on which you do not agree, such as residency of the minor children, child support, marital debt, distribution of property, spousal support, or exclusive possession of house or apartment. It is a non-substantive hearing, meaning there will be no temporary or final decisions made on your case other than scheduling deadlines.

In addition, the judge will identify other steps the parties must take to move the case toward settlement or trial, such as the child impact seminar, scheduling of mediation, appointment of a guardian *ad litem,* or other strategies to help parties work out agreements without a trial. Further, the judge will likely set deadlines and ensure that the parties have exchanged relevant information needed to prepare for a hearing.

1.26   What is an *ex parte* motion and order?

An *ex parte* court order is obtained by one party going to the judge to ask for something without giving timely notice and opportunity to respond. Typically, when a motion is filed, the clerk's office will hold the motion and wait ten days for an objection to be filed before giving it to the judge for a ruling. This step is skipped in an *ex parte* process so that an immediate order can be issued without waiting the typical ten days for a response. This action is rarely necessary, but it can be taken if, for example, there is danger of harm to a child of if there is an immediate risk of a spouse absconding with money.

You must attempt to notify your spouse by telephone, text, or otherwise of your filing of an *ex parte* motion and explain to the court your spouse's response. Judges are reluctant to sign *ex parte* orders because everyone is entitled to fair notice and an opportunity for a hearing before a court takes away parenting or property rights.

Ordinarily, even when a spouse asks for an *ex parte* order from a judge, the court can require the other side to be served or receive notice of any requests for court orders before a hearing. When an *ex parte* order is granted, the party who did not request the order has an opportunity to request a hearing be scheduled within five business days of the request, giving a judge an opportunity to determine whether the order should remain in effect, be denied or modified.

1.27   What is a *temporary hearing?*

Within the petition for divorce, a party can request a *temporary hearing* be scheduled on issues by checking the relevant boxes on the form. If a first appearance (if there are minor children) and mediation occurs and is unsuccessful, a temporary hearing will be scheduled. Note that unless additional time is requested, a thirty-minute temporary hearing will be scheduled. If you need more time, a separate motion or clear request in the mediator's report may be required. Following a temporary hearing, the court will issue orders that are legally effective and binding on you and your spouse until there is a final order entered in your case. A temporary order can be enforced the same way as a final order, by contempt or other sanctions if a party fails to follow the order.

There may be other motions necessary to handle procedural aspects of your case, such as a *motion for a continuance,* asking that a court date be changed, or a motion for an extension of time, asking that the court extend a deadline. These motions are pretty standard because you or your spouse may have a conflict with the court date, or a lawyer is legitimately unavailable. These motions are part of most cases and require cooperation from both parties and lawyers to make sure the case is run efficiently.

Other motions are more complicated and may be more difficult to agree upon with your spouse or between lawyers. For example, your attorney may file a written motion with the court asking for an order related to the temporary award of a residence to you or your spouse, an allocation of parental rights and responsibilities such as primary residence and parenting time, the appointment of a guardian *ad litem,* child support, spousal support, legal or expert-witness fees, or other financial matters, such as payment of household bills and credit card debt.

The purpose of this type of motion is to try to give the parties some structure and rules as they (and the children) adjust to the practical and emotional event of a divorce. Your lawyer should work with the other lawyer to help facilitate temporary agreements that avoid a hearing. Hearings are often expensive, and you may not be adequately prepared with financial or child-related information. This may mean that a judge will decide the facts without all the information or, worse, with inaccurate or false information.

When a judge has to decide temporary issues, you or your spouse may receive a decision that is much more difficult to unravel or change later. Like it or not, the temporary orders can set a precedent in your case. So the choice to have a temporary hearing has risks and benefits that you should carefully discuss with your lawyer before filing the motion or compromising on a temporary order that avoids a hearing.

1.28 How soon will it be before temporary issues can be heard by a judge?

As explained, a temporary hearing is a request to the court to provide some rules or structure for the divorce before there is a final settlement or a trial and the entry of a final decree of divorce. In New Hampshire, the time frame for a temporary hearing differs from county to county, depending upon the availability of the judge and the caseload in the specific court where you filed your case.

If there are minor children involved, you will not get into court for a temporary hearing until after the first appearance and likely at least one mediation session, unless you or your attorney can convince the judge to schedule a temporary hearing sooner for you. In most courts, it is typical for two to three months to pass from the time of filing for divorce and a temporary hearing. In other courts, it can be longer. Hearings may take longer to schedule if the hearing requires more than thirty minutes of time.

Having to go to mediation before a temporary hearing can work to your advantage. A mediated agreement may be closer to what works for you and your family than what a judge may decide at a hearing—and it may be less costly. Finally, it is important to know that lawyers do not control the court calendar; clerks and judges do. Your lawyer can file a motion and ask for a hearing, but your case is one among many, so that decision may take longer than you think is fair. Additionally, once the hearing occurs, you likely will have to wait between two and eight more weeks to get the decision in the mail.

1.29 How much notice will I get if my spouse seeks a temporary order?

If your spouse requests a temporary hearing, you will receive that notice in the *orders of notice* with the divorce petition and have the opportunity to respond to that with your answer within thirty days. If the request is made later and you don't agree, you will have ten days to respond, but less than that time if a party applies for an expedited or emergency hearing such as discussed in the previous question. You are entitled to reasonable notice of any and all court hearings.

1.30 If I agree to temporary orders in New Hampshire, will that decision hurt my case later?

This question is important and yet generally difficult to answer. On economic matters, judges really do understand that early agreements may not reflect informed financial information or accurate valuations or income, and that spouses are making difficult decisions about their lives quickly, such as finding new living accommodations.

What was financially true when the divorce was filed, may look nothing like the facts six or twelve months later. Moreover, judges must consider different parts of the law when entering a final order of divorce and allocating assets and debts, awarding spousal support, or deciding parental primary residence and parenting time.

It is unusual for a temporary order related to financial matters to prejudice anyone unless one spouse misrepresented finances or violated the court's orders by failing to comply. Temporary financial orders are often issued as a "band-aid" of sorts on finances while families are in transition during a divorcee.

Temporary orders related to children may be different than child support. As an example, a parenting schedule or school placement, which you agree to for an extended time, may be difficult to change later if the children have been doing well. Discuss the advantages and disadvantages of temporary orders with your lawyer so you can make informed decisions.

1.31 During my divorce, what actions am I responsible for?

Your attorney will explain what actions you should take to help you reach the most practical and beneficial possible outcome. At a minimum, you will be asked to:

- Update your attorney regarding any changes in your contact information.
- Provide your attorney with all requested documents.

24

- Provide requested information in a timely manner.
- Complete forms and questionnaires.
- Appear in court on time.
- Be direct about asking any questions you might have.
- Tell your attorney your thoughts about settlement.
- Explore what you would like the judge to order in your case.
- Remain respectful toward your spouse throughout the process.
- Keep your children out of the litigation by not discussing the divorce with them.
- Comply with any temporary court orders as best you can; do not ignore any orders.
- Advise your attorney of any personal developments that may influence your case.

By doing your part in the divorce process, you enable your attorney to partner with you for a better outcome while also lowering your attorney fees. Nevertheless, as we often tell clients, you cannot control who your spouse hires as a lawyer, and that may have consequences to your family during the process.

1.32 I'm worried that I won't remember to ask my lawyer about all of the issues. How can I be sure I don't miss anything?

Write down all of the topics you want to discuss with your attorney, including what your goals are for the outcome. The sooner you get clarification about that, the easier and less expensive it should be for your attorney to support you. Realize that your attorney may think of some issues that you may not have considered. Your lawyer's experience will be helpful in making sure nothing important is forgotten.

The following Divorce Issues Checklist will help you organize topics for discussion.

Divorce in New Hampshire

Divorce Issues Checklist

Issue	Notes
Dissolution of marriage	
Parenting rights and responsibilities of minor children (custody)	
Removal of children from jurisdiction	
Parenting plan	
Child support	
Deviation from child support guidelines	
Abatement of child support	
Travel expenses to facilitate parenting time for out-of-town/state parents	
Life insurance to fund unpaid child support	
Automatic withholding for support/wage assignment	
Child support arrearage from temporary order	
Child-care expenses	
Child-care credit	
Health insurance for minor children	
Uninsured medical expenses for minor children	
Qualified medical support order	
Private school tuition for children	
College expenses for children	
College savings accounts for benefit of children	
Health insurance on the parties	
Real property: marital residence	
Real property: rentals, cabins, and commercial property	
Time-shares	
Retirement accounts	
Federal or military pensions	

Divorce Issues Checklist (Continued)

Issue	Notes
Business interests	
Bank accounts	
Investments	
Stock options	
Stock purchase plans	
Life insurance policies	
Frequent-flyer miles	
Credit card points	
Season tickets for events	
Premarital assets	
Premarital debts	
Pets	
Personal property division: including motor vehicles, recreational vehicles, campers, airplanes, collections, furniture, electronics, tools, household goods	
Exchange date for personal property	
Division of maritial debt	
Property settlement	
Spousal support	
Life insurance to fund unpaid spousal support	
Arrearage of spousal support from temporary order	
Tax exemptions for minor children	
IRS Form 8332	
Filing status for tax returns for last/current year	
Former name restoration	
Attorney fees	

1.33   My spouse has all of our financial information. How will I be able to prepare for negotiations or trial if I do not have the proper documents?

After your divorce has been filed with the court, the timeline on the *mandatory disclosure rule* (Rule 1.25A) begins. These mandatory disclosures include a year's worth of bank account statements, retirement and investment accounts, the last three years of tax returns and documents, six months of credit card statements, as well as additional information if you are self-employed. You will also receive this information from your spouse or through his or her attorney.

If the mandatory disclosure information is not sufficient to provide you with the desired information, your attorney will proceed with a process known as *discovery*. Through discovery, your attorney can ask your spouse to provide documents and information needed to prepare your case. Your attorney can also subpoena information directly from an institution to obtain the requested documentation if necessary.

Often, the lawyers will confer with each other and cooperatively exchange all the materials needed for the divorce. The best lawyers recognize that transparency and truth-telling saves substantial time and money for clients, and that those clients who act in a trustworthy way, which is reciprocated, will have a better postdivorce relationship with family and children. Besides, it is the right thing to do.

1.34   My spouse and I want our divorce to be amicable and less costly. How can we make that happen?

You and your spouse are to be acknowledged for your willingness to cooperate while focusing on moving through the divorce process. This will not only make your lives easier and save you money on attorney fees, but it is also more likely to result in an outcome you are both satisfied with.

Find a lawyer who understands your goal to reach a settlement and encourage your spouse to do the same. Cooperate with the prompt and transparent exchange of necessary information. Then ask your attorney about options for mediation and negotiation for reaching agreement.

There is also a type of divorce that can be achieved through *collaborative law*. This approach involves couples working with lawyers, coaches, and financial experts to arrive at a settlement without litigation. If this approach interests you, be sure to find a collaboratively trained attorney. Even if you are not able to settle all the issues, these actions can increase the likelihood of agreement on many of the terms of your divorce decree.

1.35   Can I choose my judge?

You may not choose your own judge nor go *judge shopping* in New Hampshire. Judge shopping refers to a person trying to influence which judge will be assigned to their case. However, if you have concerns about a particular judge, discuss your concerns with your attorney. If you believe that a judge has a conflict of interest, such as being a close friend of your spouse, you may have a basis for asking the judge to be *recused* in order to allow another judge to hear the case. This is not something to be done lightly, however.

You can select, if your spouse agrees, a private arbitrator or referee to act as judge to decide your case outside the court system. The court can appoint a lawyer to act as a judge in complex cases. You can choose to have an arbitrator's decision binding or subject to appeal. This a very complicated choice to make, so be sure to discuss such choices with your lawyer.

1.36   How long will it take to finalize my divorce?

The more you and your spouse are in agreement about your divorce, the sooner (and less expensively) your divorce will conclude. At a minimum, assuming all issues, such as parenting, support, property, and debts, are completely settled between you and your spouse, you can waive a final hearing and you can be divorced in a matter of weeks.

1.37   What is the significance of my divorce being final?

The finality of your divorce decree is important for many reasons. It can affect your right to remarry, your eligibility for health insurance from your former spouse, and your filing status for income taxes.

1.38   When does my divorce become *final*?

Your divorce becomes final for different purposes on different dates. The date that triggers the time period for a divorce becoming final is the date that the divorce decree is signed by the judge if there is an agreement. If you had a trial, then the divorce will not be final for thirty-one days after the date of the clerk's notice unless one party files a notice of appeal with the court. If that happens, your divorce will not be final until the appeal is decided by the New Hampshire Supreme Court, and that can take approximately a year under most circumstances.

For most purposes, your divorce is final on the date the judge signs the decree. For the purposes of health insurance and other important rights like retirement benefits, pensions, or *COBRA,* you should have investigated and made plans during the case so that you are not caught off guard, and do not forfeit rights that you should have retained. With many employers, your right to stay on your spouse's health insurance ends with the divorce decree.

1.39   If I want to change my name, when can I start using my former name?

The judge can grant your name change at your final hearing or in the final decree at no cost. If you wait and decide after the divorce that you want a name change, you can obtain that change at the probate court in the county where you live for a filing fee, but it is an inconvenience that is avoidable if you do it in your divorce decree. You may begin using your former name at any time, provided you are not doing so for any unlawful purpose, such as to avoid your creditors. Many agencies and government institutions, like the Social Security Administration or the passport office, however, will not alter their records without a court order specifically granting you a change of name.

If you want your former name restored, let your attorney know so that this provision can be included in your divorce decree. There may be additional problems if you wait, so make this decision as early in the process as you can.

2

Coping with Stress
during the Divorce Process

It may have been a few years ago. Or it may have been many years ago. Perhaps it was only months. But when you said, "I do," you meant it. Like most people getting married, you planned a lifetime together.

But things happen. Life brings change. People change. Whatever the circumstances, you now find yourself considering divorce. The emotions of divorce run from one extreme to another as you journey through the process. You may feel relief and be ready to move on with your life. On the other hand, you may feel emotions that are quite painful. Anger. Fear. Sorrow. A deep sense of loss or failure. Remember, it is important to find professional or community support for coping with all these strong emotions.

Because going through a divorce can be an emotional time, having a clear understanding of the divorce process and what to expect will help you make better decisions. And when it comes to decision-making, search inside your own values and beliefs to clarify your intentions and goals for the future. Let these good and empathetic intentions be your guide.

2.1 My spouse left home weeks ago. I don't want a divorce because I feel our marriage can be saved. Should I still see an attorney?

It is a good idea to see an attorney. Whether you want a divorce or not, there may be important actions you need to consider to protect your assets, debts, credit, home, children, and support. We do not endorse the choice to go to court for no reason beyond emotion, but we do want you to carefully consider the potential consequences of the choice to divorce.

What you always want to be is an informed consumer. The courts are governed by laws and rules related to divorce so knowing those laws and rules can help you protect yourself and your family. You also want to be ready in the event that you are served with a divorce petition.

2.2   How fast can I get a temporary hearing?

As discussed earlier, an emergency or expedited hearing to address temporary issues may either be immediate or take at least a few weeks or more, depending upon the county in which your case is pending. If minor children are involved, a first appearance and mediation may be scheduled before you get a temporary hearing. The mediation may be sufficient to address your temporary concerns. Judges will usually require mediation in all divorce cases before holding a temporary hearing.

The important point is that you may need a judge to help you protect your family or your finances. Filing a motion is not complicated but deciding whether or not to ask a judge to decide temporary issues has consequences you should discuss with a lawyer.

For example, you may want a temporary hearing on child support, but your former spouse may already be paying the mortgage and the car payment. If your former spouse is voluntarily paying these bills, and the amount the former spouse is paying exceeds a child support order under the guidelines, then talk to your lawyer. Any temporary agreement should be clear about what bills will be paid and should be approved by court order. Be careful to make sure that a hearing will actually be helpful rather than put you in a worse financial position.

2.3   The thought of going to a lawyer's office is more than I can bear. I canceled my first appointment because I just could not do it. What should I do?

Many people going through a divorce are dealing with lawyers for the first time and feel anxious about the experience. Ask a trusted friend or family member to go with you. He or she can support you by writing down your questions in advance, by taking notes for you during the meeting, and by helping you to remember what the lawyer said after the meeting is concluded. It is very likely that you will feel relieved just to be better informed.

Just remember that when you speak with a lawyer, everything you tell him or her is confidential or privileged. If you have someone with you at your meeting, you need to make sure that person will respect your privacy and the advice you receive from your lawyer. The person(s) sitting there with you and your lawyer should respect your confidentiality—you need to make sure that this is clear before the meeting.

2.4   There is some information about my marriage that I think my attorney needs, but I am too embarrassed to discuss it. Must I tell the attorney?

Your attorney has an ethical duty to maintain confidentiality. Attorneys who practice divorce law are accustomed to hearing intimate information about families. Although it may be deeply personal to you, it is unlikely that anything you tell your lawyer will be a shock. It may feel uncomfortable for a short moment, but it is important that your attorney have all of the facts so that your interests can be fully protected.

It is very important that your attorney not be surprised with important facts that he or she learns from your spouse's attorney or while in a court hearing. If speaking directly about these facts in your life still seems too hard, consider putting them in a letter.

If you have a therapist who can help explain what you have experienced emotionally during your marriage, consider a conference call with your lawyer.

Be very careful with e-mail or texting or any other form of electronic communication; anything you put on the Internet or your phone is not considered private. Discuss with your lawyer what you should send or not send by e-mail to protect your confidentiality. Every law office is different.

2.5   I am unsure about how to tell our children about the divorce. What's the best way to inform children of such a situation?

How you talk to your children about your divorce will depend upon their ages, maturity levels, and developmental stage. Changes in your children's everyday lives, such as a change of residence or one parent leaving the home, are far more important to them. Information about legal proceedings and meetings with lawyers are best kept among adults.

Research suggests that simpler answers are best for young children. Avoid giving them more information than they need. Use the adults in your life as a source of support to meet your own emotional needs. If your spouse tells the children anything you don't want disclosed to them, try to resist the tendency to respond "tit for tat" because that will only make things worse for you and your family.

After the initial discussion, keep the door open to further talks by creating opportunities for your children to talk about the divorce. Use these times to acknowledge their feelings and offer support. Always assure them that the divorce is not their fault and that they are still loved by both you and your spouse, regardless of what happens. Please remember that your children may blame themselves for many reasons, so do your best to make sure that does not happen.

If appropriate, you should consider engaging a qualified therapist for a child, so they have a safe place to share their feelings. But make sure that the therapist is able to manage potential differences between you and your spouse and can protect your children from the conflict while still providing you with insights into the divorce process and the normal emotions that children must process.

Please remember that the purpose of therapy or counseling is to help children and adults make positive change and process complex and deeply held emotions and thoughts. Do not seek a licensed therapist only to have an ally against your spouse in court. That may backfire and would not help your children.

2.6   My youngest child seems depressed about the divorce, the middle one is angry, and my teenager is starting to skip school. How can I cope?

A child's reaction to divorce may vary depending upon his or her age and other factors. Some may cry and beg for reconciliation, and others may behave inappropriately or put themselves at risk. Reducing conflict with your spouse, being a consistent and nurturing parent, and making sure both of you remain involved with your children are all actions that can support them regardless of how they are reacting to the divorce.

Support groups for children whose parents are divorcing are available at many schools and religious communities. A school counselor or social worker can also provide support. If more help is needed, confer with a therapist experienced in working with children. In addition, you will find some links to support groups in the Resources section.

2.7   I am so frustrated by my spouse's *Disneyland parent* behavior. Is there anything I can do to stop this?

Feelings of guilt, competition, or remorse sometimes lead a parent to be tempted to spend parenting time in trips to the toy store and special activities. Other times these feelings can result in an absence of discipline in an effort to become the favored parent or to make the time *special*.

Shift your focus from the other parent's behavior to your own and do your best to be an outstanding parent during your time with your children. This includes keeping a routine for your children for family meals, bedtimes, chores, and homework. Encourage family activities, as well as individual time with each child, when it's possible.

During the time when a child's life is changing, providing a consistent and stable routine in your home can ease his or her anxiety and provide comfort.

2.8   Between requests for information from my spouse's lawyer and my own lawyer, I am totally overwhelmed. How do I manage gathering this detailed information by the deadlines imposed?

First, simply get started. Often the thought about a task is worse than the job itself.

Second, break it down into smaller tasks. Perhaps one evening you can gather your tax returns and on the weekend you can work on your monthly living expenses and bank statements.

Third, if you have a friend or family member you trust to respect your privacy, ask him or her to come over for an evening with a calculator to help you get organized.

Fourth, communicate with your lawyer. Your attorney or paralegal may be able to make your job easier by giving you suggestions or help. It may be that essential information can be provided now and details submitted later.

Finally, remember that these documents and any other information you provide should be as truthful as they can be. If you do not know the answer to a question or if you cannot find helpful information in this book or another resource, just tell your lawyer. You may be able to get an extension of time for a good reason, but a judge will not look kindly on a refusal to cooperate or a bending of the truth.

2.9   I am so depressed about my divorce that I'm having difficulty getting out of bed in the morning to care for my children. What should I do?

You should see your health-care provider immediately. Feelings of depression or sadness are common during a divorce. You also want to make sure that you identify any physical health concerns. Although feelings of sadness are common during a divorce, more serious depression requires professional support.

Your health and your ability to care for yourself and your children are both essential. Follow through on all recommendations by your health-care professionals for therapy, appropriate medication, or other measures to improve your wellness.

2.10   Will taking prescribed medication to help treat my insomnia or depression, for example, hurt my case?

Not necessarily. Talk to your health-care professional and follow their recommendations. Taking care of your health is of the utmost importance during this difficult time, and it will serve your best interest as well as the best interest of your children. Inform your attorney of any medications that you are taking or treatment that you are seeking. But also keep in mind that you must follow through with treatment. If you misuse medications or self-medicate with alcohol or drugs (legal or illegal), this can hurt you, your case, and your family so be transparent with your lawyer early in the case.

2.11   I know I need help to cope with the stress of the divorce, but I can't afford counseling. What can I do?

You are wise to recognize that divorce is a time for seeking support. Assuming you have no private or public health care available, you can explore a number of options, including:

- Meeting with a member of the clergy or lay chaplain

- Joining a divorce support group or, if appropriate, other groups provided, often for free, by your local domestic violence agency

- Turning to friends and family members who will respect your privacy

- Contacting a social service agency that offers counseling services on a sliding-fee scale

If none of these options are available, look again at your budget. You may see that counseling is important enough that you can find a way to increase your income or lower your expenses to support this investment in your well-being.

2.12   I'm the one who filed for divorce, but I still have loving feelings toward my spouse and feel sad about divorcing. Does this mean I should dismiss my divorce?

Strong feelings of caring about your spouse often persist after a divorce is filed. Whether or not to proceed with a divorce is a deeply personal decision. Although feelings can inform us of our thoughts, sometimes they can also cause us to not look at everything there is to see in our situation.

37

Have you and your spouse participated in marriage counseling? Has your spouse refused to seek treatment for an addiction? Are you worried about the safety of you or your children if you remain in the marriage? Can you envision yourself as financially secure if you remain in this marriage? Is your spouse involved in another relationship?

The answers to these questions can help you get clear about whether to consider reconciliation. Talk to your therapist or spiritual adviser to help determine the right path for you. On this point there is no easy answer, nor can anyone make that decision for you. What we can say is that it is important that you be sure this decision is what you want for the long term and that you have made a good-faith effort to work at your marriage.

2.13 Will my lawyer charge me for the time I spend talking with them about my feelings about my spouse and my divorce?

It depends. If you are paying your attorney by the hour, expect to be charged for the time your attorney spends talking with you, irrespective of the topic you choose to discuss. This is the reason you should always have a *written fee agreement* so you know what services may cost and what services you will be billed for. Carefully review your fee agreement so you are familiar with the billing terms. You do not want any surprises later.

2.14 My lawyer doesn't seem to realize how difficult my divorce is for me. How can I get him or her to understand?

Everyone wants support and compassion from the professionals who help them during a divorce. Speak frankly with your attorney about your concerns. It may be that your lawyer does not see your concerns as being relevant to their job of achieving your desired outcome in the divorce. Your willingness to improve communication will help your lawyer understand how best to support you in the process and will help you understand which matters are best left for discussion with your therapist or a supportive friend.

But also remember that lawyers are not trained therapists. They have to be careful not to take on that role or they could risk hurting you or their professional license. Sometimes what you are observing may simply be respect for you and not necessarily indifference to your feelings. Competent lawyers will have no problem talking about this with you, so you should ask rather than simply wonder about it or feel that you are not being heard.

2.15 I've been told not to speak ill of my spouse in front of my child, but I know my spouse is doing this all the time. Why can't I just speak the truth?

Let us begin with a simple fact. What parents in divorce believe is the truth may be more one-sided opinion than any truly objective story. It can be devastating for your child to hear you bad-mouthing the other parent. For children, few things can cause more long-term emotional and psychological harm than creating a loyalty conflict for that child. What your child needs is permission to love both of you, regardless of any poor parental behavior. The best way to support your child during this time is to encourage a positive relationship with the other parent.

If behaviors that are demeaning to you and harmful to your child continue, however, you may need to have your lawyer file a motion with the court for assistance. Under New Hampshire's *best-interest-of-the-child law,* a judge may consider these behaviors when allocating parenting time. We can tell you from many years of experience that lack of cooperation and behavior that demeans the other parent is something that judges will pay very careful attention to at a final hearing. In some extreme cases, these behaviors may even amount to a form of child or spousal abuse.

2.16 Nobody in our family has ever been divorced before, and I feel really ashamed. Will my children feel the same way?

Making a change in how you see your family identity is huge for you. The best way to help your children is to establish a sense of safety and stability so they can look forward to the future with a real sense of confidence. It is important to remember that children today have very different experiences with divorced families than they did thirty years ago. They see divorced couples on TV and in movies and they hear and read stories on social media. Often their biggest concerns are losing their family and friends, their house, or their room.

Sometimes that is a rational fear because it might be real, but sometimes it is what they are hearing or thinking and you may not know why they are scared. If you are not sure, ask the school counselor to talk with your children, or contact your church or other local agency for help. There are groups and parent education programs that can provide excellent resources to you and your children. But do not let this fester because children can be hurt by stress.

Your children will have an opportunity to witness you overcoming obstacles, demonstrating independence, and moving forward in your life notwithstanding challenges. You can be a great teacher to them during this time by demonstrating pride in your family and in yourself.

2.17 I am terrified of having my deposition taken. My spouse's lawyer is very aggressive, and I'm afraid I'm going to say something that will hurt my case. What can I do?

A *deposition* (like all the forms of discovery) is an opportunity for your spouse's attorney to gather information and to assess the type of witness you will be if the case proceeds to trial. A deposition is testimony given under oath, often at an attorney's office, which is then transcribed into written form of questions and answers and used in your case. Feeling anxious about your deposition is normal. However, regardless of the personality of the lawyers, most depositions in divorces are quite uneventful.

Think of it as an opportunity, and enlist your lawyer's support in being well prepared. Remember that your attorney will be seated by your side at all times to support you. Ask to meet with your lawyer in advance to prepare for the deposition. If you are worried about certain questions that might be asked, talk to your attorney about them. Be frank about your concerns. The deposition itself is not a good place to resolve surprises.

This advice is standard, but it is helpful to read it carefully so you may better understand the procedures before you arrive.

2.18 I am still so angry at my spouse. How can I be expected to sit in the same room during mediation or a settlement conference?

If you are still angry at your spouse, it may be beneficial to postpone the conference for a time. You might also consider seeking some counseling to help you cope with your feelings.

Another option might be *shuttle* negotiations. If you use this method, you and your attorney will remain in one room while your spouse and his or her attorney stay in another. The mediator or settlement judge then relays any settlement offers or ideas between attorneys throughout the negotiation process. By shifting your focus from your angry feelings to your goal of a settlement, it may be easier to proceed through the process.

In the end, a judge cannot help you feel better about those emotions; a judge can only enter orders concerning money or children. Clients sometimes find that frustrating because they want to feel that someone actually listened to how they were badly treated or harmed during the marriage.

2.19 I'm afraid I can't make it through the court process without having an emotional breakdown. How do I prepare?

A divorce trial can be a highly emotional time, calling for lots of support. Some of these ideas may help you through the process:

- Meet with your lawyer or the firm's support staff in advance of your court date to prepare you for court.

- Ask your lawyer whether there are any documents you should review in preparation for court, such as your deposition.

- Visit the courtroom in advance to get comfortable with the surroundings.

- Ask your lawyer about having a support person with you on your court date. This would be a person who should not be on either party's witness list.

- Ask yourself what the worst thing that could happen would be and consider what options you would have if it did.

- Avoid alcohol or non-prescription drug use, eat healthfully, exercise, and get plenty of rest during the period of time leading up to the court date. Each of these recommendations will help you to prepare for the emotions of the day.

- Plan what you intend to wear in advance. Small preparations made ahead of time will lower your stress.

- Visualize the experience going well. Picture yourself sitting in the witness chair and giving clear, confident, and truthful answers to easy questions.

- Arrive early to the courthouse and make sure you have a plan for parking your car if you are not familiar with the area.

- Take slow, deep breaths. Breathing deeply will steady your voice, calm your nerves, and improve your focus.

Your attorney will be prepared to support you throughout the proceedings. By taking these steps, you can increase the ease of your experience.

2.20   I am so confused. One day I think divorce is a mistake, the next day I know I can't go back, and later I can hardly wait to be single. What's happening?

Denial, transition, and acceptance are common passages for a person going through a divorce. One moment you might feel excited about your future, and a few hours later you think your life is ruined.

What can be helpful to remember is that you may not pass from one stage to the next in a direct line. Feelings of anger or sadness may well up in you long after you thought you had moved on. Similarly, your mood might feel bright one day as you think about your future plans, even though you still miss your spouse.

Taking good care of yourself is essential during this period of your life. What you are going through requires a tremendous amount of energy. Allow yourself to experience your emotions, but also continue moving forward with your life. These steps will help your life get easier day by day.

3

Working with Your Attorney

If there is one thing you can be sure of in your divorce, it is that you will be given plenty of advice. Well-intentioned neighbors, cousins, siblings, adult parents, grandparents, stepfamily members, therapeutic professionals, spiritual advisers, and even complete strangers will be happy to tell you war stories about their ex or about their sister who got divorced in Canada. Many will insist they know what you should do, even though they know nothing about the facts of your case or the law in New Hampshire.

But there is one person whose advice should matter most to you: your attorney. Your lawyer should be your trusted and supportive advocate at all times throughout your divorce. The counsel, skill, and loyalty of your attorney can affect your life for years to come. Therefore, you should take the time and energy to choose the right one for you.

You should see your relationship with your attorney as a partnership for pursuing what is most important to you. With clear and open attorney-client communication, you will gain the best outcome possible and your entire divorce will be less stressful.

One last but rather important cautionary reminder, however. Lawyers are not licensed clinicians or therapists. They are not trained to do more than listen carefully and advocate for you within the ethical and legal rules that pertain to divorce. You cannot ask your lawyer to do anything unethical, like hide documents or assets, or use your children as leverage to gain an advantage for money. Good lawyers will tell you what they cannot do as much as tell you what they can do in your case.

Pay very careful attention to the behavior of your lawyer. If you believe that your representation is more about a battle between lawyers, with lots of letter writing and name-calling, then think carefully about whether this lawyer is properly representing you, or is he or she hurting your family. Once again, your lawyer works for you but is bound by law and ethical duty, so you have to be a partner who expects dignity and honesty from your lawyer and yourself, no matter the behavior of your spouse or the other lawyer.

3.1 Where do I begin looking for an attorney for my divorce?

There are many ways to find a divorce attorney. Ask people you trust—friends and family members who have gone through a divorce—if they thought they had a good lawyer (or if their former spouse did!). If you know professionals who work with attorneys, ask for a referral to one who is experienced in family law.

Consult your local bar association or the state bar association to find out whether they have a referral service. Be sure to specify that you are looking for an attorney who handles divorces.

Go online. Many attorneys have websites that provide information on their areas of practice, professional associations, experience, and philosophy.

Check out organizations like the International or American Academy of Matrimonial Lawyers, as well as the Family Law Section of the New Hampshire Bar Association. Contact information is in the Resources section.

Ask therapists, mediators, or other local professionals who they think has integrity and competence in this field.

3.2 How do I choose the right attorney?

Choosing the right attorney for your divorce is an important and complex decision. Your attorney should be a trusted professional with whom you feel comfortable sharing information openly. He or she should be a person you can trust and an intelligent and efficient advocate for your interests. However, there is one warning or caveat you should consider: Do not confuse posturing or promises made in a lawyer's office with intelligent and effective advocacy. You will rely upon your attorney to help you make many decisions throughout your divorce. You will also entrust your legal counsel to make a range of strategic and procedural decisions on your behalf.

The best lawyers will not tell you what you want to hear, but what you need to hear about the legal process and the range of potential outcomes. A promise of certainty or derogatory references about your spouse or the other lawyer should cause you to stop and reflect—really stop and reflect—about whether this is the right lawyer for you.

The initial consultation for a divorce might be your first meeting with a lawyer. Know that attorneys want to be supportive and fully inform you of what they know. Feel free to seek all of the information you need to help you feel secure in knowing you have made the right choice.

Find an attorney who practices primarily in the family law area. Although many attorneys handle divorces, it is likely you will have more effective representation at a lower cost from an attorney who already knows the fundamentals of divorce law and procedure in New Hampshire.

Also, determine the level of experience you want in your attorney. For example, if you have had a short marriage, no children, and few assets, an attorney with lesser experience might be a good value for your legal needs. However, if you are anticipating a parental rights dispute or have complex or substantial assets, a more experienced attorney might better meet your needs.

Consider the qualities in an attorney that are important to you. Even the most experienced and skilled attorney is not right for every person. Ask yourself what you are really looking for in an attorney so that you can make your choice with these standards in mind.

It is important that you be confident in the attorney you hire. If you're unsure about whether the lawyer is really listening to you or understanding your concerns, keep looking until you find one who will. Your divorce is a very important matter. It's critical that you have a professional you can trust and with whom you have rapport.

3.3   Should I hire a *bulldog* —a very aggressive attorney?

Again, consider the qualities in an attorney that are important to you. A *bulldog* or *bomb thrower* may promise to be overly aggressive and take your spouse for *everything* he or she is worth (which, by the way, may not actually be much net after paying legal fees if you go in this direction).

However, it may be important to you to create a mutually respectful relationship with your spouse during and after the divorce, especially if there are minor children involved.

Additionally, expect the cost of your divorce to increase exponentially if your attorney is unwilling to negotiate and drags your spouse into court at every opportunity. Look for a lawyer who can represent you while at the same time maintaining a high level of courtesy, professionalism, and integrity.

Ask yourself a simple question: Would this lawyer give the same advice if he or she was representing my spouse? Good, ethical lawyers do not change the integrity of their advice because of who the client is. The law is the same, and the facts are usually not that different. Advocacy may mean different things for different clients, like who may pay spousal or child support, but integrity and the law do not change according to the client. So if you were on the other side, how would you like the way your lawyer is behaving?

3.4   Should I interview more than one attorney?

Be willing to interview more than one attorney. Every lawyer has different strengths, and it is important to find the one that is right for you. Sometimes it is only by meeting with more than one attorney that you can see clearly who is best able to help you reach your goals in the way you want.

Changing lawyers in the middle of litigation can be stressful and costly. It is wise to invest energy at the outset in making the right choice. This does not mean you may not change lawyers later, but you should at least make the first decision as carefully and as well informed as you can be at the time.

3.5   My spouse says because we're still friends we should use the same attorney for the divorce. Is this a good idea?

Even the most amicable of divorcing couples usually have differing interests. For this reason, it is never recommended that an attorney represent both parties to a divorce. In most cases, an attorney is ethically prohibited from representing two people with conflicting interests who are in dispute.

Sometimes, couples have reached agreements without understanding all of their rights under the law, or, worse, without knowing that they may incur tax consequences or lose valuable rights like survivorship benefits in a pension or health insurance coverage. You will always benefit from receiving further legal advice on matters such as tax considerations, retirement options, and health insurance issues.

It is not uncommon for one party to retain an attorney and for the other party not to do so. In such cases, the party with the attorney prepares the petition, and agreements reached between the parties are typically sent to the spouse for approval and signing. If your spouse has filed for divorce and said that you do not need an attorney, you should nevertheless meet with a lawyer for advice on how proceeding without a lawyer could affect your legal rights.

3.6   What is *unbundling* or *limited representation* and how is it used?

Lawyers must follow specific rules of disclosure in a fee agreement or engagement letter under the New Hampshire Rules of Professional Conduct. For example, *limited representation* or *unbundling* is an ethical way for a lawyer to help you with a part of your case but not the whole case. The lawyer must provide you with a specific written fee agreement that clearly identifies the terms of representation. If you do not receive such a fee agreement, you should ask the lawyer you have met with to send it to you to review.

With unbundling, you can hire a lawyer to review your settlement documents and assist you with negotiations and drafting, but that lawyer may not represent you in court. Or a lawyer may represent you at a temporary hearing but not at the final trial. But be very careful. Some clients who have not clearly understood what unbundling meant found themselves on the eve of trial without a lawyer because they thought the lawyer was representing them with the whole case and this was not true. Also, having a lawyer jump in and out of a case can be challenging for the lawyer to "catch up" to where things are. It is helpful to be organized and keep all documents in your court case to save your attorney time and save you money.

When done properly, unbundling can save you money, but be sure that you know what you are specifically hiring the lawyer to do and what you are *not* hiring the lawyer to do.

3.7 What information should I take with me to the first meeting with my attorney?

Attorneys differ on the amount of information they like to see at an initial consultation. If a court proceeding, either for a divorce or for a restraining order, has already been initiated by either you or your spouse, it is important to take copies of any court documents, such as the following:

- If you have a prenuptial or postnuptial agreement with your spouse, that is another important document for you to bring at the outset of your case.

- If you intend to ask for support, either for yourself or for your children, documents evidencing income of both you and your spouse will also be useful. These might include:

  - Recent pay stubs
  - Individual and business tax returns, W-2s, and 1099s
  - Bank statements showing deposits
  - A statement of your monthly budget

Your attorney may ask you to complete a questionnaire at the time of your first meeting. Ask whether it is possible to do this in advance of your meeting. This can allow you to provide more complete information and to make the most of your appointment time with the lawyer.

If your situation is urgent or you do not have access to these documents, don't let it stop you from scheduling your appointment with an attorney. Prompt legal advice about your rights is often more important than having detailed financial information at the beginning. Your attorney can explain to you your options for obtaining these financial records if they are not readily available to you.

3.8 What unfamiliar words might an attorney use at the first meeting?

The law has a language all its own, and attorneys sometimes lapse into *legalese,* forgetting that nonlawyers may not recognize words used daily in the practice of law. Some words and phrases you might hear include:

- *Dissolution of marriage*—the divorce
- *Petitioner*—the person who files the divorce petition
- *Respondent*—the person who did not file the divorce petition
- *Jurisdiction*—the authority of a court to make rulings affecting a party or children
- *Service*—the process of officially notifying a party about a legal filing
- *Discovery*—the formal process for sharing information
- *Interrogatories*—a part of discovery, where questions are answered under oath in writing to the other party
- *Deposition*—a part of discovery, where questions are answered under oath and the words are transcribed onto a transcript
- *Decree*—the final order entered in a divorce case

Never hesitate to ask your attorney the meaning of a term. Your complete understanding of your lawyer's advice is essential for you to partner with your advocate as effectively and efficiently as possible.

3.9 What can I expect at an initial consultation with an attorney?

Most attorneys will ask you to complete a questionnaire prior to the meeting. With few exceptions, attorneys are required to keep confidential all information you provide.

The nature of the advice you get from an attorney at an initial consultation will depend upon whether you are still deciding whether you want a divorce, whether you are planning for a possible divorce in the future, or whether you are ready to file for divorce right away. During the meeting, you should expect to provide the following information:

- A brief history of the marriage
- Background information regarding yourself, your spouse, and your children
- Your immediate situation
- Your intentions and goals regarding your relationship with your spouse
- What information you are seeking from the attorney during the consultation

You can expect the attorney to identify the following information to you:

- The procedure for divorce in New Hampshire, including timelines
- The issues important in your case
- A preliminary assessment of your rights and responsibilities under the law
- Background information regarding the firm and counsel
- Information about fees and filings

Although some questions may be impossible for the attorney to answer at the initial consultation because additional information or research is needed, the initial consultation is nevertheless an opportunity for you to ask all the questions you have at the time of the meeting.

3.10 Will the communication with my attorney be confidential?

Yes. Your lawyer has an ethical duty to maintain your *confidentiality,* which is often referred to as the *attorney-client privilege.* This duty of confidentiality also extends to the legal staff working with your attorney. The privileged information that you share with your attorney will remain private and confidential, unless such privilege is waived by voluntarily disclosing it to third parties.

Just to be very clear, however: Confidentiality, or the attorney-client privilege, *relies on you as well as your lawyer.* If you decide to tell people what you talked about with your lawyer, share e-mails or correspondence from your lawyer, post his or her advice on your Facebook page, or tweet it on your Twitter account, you have waived that confidentiality as well as some or all of your attorney-client privilege. Be very careful with all information from your lawyer during your case so as not to break the privilege.

3.11 Is there any way that I could accidentally waive the attorney-client privilege?

Yes, there is. To ensure that communications between you and your attorney remain confidential, and to protect against the voluntary or involuntary waiver of your attorney-client privilege, the following are some tips:

- Refrain from disclosing the content of communications with your attorney, or discussing in substantive detail those communications with third parties, which include friends, personal relationships, coworkers, or family members.

- If you decide to date during your divorce and that relationship does not last, your private information may find its way into the hands of your spouse if that person is angry at you later. This really does happen!

- Social media provides the potential for waiving the attorney-client privilege by your publicly disclosing confidential information. Do not post information or send messages relating to your case or communications with your attorney on Facebook, Twitter, a personal or video blog, in online chat rooms, on online message boards, or any other social media websites.

- Do not use your work-related e-mail account to communicate with your attorney or to discuss your case.

- Depending upon your employer's policy relating to electronic communication, the attorney-client privilege may be waived by communicating with your attorney or by discussing your case even through your personal e-mail account if it is done on a company computer. To ensure your communications remain confidential, it is best to communicate via e-mail only from your private e-mail address from your home computer or personal device.

3.12 Can I take a friend of family member to my initial consultation with an attorney?

Yes. Having someone with you during your initial consultation can be a source of great support. You might ask him or her to take notes on your behalf so that you can focus on listening and asking questions. However, remember that this is your consultation, and it is important that an attorney hears the facts of your case directly from you. Also, ask your attorney how having a friend or relative with you could impact the confidentiality of the attorney-client privilege.

3.13 What exactly will my attorney do to help me get a divorce?

Your attorney will play a critical role in helping you get your divorce. You will be actively involved in some of the work, while other actions will be taken behind the scenes at the law office or the courthouse, such as the following:

- Assess the situation to determine which court has jurisdiction to hear your case.
- Develop a strategy for advising you about all aspects of your divorce, including the treatment of assets and matters concerning children.
- Prepare legal documents for filing with the court.
- Conduct discovery to obtain information from the other party, which could include depositions, requests for production of documents, and written interrogatories.
- Appear with you at all court appearances, depositions, and conferences.
- Schedule all deadlines and court appearances.
- Support you in responding to information requests from your spouse.
- Inform you of actions you are required to take.

- Perform financial analyses of your case.

- Conduct legal research.

- Prepare you for court appearances and depositions.

- Prepare your case for hearings and trial, including preparing proposed documents and exhibits and interviewing witnesses.

- Advise you regarding your rights under the law.

- Counsel you regarding the risks and benefits of negotiated settlement as compared to proceeding to trial.

As your advocate, your attorney is entrusted to take steps necessary to represent your interests in the divorce. But keep in mind that you need to assess the costs and benefits of some strategies, so before you make a decision be careful to ask how much it will cost and what the benefits may be. No client likes surprise costs.

3.14 What professionals should I expect to work with during my divorce?

Depending upon the issues identified by your attorney, you can expect to work with various types of professionals, such as appraisers, financial professionals, real estate agents, and mental health experts.

Additionally, in some cases where parental rights or parenting time issues are seriously disputed, the court may appoint a *guardian ad litem (GAL)*. This person, who may be a lawyer or other licensed professional in New Hampshire, has the duty to represent recommendations about what is in the best interest of a child; this information should be presented both orally and in a written report. A guardian *ad litem* has the responsibility to investigate both you and your spouse as well as the needs and desires of your child. The GAL may then be called as a witness at trial to testify regarding any relevant observations. You will find some helpful contacts in the Resources at the end of this book that will provide important information concerning the benefits and consequences of a GAL.

Another expert who could be appointed by the court is a psychologist. The role of the psychologist depends upon the purpose for which she or he was appointed. For example, the psychologist may be appointed to perform a *family systems evaluation,* which involves assessing both parents and the children. Or, the expert may be ordered to evaluate just one parent to assess the child's safety while spending time with that parent.

3.15 I've been divorced before and I don't think I need an attorney this time, but my spouse is hiring one. Is it wise to go it alone?

Having gone through a prior divorce, it's likely that you have learned a great deal about the divorce process as well as your legal rights. However, there are many reasons why you should be extremely cautious about proceeding without legal representation.

It is important to remember that every divorce is different. The length of the marriage, whether there are children, the relative financial situation for you and your spouse, as well as your age and health can all affect the financial outcome in your divorce.

The law may also have changed since your last divorce. Some aspects of divorce law are likely to change each year. New laws get passed and new decisions get handed down by the New Hampshire Supreme Court, which affect the rights and responsibilities of people who divorce, including the support and parenting responsibilities for minor children. The New Hampshire Legislature may have also amended the law in ways that are very different from the law during your first divorce.

In some cases, the involvement of your lawyer could be minimal. This might be the case if your marriage was short, your financial situation is very similar to that of your spouse, there are no children, and the two of you remain amicable. At a minimum, however, an initial consultation with an attorney to discuss your rights and having an attorney review any final agreement is advisable.

3.16 Can I take my children to meetings with my attorney?

It is best to make other arrangements for your children when you meet with your attorney. Your attorney will be giving you a great deal of important information during your conferences, and it will benefit you to give your full attention to the process. You should be very wary of any lawyer who suggests you bring your children to meet with them. This can influence your case and may annoy a judge or other parent. Be careful.

It is also recommended that you take every measure to keep information about the legal aspects of your divorce away from your children. Knowledge that you are seeing an attorney can add to your child's anxiety about the process. It can also make your child a target for questioning by the other parent about your contact with your attorney.

Most law offices are not designed to accommodate young children; they are ordinarily not "childproof". For both your child's well-being and your own peace of mind, explore options for someone to care for your child when you have nonemergency meetings with your attorney.

3.17   What is the role of the *paralegal* or *legal assistant?*

A *paralegal,* or *legal assistant,* is a trained legal professional whose duties include providing support for you and your lawyer. Working with a paralegal can make your divorce more efficient because he or she is likely to be much more available than your attorney to help you with many matters. It can also lower your legal costs, as the hourly rate for paralegal services is less than the rate for attorneys.

A paralegal is prohibited from giving legal advice. It is important that you respect the limits of the role of the paralegal if he or she is unable to answer your questions because they call for giving a legal opinion. However, a paralegal can answer many questions and provide a great deal of information to you throughout your divorce.

Paralegals can help you by receiving information from you, reviewing documents with you, providing you with updates on your case, and answering any questions about the divorce process that do not call for specific legal advice.

3.18   My attorney is not returning my phone calls or e-mails. What can I do?

You have a right to expect your phone calls or e-mails to be returned by your lawyer in a timely manner. Here are some options to consider:

- Ask to speak to the paralegal or assistant in the office.

- Send an e-mail or fax telling your lawyer that you have been trying to reach him or her by phone and explaining the reason it is important that you receive a return call promptly.

- Ask the receptionist or assistant to schedule a phone conference for you to speak with your attorney at a specific date and time.

- Schedule a face-to-face meeting with your attorney to discuss both the issue needing attention as well as your concerns about their communication.

Your attorney wants to provide good service to you. If your calls are not being returned, take action to get the communication with your lawyer back on track. Often there is a reasonable explanation, such as being tied up at a family emergency or a trial appearance, but you are still entitled to an answer when these situations arise. Please remember to be polite. The staff at family law firms is trained to help, but they are also employees and cannot make decisions without the authority of the lawyer.

3.19   How do I know when it's time to change lawyers?

Changing lawyers is costly. You will incur legal fees for your new attorney to review information that is already familiar to your current attorney. You will spend time giving much of the same information to your new lawyer that you gave to the one you have discharged. A change in lawyers may also result in delays in the divorce.

The following are questions to ask yourself when deciding whether to stay with your attorney or seek new counsel:

- Have I spoken directly to my attorney about my concerns?

- When I expressed concerns, did my lawyer take action accordingly?

- Is my lawyer open and receptive to what I have to say?

- Am I blaming my lawyer for the bad behavior of my spouse or opposing counsel?

- Have I provided my lawyer with the information needed for taking the next action?

- Does my lawyer have control over the complaints I have, or are they controlled by the law or the judge?

- Is my lawyer keeping promises made for completing action on my case?

- Do I trust my lawyer?

- What would be the advantages of changing lawyers when compared to the cost?

- Do I believe my lawyer will support me to achieve the outcome I'm seeking in my divorce?

Every effort should be made to resolve concerns with your attorney. If you have made this effort and the situation remains unchanged, it may be time to change lawyers. Interview carefully and make sure that you have a good fit with the new lawyer, as well as learn what the anticipated cost will be for him or her to read and understand your file. In family law, more than any other area of the practice of law, clients often change lawyers, so this is not unusual.

3.20   Are there any expectations that I should have when working with my legal team?

Yes, your legal team should be able to provide you with support and guidance during the divorce process. There are certain actions you can expect your legal team to do for you during your divorce. A list of some of them follows.

Meet with you prior to the filing of a court action to advise you on actions you should take first. There may be important steps to take before you initiate the legal process. Your legal team can support you to be well prepared prior to initiating divorce.

Take action to obtain a temporary court order or to enforce existing orders. Temporary court orders are often needed to ensure clarity regarding rights and responsibilities while your divorce is pending. Your legal team can help you obtain a temporary order and ask the court to enforce its orders if there is a violation.

Explain the legal process during each step of your case. Understanding the legal process reduces the stress of your divorce.

Listen to your concerns and answer any questions. Although only the attorneys can give you legal advice, everyone on your team should be available to listen, to provide support, and to direct you to the right person who can help.

Support you in developing your parenting plan. Many parents do not know how to decide what type of parenting plan is best for their children. Your legal team can help you look at the needs of your children and offer advice based on their experience in working with families.

Support you with the completion of your discovery responses and preparing for depositions. The discovery process can be overwhelming for anyone. You will be asked to provide detailed information and many documents. Your legal team can make this job easier. Just ask. If your case involves depositions, your legal team will support you to be fully prepared for the experience.

Identify important issues, analyze the evidence, and advise you. Divorce is complex. Often there is a great deal of uncertainty. Your legal team can analyze the unique facts of your case and help you make efficient and cost-effective decisions based upon the law and their expertise.

Communicate with the opposing party's attorney to try to resolve issues without going to court, and to keep your case progressing. Although your attorney cannot control the actions of the opposing party or their lawyer, your attorney can always initiate communication as your advocate. Phoning, e-mailing, or writing to opposing counsel are actions your legal team can take to encourage cooperation and to keep your divorce moving forward at the pace you want without the expense of contested litigation.

Think creatively regarding challenges with your case and provide options for your consideration. At the outset, you may see many obstacles to reaching a final resolution. Your legal team can offer creative ideas for resolving challenges and help you to explore your options to achieve the best possible outcome.

Facilitate the settlement process. Although your legal team can never make the other party settle, your attorney can take actions that promote an environment for settlement by preparing settlement proposals, inviting settlement conferences, and negotiating rationally and realistically on your behalf.

Send you copies of all data relevant to your case. Your lawyer should promptly send you copies of all pleadings, orders, documents, or electronic or paper communications of any kind concerning your case (unless there is a court order forbidding the lawyer to do so, such as with psychiatric records).

3.21 Are there certain things my legal team will not be able to do?

Yes—and this is actually a very important set of things for you to know. Although there are many ways your legal team can support you during your divorce, there are also things your legal team will not be able to accomplish. A list of some of them follows:

Force the other parent to exercise their parenting time. Your lawyer cannot force a parent to exercise parenting time. However, be mindful that chronic neglect of parenting time may be a basis for modifying your parenting plan later. Tell your attorney if the other parent is repeatedly failing to exercise their parenting time.

Force the other party to respond to a settlement proposal. Your attorney may send proposals or make requests to opposing counsel; however, there is no duty for them to respond. After repeated follow-ups without a response, it may be clear no response is coming. This may be the decision of your spouse or the other lawyer. Some lawyers are slow to tell their clients about proposals. Your attorney will decide whether the issues merit court action. Both parties must agree on all terms for a case to be settled without a trial. If one party wants to proceed to trial, even over a single issue, he/she will be able to do so.

Communicate with your spouse directly. Clients often ask about this. Your lawyer cannot speak with your spouse if he or she is represented by a lawyer. This is unethical conduct and could get the lawyer sanctioned. (And the reverse is also true: Your spouse's lawyer can't speak with you.) You can communicate directly with your spouse, but you need to be very careful.

Control the tone of communication from opposing counsel or communications from the other party, or their family members. Unfortunately, communication from the opposing attorney may sometimes appear rude, condescending, or demanding. Your legal team cannot stop an attorney from using these tactics. Absent a pattern of harassment, your lawyer also cannot stop the other party or third parties from contacting you. If you do not want this type of contact, talk with your attorney about how to best handle the situation. Of course, appropriate communication regarding your children is always encouraged.

Ask the court to compensate you for every wrong done to you by the other party over the course of your marriage. Although your attorney will empathize with valid complaints, please understand that focusing on the most important issues may better yield the best and most cost-effective outcome in the end. Raising numerous small issues may distract from your most important goals—and increase your bill dramatically.

Remedy poor financial decisions made during the marriage. With few exceptions, the court's duty is to divide the marital estate and income as it currently exists. The judge will not attempt to remedy all past financial wrongs, such as overspending or poor investments by your spouse. If there is significant debt, consult with a debt counselor or bankruptcy lawyer. Fraudulent decisions about money or assets are not the same in the eyes of the law as poor business decisions or unpredictable shifts in the economy. This is often quite sad, but irreversible. Courts and the lawyers cannot go back in time and fix economic or parenting decisions from the past.

Control how the other party parents your children during his/her parenting time. Each parent has strengths and weaknesses. Absent special needs of a child, most judges will not issue orders regarding bedtimes, number of hours spent watching TV or playing video games, discipline methods, clothing, or diet. Of course, any suspected abuse should be reported immediately to the appropriate authorities.

Demand an accounting of how a parent uses court-ordered child support. Absent extraordinary circumstances, the court will not order the other parent to provide an accounting for the use of child support. This is the law as it currently exists.

Leverage money for rights regarding your children. Tactics oriented toward asserting parental rights as leverage toward attaining financial goals will be discouraged. Your lawyer should negotiate parenting issues based solely on considerations related to your child, then separately negotiate child support based on financial considerations. Nevertheless, this type of behavior does take place, so be prepared to stop it at the earliest stages of your case.

Guarantee payment of child support and spousal support. Enforcement of payment of support is only possible when it is court ordered. However, even with a court order, you may experience inconsistent timing of payments due to job loss, refusal to pay, or bad faith. Talk with your attorney if a pattern of repeated missed payments has developed. But getting a court order is much different from collecting the money under the court order.

Collect child care and uninsured medical expenses if provisions of the order are not complied with. If your order requires you to provide documentation of payment of expenses to the other party and you fail to, you could be prohibited from collecting reimbursement for those expenses. Follow the court's orders regarding documentation to the other parent, even if they do not pay. Always keep records of these expenses and payments, and keep copies of any communication with the other parent regarding payment/reimbursement. It is much easier to keep these records on an ongoing basis than to get copies of old checks, day-care bills, medical bills, and insurance documents later.

4

Attorney Fees and Litigation Costs

Any time you make a major investment, you usually want to know what the cost is going to be and what you are getting for your money. Investing in quality legal representation for your divorce is no different.

The cost of your divorce might be one of your greatest concerns. Because of this, you will want to be an intelligent consumer of legal services. You want quality, but you also want to get the best value for the fees you are paying.

Legal fees for a divorce can be costly and the total expense not always predictable. But there are many actions you can take to control and estimate the cost. Develop a plan early on for how you will finance your divorce. Speak openly with your lawyer about fees from the outset. Learn as much as you can about how you will be charged.

Most importantly: *Insist on a written fee agreement.* If you are hiring a lawyer for a flat fee, the agreement should be very specific as to what is included and what is not for the services. If you are negotiating an hourly rate, then the rate and terms for billing should be explicit and written in a language you can understand.

Unless there are very unusual circumstances, never hire a lawyer who does not use written fee agreements. By being informed, aware, and wise, your financial investment in your divorce will be money well spent to protect your future.

4.1 Can I get free legal advice from a lawyer over the phone?

Every law firm and state bar association has its own policy regarding lawyers talking to people who are not yet clients of the firm. Most questions about your divorce are too complex for a lawyer to respond to with a meaningful answer during a brief phone call.

Questions about your divorce require a complete look at the facts, circumstances, and background of your marriage. To obtain good legal advice, it really is best to schedule an initial consultation with a lawyer who handles divorces.

4.2 Will I be charged for an initial consultation with a lawyer?

It depends. Some lawyers offer free consultations, while others charge a fee. When scheduling your appointment, you should be told the amount of the fee. Payment is ordinarily due at the time of the consultation.

Some lawyers use a small fee like $200 as a way to screen people who are just shopping around for advice but never intend to hire a lawyer or are trying to create a conflict of interest so a lawyer cannot take the case on behalf of their spouse. In small communities this can be a problem, so the fee is intended to screen serious potential clients from those who are not.

Just remember that you are hiring a professional, so a small fee is often a sign of the seriousness of the lawyer about his or her craft.

4.3 If I decide to hire an attorney, when must I pay him or her?

If your attorney charges for an initial consultation, be prepared to make that payment at the time of your meeting. At the close of your consultation, the attorney may tell you the amount of the retainer needed by the law firm to handle your divorce. However, you are not expected to pay the retainer at the time of your first meeting. Rather, the retainer is paid after you have decided to hire the lawyer, the lawyer has accepted your case, you are ready to proceed, and you have signed a written fee agreement.

4.4   What exactly is a *retainer,* and how much should it be?

A *retainer* is a sum paid to your lawyer in advance for services to be performed and costs to be incurred in your divorce. It is customary for family law attorneys to request a retainer, also known as a *fee advance,* prior to beginning work on your case.

This will be either an amount paid toward a flat fee for your divorce, or an advance credit for services that will be charged by the hour. Be sure to ask your attorney what portion, if any, of the retainer is refundable if you do not continue with the case or if you terminate your relationship with the attorney.

If your case is accepted, you should expect the attorney to request a retainer. The amount of the retainer may vary from hundreds of dollars to several thousand dollars or more depending upon the nature of your case. Parenting cases, divorces involving businesses, or high-conflict disputes, for example, are all likely to require higher retainers. Other factors that can affect the amount of the retainer include the nature and number of the disputed issues between you and your spouse.

4.5   Will my attorney accept my divorce case on a contingency-fee basis?

No. A *contingency fee* is one that only becomes payable if your case is successful. In New Hampshire, lawyers are prohibited from entering into a contingent fee contract in any divorce case. Your lawyer may not accept payment based upon securing your divorce, the amount of spousal support or support awarded, or the division of the property settlement. On rare occasions, attorneys may agree to await receipt of payment in full until an asset is divided or a court orders attorneys fees be paid. This is entirely up to an attorney's discretion and not all attorneys are able to offer this option to clients.

4.6   How much does it cost to get a divorce, including expert witnesses?

It is important that your discussion of the cost of your divorce begin at your first meeting with your attorney. The cost of your divorce depends upon many factors, including the behavior of the parties, the influence of third parties, the complexity of tax and valuation issues, the willingness of the parents to co-parent, the presence of alcohol or substance abuse issues, mental health of one or both parties, the willingness of parties to settle personal property and debts collaboratively, and participation in mediation or other dispute resolution methods without lawyers or in collaboration with lawyers.

Please remember, however, that you are only half of the equation. You or your spouse may elect to litigate every point at great expense, so you want to be careful and selective about the things that really matter to you.

Finally, it is important to have a discussion about any experts you may need for your case, such as a *forensic accountant,* clinical or forensic psychologist, guardian *ad litem,* real estate appraiser, or other professionals required to help with obtaining factual or opinion evidence for your case. Most of the time, these costs will be paid separately by you or from some other marital funds or sources and not from the retainer. Sometimes, divorcing couples cooperate with experts and sometimes they do not. There are important tactical considerations for that choice.

Lawyers cannot always predict what experts are needed. For example, a client may tell us that she is confident the tax returns honestly reflect all income, but we then learn that there is a significant difference in expenses billed to the family business. These types of expenses can reduce the income of the business that is available to pay support or reduce the fair market value of the business if a valuation is done later.

4.7 What are typical hourly rates for a divorce lawyer?

Some attorneys perform divorces for a flat fee, but most charge by the hour. A *flat fee* is a fixed amount for the legal services being provided. A flat fee is more likely to be used when there are no children of the marriage and the parties have agreed upon the division of their property and debts.

In New Hampshire, attorneys who practice divorce law charge from $150 per hour to more than twice that rate. Paralegals may charge at a rate of $60 and up. The rate your attorney charges may depend upon factors such as skills, reputation, experience, exclusive focus on divorce law, and what other attorneys in the area are charging. An hourly rate typically means that the lawyer will charge based upon increments of one-tenths of an hour. Often this may mean at least two-tenths whenever you call your lawyer, so be sure to ask.

The most important point is not the hourly rate *by itself,* but the efficiency of the lawyer. For example:

- Are you charged for multiple lawyers looking at some point of law?

- Does the lawyer engage in expensive letter-writing campaigns with the other lawyer at no gain to your case?

- Does the lawyer write clear responses to court motions and objections in a few pages (unless the issue is complex, of course)?

- Does the lawyer make good use of form pleadings and documents, and how are you charged for that kind of work?

- Do the bills make sense to you when you are given copies of the work?

If you have a concern about an attorney's hourly rate, but you would like to hire the firm with which the attorney is associated, consider asking to work with an associate attorney in the firm, who is likely to charge a lower rate. Associates are attorneys who ordinarily have less experience than the senior partners. However, they often are trained by the senior partners, are still very experienced, and are very likely fully capable of handling your case.

4.8   If I can't afford to pay the full amount of the retainer, can I make monthly payments to my attorney?

Every law firm has its own policies regarding payment arrangements for divorce clients. Often these arrangements are tailored to the specific client. Most attorneys will require a retainer to be paid at the outset of your case. Some attorneys may accept monthly payments in lieu of the retainer. Most will require monthly payments in addition to the initial retainer, or request additional retainers as your case progresses.

Ask frank questions of your attorney about your responsibility for payment of legal fees. You have the right to not hire the lawyer, but once you sign the fee agreement, that is a binding contract so make sure you can meet those obligations.

4.9 I agreed to pay my attorney a substantial retainer. Will I still have to make monthly payments?

Ask your attorney what will be expected of you regarding payments on your account while the divorce is in progress. Clarify whether monthly payments on your account are expected, whether it is likely that you will be asked to pay additional retainers, and whether the firm charges interest on past-due accounts. Regular payments to your attorney can help you avoid a burdensome legal bill at the end of your case.

Additionally, you may also be required to keep a minimum credit balance in your account to ensure your case is adequately funded for ongoing work by your legal team. Just be clear at the beginning and pay attention to what is going on in your case. Many law firms accept credit cards, but you should also discuss that with your lawyer.

4.10 My lawyer gave me an estimate of the cost of my divorce and it sounds reasonable. Do I still need a *written fee agreement?*

Absolutely. Insist upon a *written fee agreement* with your attorney, and do not hire any lawyer who will not give you one, even if it is just a letter confirming the terms of the agreement for you to sign. This is essential not only to define the scope of the legal services but also to ensure that you are clear about matters such as your attorney's hourly rate, whether you will be billed for certain costs such as copying and travel, and when and how you can expect to receive statements on your account.

A clear fee agreement written in plain English reduces the risk of misunderstandings between you and your lawyer so you can both focus on the legal services rather than on disputes about your fees.

4.11 How will I know how the fees and charges are accumulating?

Be sure your written fee agreement is completely clear about how you will be informed regarding the status of your account. If your attorney agrees to handle your divorce for a flat fee, your fee agreement should clearly set forth what is included in the fee. If it is an hourly rate, then be sure your written fee agreement includes a provision for the attorney to provide you with regular statements of your account.

It is reasonable to ask that these statements be provided monthly. Review the statement of your account promptly after you receive it. Check to make sure there are no errors, such as duplicate billing entries or copying costs that seem too high for what you received in the mail. This happens with any business making hundreds of data entries a month so it is often an honest mistake.

If your statement reflects errors or work that you were unaware was performed, call for clarification. Your attorney's office should welcome any questions you have about the services it provided. By doing this each month, you should avoid surprises concerning fees.

Your statement might also include filing fees, court reporter fees for transcripts of court testimony or depositions, copy expenses, or interest charged on your account, for example. If a month passes and you have not received a statement on your account, call your attorney's office manager or billing person to request one. Legal fees can mount quickly, and it is important that you stay aware of the status of your expenses.

4.12 What other expenses are related to the divorce litigation besides lawyer fees?

Talk to your attorney about other non-fee costs. Ask whether it is likely there will be filing fees, court reporter expenses, or subpoena, mediation, or parenting class fees.

Expert-witness fees are a different category because these can be a substantial expense, ranging from hundreds to thousands of dollars, depending upon the type of expert and the extent to which he or she is involved in your case. Experts should also provide you or your lawyer with a fee agreement or statement for services. For example, a standard residential real estate appraisal may be $450, but a commercial or rental property appraisal can cost $2,500 or more. The complete appraisal of a business that includes an analysis of its books can cost $10,000 to $25,000. Psychological evaluations for parents and children can cost $2,500 to $10,000, depending upon the case, and are not covered by health insurance. A pension expert can cost $750 to $1,500 if a domestic relations order is needed.

These really are just ballpark figures. The complexity and nature of the services may require more-expensive fees or the lawyers may agree to a limited approach that can lower the cost.

These costs usually do not include testifying in court, so just be clear and ask. Any reputable expert will know what he or she charges. The expert should be quite transparent with the information and tell you what he or she will or will not do for a reduced fee.

Speak frankly with your attorney about these costs so that together you can make the best decisions about how to use your budget for the litigation. It does you little good to proceed with an expert, get a report, and then find out you do not have the funds to pay that expert to travel and testify in court.

4.13 Who pays for the experts such as appraisers, accountants, and mediators?

Costs for the services of experts, whether appointed by the court or hired by the parties, are paid for by the parties. Whether these costs are shared or not is a tactical decision between you and your lawyer. Sometimes you may want an expert of your own because you are concerned about the truthfulness of the information and want an independent opinion from an expert paid by you. Sometimes, as with residential appraisals, lawyers who often work together have an expert they mutually use and trust, so the fee can be split and the work done more efficiently.

In the case of a guardian *ad litem* (GAL), who may be appointed to represent the best interest of your children, the amount of the fee will depend upon how much time this professional spends. New Hampshire law has some special rules for GALs, described in question 8.8 in chapter 8. The judge often orders this fee to be shared by the parties. However, depending upon the circumstances, one party can be ordered to pay the entire fee. In New Hampshire, there are no public funds for GALs in private parenting cases, so if you cannot afford it, you likely will be unable to have the benefit of a GAL investigation in your case.

Psychologists either charge by the hour or set a flat fee for a certain type of evaluation. Again, the court can order one party to pay this fee or both parties to share the expense. It is not uncommon for a psychologist to request payment in advance and hold the release of an expert report until fees are paid.

Mediators either charge a flat fee per session or an hourly rate fee. Generally each party will pay one half of the mediator's fees prior to your mediation sessions.

The fees for many experts, including appraisers and accountants, will vary depending upon whether the individuals are called upon to provide only a specific service such as an appraisal, or whether they will need to prepare for giving testimony and appear as a witness at trial.

4.14 What factors will impact how much my divorce will cost?

Although it is difficult to predict how much your legal fees will be, the following factors will affect your costs:

- Whether there are children
- Whether parenting is agreed upon
- Whether there are unusual legal questions or special circumstances to be addressed
- Whether a pension plan or retirement plan will be divided between the parties
- The nature of the issues contested, including the complexity of properties or a demand for spousal support
- The number of issues stipulated to or agreed to by the parties
- The level of cooperation between the opposing party and opposing counsel
- The frequency of your communication with your legal team
- Whether a party has made a claim for fault-based divorce.

- The ability of the parties to communicate with each other, as well as the client's ability to communicate well with his or her attorney
- The promptness with which information is provided and/or exchanged between clients and attorneys
- Whether there are litigation costs, such as fees for expert witnesses
- The hourly rate of the attorney, associates, and staff
- The time it will take to conclude your divorce in terms of court availability

Communicating with your lawyer regularly about your legal fees and potential costs will help you to have a better understanding as your case proceeds. Just keep track of your monthly bills and make sure you are targeting the issues of most importance to you.

4.15 Will my attorney charge for phone calls, e-mails, or other communications?

Unless your case is being handled on a flat-fee basis, you should expect to be billed for any communication with your attorney. Many of the professional services provided by lawyers are done by phone and e-mail. This time can be spent giving legal advice, negotiating, or gathering information to protect your interests. These calls and e-mails are all legal services for which you should anticipate being charged by your attorney.

To make the most of your time during attorney phone calls, plan your call in advance. Organize the information you want to relay, your questions, and any concerns to be addressed. This will help you to be clear and focused during the phone call so that your fees are well spent.

4.16 Will I be charged for talking to the staff at my lawyer's office?

It depends. Check the terms of your fee agreement with your lawyer. Whether you are charged any fees for talking to nonlawyers may depend upon their role in the office. For example, many law firms charge for the services of paralegals and law clerks but not receptionists or legal assistants.

Remember that nonlawyers cannot give legal advice, so it is important to respect their roles. Do not expect the receptionist to give you an opinion regarding whether you will win custody or receive spousal support.

Your lawyer's support staff will be able to relay your messages and receive information from you. They may also be able to answer many of your procedural questions. Allowing this type of support within the firm is an important way to control your legal fees, too.

4.17 What is a *litigation budget,* and how do I know if I need one?

If your case is complex and you are anticipating substantial legal fees, ask your attorney to prepare a *litigation budget* for your review. This can help you to understand the nature of the services anticipated, the time that may be spent, and the overall amount it will cost to proceed to trial. The litigation budget will likely be comprised of a combination of your attorney's and your legal team's hourly rates. It can also be helpful for budgeting and planning for additional retainers and expert fees. Knowing the anticipated costs of litigation can help you to make meaningful decisions about which issues to litigate and which to consider resolving with settlement negotiations.

4.18 What is a *trial retainer,* and will I have to pay one?

The purpose of the *trial retainer* is to fund the work needed to prepare for trial and for services during the trial. A trial retainer is a sum of money paid on your account with your lawyer when it appears as though your case may not settle and is at risk for proceeding to trial.

The payment for a trial retainer should be part of your original fee agreement so that you can plan accordingly. This may also partially guide your decision to settle or proceed to trial. Trials are very expensive because preparation and attendance at trial for experienced lawyers is critical to success and, therefore, time-consuming.

Confirm with your attorney that any unearned portion of your trial retainer will be refunded if your case settles. Ask your lawyer whether and when a trial retainer might be required in your case so that you can avoid surprises and plan your budget accordingly.

4.19 How do I know whether I should spend the fees required for trial?

Deciding whether to take a case to trial, or to settle, is often the most challenging point in the divorce process. When the issues in dispute are primarily financial, often the decision about settlement is related to the costs of going to trial as opposed to the amount you may win in your "best" case and the amount you could lose in your "worst" case.

We often tell clients that the decision to reject a settlement offer and proceed to trial depends upon whether the amount of the offer significantly affects your life. Think about why you are rejecting the offer—really think about it. Realize that the risk for you in going to trial is to potentially lose some of what would be the settlement amount due to trial costs or the outcome decided by a judge. Clarify just how far apart you and your spouse are on financial matters. Compare this to the estimated or tangible costs (like fees and expert costs) of going to trial. Do not forget intangible costs, as well, such as the emotional consequences to you and your family and the delay in a final outcome you cannot control. By comparing these amounts, you can decide whether a compromise on certain financial issues and having certainty about the outcome would be better than paying legal fees and not knowing how your case will resolve.

Keep in mind that the judge takes the case under advisement and you may receive a written decision weeks or months later. Clients can be confused by television drama shows, that usually have a jury trial, a short jury deliberation, and an immediate verdict—all in an hour. In real life, a judge is required to write a decision and explain his or her reasoning, and that can delay the outcome of your case. Moreover, a decision by a judge may require the lawyers to file even more paperwork to protect your rights.

4.20 Is there any way I can reduce some of the expenses of getting a divorce?

Litigation of any kind can be expensive, and divorce is no exception. The good news is that there are many ways that you can control these expenses. Here are some suggestions:

Put it in writing. If you need to relay information that is important but not urgent, consider providing it to your attorney by mail, fax, or e-mail. This creates a prompt and accurate record for your file and takes less time than exchanging phone messages or talking on the phone.

Keep your attorney informed. Just as your attorney should keep you up to date on the status of your case, you need to do the same. Keep your lawyer advised about any major developments in your life, such as plans to move, have someone move into your home, change your employment status, or buy or sell property.

During your divorce, if your contact information changes, be sure to notify your attorney immediately. Your attorney may need to reach you with information, and reaching you in a timely manner may help avoid more costly fees. Lawyers and their staff are busy, so you have to make sure you can be contacted quickly when needed.

Obtain copies of documents. An important part of litigation includes reviewing many documents such as tax returns, account statements, report cards, or medical records. Your attorney will ordinarily be able to request or subpoena these items, but many can be made readily available to you directly upon request, saving you money in attorney fees.

Consult your attorney's website. If your lawyer has a website, it may be a great source of useful information. The answers to commonly asked questions about the divorce process can often be found there. Be careful, however, because simple answers may not fit your case or needs at that moment.

Utilize support professionals. Get to know the support staff at your lawyer's office. Although only attorneys are able to give you legal advice, the receptionist, paralegal, legal secretary, or law clerk may be able to answer your questions regarding the status of your case. All communication with any professionals in a law firm is strictly confidential.

Consider working with an associate attorney. Although the senior attorneys or partners in a law firm may have more experience, you may find that working with an associate attorney is a good option for you. Hourly rates for an associate attorney are typically lower than those charged by a senior partner. Frequently the associate attorney has trained under a senior partner and developed excellent skills as well as knowledge of the law. Many associate attorneys are also very experienced.

Discuss with the firm the benefits of working with a senior versus an associate attorney in light of the nature of your case, the expertise of the respective attorneys, and the potential cost savings to you.

Leave detailed messages. If your attorney knows the information you are seeking, she or he can often get the answer before returning your call. This not only gets your answer more quickly, but it may also reduce costs. But remember that it is usually more efficient to schedule a conference call or appointment if the question is complex.

Discuss more than one matter during a call. It is not unusual for clients to have many questions during litigation. If your question is not urgent, consider waiting to call your attorney until you have more than one inquiry. However, never hesitate to call to ask any legal questions. Schedule a conference call when you and your lawyer have quiet time rather than play "telephone tag" or have to leave a meeting or have the kids in the car when you are already under stress.

Provide timely responses to information requests. Whenever possible, provide information requested by your lawyer in a timely manner. This avoids the cost of follow-up action by your lawyer and the additional expenses of extending the time in litigation.

Carefully review your monthly statements. Scrutinize your monthly billing statements closely. If you believe an error has been made, contact your lawyer's office right away to discuss your concerns.

Keep an open mind about settlement. Recognize that when your disagreement concerns financial matters, the value of the money in dispute may be less than the amount it would cost to go to trial. Try to remember that a judge will make a decision based upon little information and that the outcome may be worse than compromise. There is rarely a perfect solution. Sometimes a settlement offer is the best possible solution and sometimes it is the least worst solution. The key is to try to avoid the worst outcome.

By doing your part, you can use your legal fees wisely and control the costs of your divorce.

4.21 I don't have any money and I need a divorce. What are my options?

If you have a low income and few assets, you may be eligible to obtain a divorce at no cost or minimal cost through one of the following organizations:

- New Hampshire *Pro Bono* Services (volunteer lawyers)
- New Hampshire State Bar Association Lawyer Referral Service, Reduced Fee Program

These organizations have a screening process for potential clients, as well as requirements as to the nature of the cases they can accept. The demand for their services is also usually greater than the number of attorneys available to handle cases. If you believe you might be eligible for participation in one of these programs, inquire early to increase your opportunity to get the legal help you are seeking, and anticipate being on a waiting list for a period of time.

In short, if you have very little income and few assets, you are likely to experience some delay in obtaining a lawyer. Contact information is contained in the Resources section.

If possible, consider borrowing the legal fees from friends or family. Often those close to you are concerned about your future and would be pleased to support you in your goal of having your rights protected. Although it may be uncomfortable to ask for assistance, remember that most people will appreciate that you trusted them enough to request their help. You may want to consider treating this as a loan, putting it in writing so it is clear it is not a gift. You may feel better, and the court will know the source of your fees. You may also:

- Charge the legal fees on a low-interest credit card or consider a loan.

- Start saving. If your case is not urgent, consider developing a plan for saving the money you need to proceed with a divorce. Your attorney may be willing to receive and hold monthly payments until you have paid an amount sufficient to pay the initial retainer.

- Talk to your attorney about using money held in a joint account.

- Find an attorney who will work with you on a monthly payment basis.

- Ask your attorney about your spouse paying for your legal fees, as the law allows the court to order fees, but this requires a motion and the appropriate facts to support the motion.

- Ask your attorney about being paid from the proceeds of the property settlement at the end of the case. If you and your spouse have acquired substantial assets during the marriage, you may be able to find an attorney who will wait to be paid until the assets are divided at the conclusion of the divorce. This is *not* a contingent fee, and your fee agreement should be very clear about any such arrangement. Lawyers in New Hampshire cannot take liens or mortgages to secure payment for a divorce before the case is done.

- Closely examine all sources of funds readily available to you, as you may have overlooked money that might be easily accessible to you.

Even if you do not have the financial resources to proceed with your divorce at this time, consult with an attorney to learn your rights and to develop an action plan for steps you can take between now and the time you are able to proceed.

4.23 Is there anything I can do on my own to get support for my children if I don't have money for a lawyer?

Yes. If you need child support, contact the New Hampshire Department of Health and Human Services Bureau of Child Support Services (BCSS) for help obtaining a child support order. (*See* Resources at the end of this book for contact information.) Although BCSS cannot help you with matters such as parenting or property division, it can pursue child support from your spouse or former partner for your children.

4.24 If my parent pays my legal fees, will my lawyer give her private information about my divorce?

If someone else is paying your legal fees, discuss any expectations that your lawyer will honor the ethical duty of confidentiality *to you only*. Without your permission, your attorney should not disclose information to others about your case, whether or not they are paying your legal fees.

However, if you authorize your attorney to speak with your family members, be aware that you will also be charged for these communications. Regardless of the opinions of the person who pays your attorney fees, your lawyer's duty is to remain your ethical advocate—and yours alone.

4.25 Can I ask the court to order my spouse to pay my attorney fees?

Yes. Under New Hampshire law, if you want to ask the court to order your spouse to pay any portion of your legal fees, be sure to discuss this with your attorney at the first opportunity. Most lawyers will treat the obligation for your legal fees as yours alone until the other party has made payment under a court order. Sometimes a judge will defer the allocation of your fees until the end of the case, so you should be prepared for that possibility as well. If there are limited resources, the court may allow access to assets for both parties or decline to order any fees until the end of the case.

If your case is likely to require costly experts and your spouse has a much greater ability to pay these expenses, talk to your lawyer about the possibility of filing a motion with the court asking your spouse to pay toward these costs while the case is pending.

4.26 What happens if I don't pay my attorney the fees I promised to pay?

The ethical rules for lawyers allow your attorney to file a *motion to withdraw from representation* if you do not comply with your fee agreement. If you are having difficulty paying your attorney fees, talk with your attorney about payment options. Consider borrowing the funds, using your credit card, or asking for help from friends and family.

Above all, do not avoid communication with your attorney if you are having challenges making payments. Keeping in touch with your attorney is essential for you to have an advocate at all stages of your divorce.

5

The Discovery Process

Discovery is one of the least talked about steps in divorce, but it is often the most important, and if done with malice or intent to impede the truth, it can be the most expensive (even more than the cost of a trial in some cases). *Discovery* is the pretrial phase in all civil lawsuits during which each party can obtain information and documents from the opposing party. The purpose of discovery is to ensure that both you and your spouse have access to the same information. As was noted many years ago, the purpose of discovery is to "avoid the sporting theory of justice."

In this way, you can either negotiate a fair agreement or obtain all of the relevant facts to present to a judge at trial. Discovery enables you and your spouse to meet on a more level playing field. You and your spouse both need the same information if you hope to reach agreement on any of the issues in your divorce. Similarly, a judge must also know all of the relevant facts to make a fair decision.

The discovery process may seem tedious at times because of the need to obtain and provide a great deal of detailed information. Completing it, however, can give tremendous clarity to your own lawyer and help to efficiently prepare your case. Most documents are needed by both parties so the more you cooperate, the better off you are.

Try to avoid the game of tit for tat. Just because one side does discovery that is onerous or irrelevant does not mean you should do so in return. Target what you need, be honest about your information, and stay on task without distractions.

Trust your lawyer's advice about the importance of having the necessary evidence in order to reach your goals in your divorce. And always remember this simple truth: If married people were honest, transparent, and cooperative with discovery and financial disclosure, lawyers would have much less to do and cases would be much less expensive.

5.1   Are there any rules related to discovery?

There are some rules of family law procedure in New Hampshire that are unique and that you should understand and discuss with your lawyer.

In New Hampshire, Rule 1.25-A requires mandatory discovery of a variety of financial information for a period of time leading up to the filing of the divorce action. These documents include, but are not limited to:

- A sworn financial affidavit
- The past three years of tax returns and schedules
- Twelve months of bank statements and retirement account statements
- Six months of credit card statements
- Information about health insurance for the family, and the associated costs.
- Information about self-employment if applicable, and any credit applications submitted in recent months

Although this step may appear and feel cumbersome, it is very important and helpful to the attorneys to have this information. It is also possible if both parties and/or counsel agree to waive this requirement. For example, if all accounts are joint, or known to both parties, there is no need to exchange this information.

The best lawyers will cooperate with the exchange of information and require their clients to share that information transparently. Be wary of anyone who wants to play games with either the process or the information.

5.2 What types of discovery might be requested, and how long does the discovery process take?

If discovery is necessary, the forms of discovery available to both parties are:

- *Interrogatories*—written questions propounded by the other lawyer that must be answered under oath by you

- *Requests for production of documents*—asking that certain documents be provided by you or your spouse

- *Requests for admissions*—asking that certain facts be admitted or denied

- *Subpoena of persons or documents*—a process for compelling a person or institution to appear at an office to testify under oath in response to questions from your lawyer, or to produce documents, such as bank or accounting records

- *Depositions*—the asking and answering of questions under oath, outside of court, but in the presence of a court reporter

All of these forms of discovery can be used in court on cross-examination or as evidence in your case to prove facts that are relevant to the divorce. Factors that may influence the type of discovery conducted in your divorce can include:

- The types and complexity of issues in dispute

- How much access you and your spouse have to needed information

- The level of cooperation in sharing information

- The budget available for performing discovery

- The need of your experts for specific information to investigate and prepare a report

Discovery can take anywhere from a few weeks to many months, depending upon factors such as the complexity of the case, the cooperation of both you and your spouse, and whether expert witnesses are involved. The rules of procedure for discovery do provide that interrogatories, requests for production of documents, and requests for admissions be responded to within thirty days.

In some cases, however, your lawyer may have to request the judge's help to order compliance with discovery, either because your spouse failed to respond at all or because the responses were vague or incomplete. This can delay discovery, but it is necessary if a party is obstructing the disclosure of honest or relevant information.

5.3   My lawyer insists that we conduct discovery, but I don't want to spend the time and money on it. Is it really necessary?

This is a tricky question to answer without the details of a specific case. Lawyers may advise discovery as a means of self-protection if you are unclear about the economic facts in your family, you did not have access to the information because your spouse controlled all the information, or you are a victim of abuse and may be threatened or manipulated during the divorce through your children or family members. This happens much too often, so these factors may govern the advice you are getting.

The discovery process can be critical to a successful outcome in your case for many reasons, including the following:

- Discovery increases the likelihood that any agreements reached are based on accurate information.

- It provides necessary information for deciding whether to settle or proceed to trial.

- It supports the preparation of defenses by providing information regarding your case (and you should not underestimate the value of this information to your protection at trial).

- It avoids surprises at trial, such as unexpected witnesses or economic information.

- It ensures all potential issues are identified by your attorney.

Discuss with your attorney the intention and purpose behind the type of discovery being conducted in your case to ensure it is consistent with your goals and a meaningful investment of your legal fees.

If your lawyer cannot explain the specific need for discovery and the cost of it, you should require more of an explanation.

5.4 I just received interrogatories and requests to produce documents. My lawyer wants me to respond within two weeks. I'll never make the deadline. What can I do?

This happens all the time. People today lead busy lives. Answering your discovery promptly, however, will help move your case forward and help control your legal fees. In addition, a prompt response will prevent emotional or mental gridlock because we, as humans, tend to avoid that which we do not want to do.

Discovery is almost always a challenge, so your response is understandable. If there is a legitimate reason for delay, however, the lawyers can cooperate or a judge can help (within reason). Extensions are common on answers to interrogatories. But before you reach this stage, you can take the following steps to make this task easier:

First, look at all of the questions. Many of them will not apply, or your answers will be a simple "yes" or "no."

Ask a friend to help you. It is important that you develop the practice of letting others help you while you are going through your divorce. Chances are that you will make great progress in just a couple of hours with a friend helping you. Remember that the attorney-client privilege does not apply to your friend, so be careful whom you trust and how much you share concerning your personal information.

Break it down into smaller tasks. If you answer just a few questions a day, the job will not be so overwhelming.

Call your lawyer. Ask whether a paralegal in the office can help you organize the needed information, or determine whether some of it can be provided at a later date.

Delay in the discovery process often leads to frustration by clients and lawyers. Do your best to provide the information in a timely manner with the help of others. You can always supplement or amend the discovery later or as new information comes in to you.

5.5   I don't have access to my documents, and my spouse is being uncooperative. Can my lawyer request information directly from an employer, financial institution, or other third party?

Yes, it may be possible to issue a subpoena directly to an employer or financial institution, for example. A *subpoena* is a court process directing an individual or corporate representative to appear before the court or to produce documents in a pending lawsuit.

In the discovery process, a subpoena is used to compel an individual or corporation to produce documents, papers, books, or other physical exhibits that constitute or contain evidence that is relevant to your case. Often this can be the cheapest and most efficient way to get honest information that is not filtered through a spouse or their lawyer.

5.6   My spouse's lawyer intends to subpoena my medical or therapeutic records. Aren't these records private or protected information?

Whether or not your records are relevant will depend upon the issues in dispute. If you are requesting spousal support, if your mental or physical health is an issue in the dispute concerning rights and responsibilities for a child, or if fault grounds are pled that relate to your mental health, these records may be relevant.

If a guardian *ad litem* or psychological evaluator is requesting records from you or concerning your child, you may be required to sign a release, but you still have a right to secure the privacy of that material.

You should immediately talk with your lawyer about your rights and your privacy. There are records, such as those concerning reproduction or substance abuse, that are governed by specific federal and state laws and require a release from you.

There are a number of options that may be available to prevent the disclosure of your information. One option is to require a *confidentiality agreement* and a protective order signed by the parties and lawyers and approved by a judge. This may help you ensure the privacy of your information with the threat of contempt if a party violates the order.

5.7   I own my own business. Will I have to disclose my business records?

Yes, you may be required to provide extensive records of your business in the discovery process. However, it is common for the court to protect the confidentiality of these records. You should discuss a confidentiality agreement and a protective order with your lawyer. A *protective order,* which is signed by a judge, prevents a spouse from sharing private information. A judge may allow the lawyers or an expert, such as a business valuation expert or appraiser, examine the records as part of the case. If client lists or your computer files are a part of your business or, for example, if you have trade secrets or patents and that information might be valuable to a third-party competitor, you have a right to protect it from being disclosed to other businesses.

If your former spouse refuses to cooperate, a judge can help. You should always ensure that your records are protected from your competition or from public disclosure. It is important, however, to make sure you ask for help from the judge—get the order before you turn over confidential business or personal records. Waiting until afterward might be too late to protect the information.

5.8   It's been two months since my lawyer sent interrogatories to my spouse, and we still don't have his or her answers. I answered mine on time. Is there anything that can be done to speed up the process?

The failure or refusal of a spouse to follow the rules of discovery can add to both the frustration and expense of the divorce process. If your spouse or your spouse's lawyer has not been cooperative in providing the requested information, talk with your attorney about asking the court to order your spouse to provide the information requested. The court should also spell out the consequences for your spouse for not providing the information.

Your lawyer can seek a court order for your spouse to provide the requested information by a certain date. A request for attorney fees for having to file the motion may also be appropriate.

You may also ask your lawyer whether a subpoena of information from an employer or a financial institution would be a more cost-effective way to get needed facts and documents if your spouse remains uncooperative or if you do not trust the information from your spouse.

5.9   What is a *deposition*?

A *deposition* is the asking and answering of questions under oath, outside of court, but in the presence of a court reporter. A transcript of your testimony may be printed and used in court by the other lawyer.

A deposition may be taken of you, your spouse, or potential witnesses in your divorce case, including experts. Both attorneys will be present for this process. You and your spouse also have the right to be present during the taking of depositions of any witnesses in your case.

Depositions are not performed in every divorce as these are expensive, given the lawyer preparation and attendance time and the cost of the court reporter and transcripts. In New Hampshire, depositions are most common in cases involving complex financial issues and expert witnesses, and they can be essential tools, especially when a case is likely to proceed to trial.

After your deposition is completed, the questions and answers will be transcribed, that is, typed up by the court reporter exactly as given, and sent to you. You have a chance to review the transcript to correct typographical errors, but you cannot make substantive changes in your testimony (for example, a "yes" cannot become a "no").

5.10   What is the purpose of a deposition?

A deposition can serve a number of purposes such as:

- Supporting the settlement process by providing valuable information
- Helping your attorney determine who to use as a witness at trial
- Aiding in the assessment of a witness's credibility, that is, whether the witness appears to be telling the truth

- Helping avoid surprises at the trial by learning the testimony of witnesses in advance (this is particularly true of expert witnesses)

- Preserving testimony in the event the witness is unavailable for trial

- Identifying and authenticating documents that may be disputed at trial. In this day and age of e-mails, texts, and social media, it is not simple to verify who sent what to whom. By finding out whether someone denies that they sent an e-mail or a text, or whether they posted financial information, you can better prepare.

5.11   Will what I say in my deposition be used against me when we go to court?

Usually, a deposition is used to develop trial strategy and obtain information in preparation for trial. In some circumstances, a deposition may be used at trial.

When you testify, *if* you give testimony contrary to your deposition, your deposition can be used to impeach you by showing the inconsistencies in your testimony under oath. This could cause you to lose credibility with the court, rendering your testimony less valuable.

It is important to review your deposition prior to your live testimony to ensure consistency and prepare yourself for the types of questions you may be asked.

5.12   Will the judge read the depositions?

Unless a witness becomes unavailable for trial or gives conflicting testimony at trial, or the deposition is offered by a lawyer by agreement with both lawyers, it is unlikely that the judge will ever read the depositions.

5.13   How should I prepare for my deposition?

To prepare for your deposition, review the important documents in your case, such as the complaint, your answers to interrogatories, your financial affidavit, any temporary hearing affidavits, and any other relevant communications you may have had with others that you sent or were sent to you.

Gather all documents you've been asked to provide at your deposition. Deliver them to your attorney in advance of your deposition for copying and review. Talk to your attorney about the types of questions you can expect to be asked. Discuss with him or her any questions you are concerned about answering.

Your lawyer may want to object to some documents or testimony as irrelevant or inappropriate for the case or that may require a *protective* or *confidentiality order* if the documents involve a third person, such as a family member or significant other with whom you may be involved. A protective order is entered by a judge and may require the parties and the lawyers to keep any records private except for expert witnesses or trial. A violation of a protective order can result in the punishment of a spouse or their lawyer or both, so these are serious orders.

You do not want your lawyer to be surprised with information at the deposition. He or she may not be able to help you fix a problem this could cause or protect your rights. Always remember this about discovery and depositions: *There are no do-overs!*

5.14 What will I be asked? Can I refuse to answer questions?

Questions in a deposition can cover a broad range of topics, including your education, work, income, and family history. The attorney is allowed to ask anything that is reasonably calculated to lead to the discovery of admissible evidence. If the question may lead to relevant information, it can be asked in a deposition, even though it may be inadmissible at trial. If you are unsure whether to answer a question, ask your lawyer and follow his or her advice.

Your attorney also may *object* to inappropriate questions. If there is an objection, say nothing until the attorneys discuss the objection. You will be directed whether or not you should answer, and the lawyers may have to resolve that conflict with the help of a judge later.

5.15 What if I unintentionally give incorrect information at my deposition?

You will be under oath during your deposition, so it is very important that you be truthful. If you give incorrect information by mistake, contact your attorney as soon as you realize the error so he or she can correct the error early, not later. If you lie during your deposition, you risk being impeached by the other lawyer during your divorce trial. This could cause you to lose credibility with the court, rendering your testimony less valuable.

5.16 What if I don't know or can't remember the answer to a question?

You may be asked questions about which you have no knowledge. It is always acceptable to say "I don't know" if you do not have the information. Similarly, if you cannot remember, simply say so.

5.17 What else do I need to know about having my deposition taken?

The following suggestions will help you to give a successful deposition:

- Prepare for your deposition by reviewing and providing necessary documents and talking with your lawyer.

- Get a good night's sleep the night before. Eat a meal with protein to sustain your energy, as the length of depositions can vary.

- Arrive early for your deposition so that you have time to get comfortable with your surroundings.

- Relax. You are going to be asked questions about matters you understand. Your deposition is likely to begin with routine matters such as your educational and work history.

- Tell the truth, including whether you have met with an attorney or discussed preparation for the deposition.

- Stay calm. Your spouse's lawyer will be judging your credibility and demeanor. Do not argue with the attorneys.

- Listen carefully to the entire question. Do not try to anticipate questions or start thinking about your answer before the attorney has finished asking the question.

- Answer the question directly. If the question calls only for "yes" or "no," provide such an answer without further details.

- Do not volunteer information. Answer a simple question with a simple answer. If the lawyer wants to elicit more information, he or she will do so in following questions.

- If you do not understand the question clearly, ask that it be repeated or rephrased. Do not try to answer a question if you are not sure what was asked.

- Take your time and carefully consider the question before answering. There is no need to hurry.

- If you do not know or cannot remember the answer, say so. That is an adequate answer.

- Do not guess.

- Do not try to be funny or sarcastic. It does not work and will backfire on you when your answer is read out loud in a courtroom.

- If your answer is an estimate or approximation, say so. Do not let an attorney pin you down to anything you are not sure about. For example, if you cannot remember the number of times an event occurred, say so. If the attorney asks you if it was more than ten times, answer only if you can. If you can provide a range with reasonable certainty (such as more than ten but fewer than twenty), you may do so.

- If an attorney mischaracterizes something you said earlier, say so.

- Speak clearly and loudly enough for everyone to hear you.

- Answer all questions with words, rather than gestures or sounds. "Uh-huh" is difficult for the court reporter to distinguish from "unh-unh" and may result in inaccuracies in the transcript.

- If you need a break at any point in the deposition, you have the right to request one. You can talk to your attorney during such a break.

- Discuss with your lawyer in advance of your deposition if you should review the transcript of your deposition for its accuracy or if you should waive your right to review and sign the deposition.

Remember that the purpose of your deposition is to support your case by providing clear and truthful information that you may need to use at trial as well. Completing it may actually help your case move forward to settlement.

5.18 Are depositions always necessary? Does every witness have to be deposed?

Depositions are less likely to be needed if you and your spouse reach an agreement on most of the issues and are moving toward settlement. They are more likely to be needed in cases where there are complex financial issues. Although depositions of all witnesses are usually unnecessary, it is common to take depositions of expert witnesses. This can help your lawyer prepare your case and may facilitate settlement by transparently exposing weaknesses or strengths to both lawyers and clients.

5.19 Will I get a copy of any depositions in my case?

Ask your attorney for copies of the depositions. It will be important for you to carefully review your deposition, in particular, if your case proceeds to trial.

6

Mediation and Negotiation

If your marriage had significant or chronic conflict, you might be asking how you can make that stop. You may picture your divorce as having lawyers argue, an angry spouse, and screaming matches between family members. You may wonder if there is a way out of this potential nightmare for you and your children.

Or perhaps you and your spouse are parting ways amicably. Although you are in disagreement about how your divorce should be settled, you are clear that you want the process to be respectful and without hostility. You'd rather spend your hard-earned money on your retirement or your children's college education than legal fees.

What matters with either scenario is that doing costly discovery and going to trial so that a judge makes all of the decisions in your divorce is not inevitable. In fact, most New Hampshire divorce cases settle without the need for a trial. Mediation and negotiation (also known as *alternative dispute resolution,* or *ADR*) can help you and your spouse resolve disputed issues and reach your own agreements without taking your case before a judge. ADR can include co-parenting counseling, neutral case evaluation by a judge, advisory opinions from an experienced former judge or neutral party, or regular mediation strategies.

Resolving your divorce through a mediated or negotiated settlement has many advantages. You can achieve a mutually satisfying agreement, a known outcome, no appeal, and, often, significantly lower legal fees and expert costs. Despite the circumstances that led to the end of your marriage, it might be possible for your divorce to conclude peacefully with the help of these tools.

6.1 What is the difference between *mediation* and *negotiation*?

Both mediation and negotiation are methods used to help you and your spouse settle your divorce by reaching agreement rather than going to trial and having the judge make decisions for you. *Negotiation* involves lawyers for both you and your spouse sharing ideas and structures for settlement either formally or informally by meeting or by letter.

In some cases, you and your spouse may elect to negotiate by yourselves; this can become contentious, however, so be careful. Even the most well-meaning and experienced professionals recognize that they need a neutral party to help keep the discussions respectful and on target.

Mediation uses a trained mediator who is an independent, neutral third party. Sometimes the mediator is a lawyer who specializes in economic valuations and support or other financial matters, or he or she may be a social worker or psychologist who can help with parenting plans. On occasion, former judges can serve as mediators and can be quite helpful in resolving cases. Lawyers for the spouses may be present during mediation.

A skilled professional can assist you and your spouse with the process of developing creative solutions to problem solving. In many cases, the parties may want close to the same outcome but are not finding the solution. For example, a spouse may need a particular amount of total support but the other spouse does not believe he has the cash flow to meet that obligation. A skilled mediator may be able to assist with creative options to resolve these disputes.

6.2 How are mediation and negotiation different from a collaborative divorce?

Collaborative law is a method of resolving a divorce case in which each party hires an attorney trained in the collaborative law process. Additionally, the collaborative process involves a team approach to resolving your case, in which you may have a mental health professional known as a *divorce coach* to assist you with the emotional issues in your divorce and a *financial neutral,* who is a certified divorce financial planner; such a planner can assist both spouses with crunching numbers and approaching financial resolution. You and your lawyers and other members of the team enter into an agreement that provides that if either you or your spouse decides to take the case to court, both of you must terminate legal services with your collaborative lawyers and other professionals and start anew in litigation.

Although the process may be lengthy, it enables the focus to shift away from the conflict and toward finding solutions. The attorneys become a part of a team supporting a settlement rather than advocates adding to the conflict. When the collaborative approach works, it can be transformative for a family who likely will need to continue on as co-parents long after the divorce is behind them.

Talk to your lawyer about whether your case would be well suited to the collaborative law process. Keep in mind not every lawyer is collaboratively trained. The New Hampshire Collaborative Law Alliance keeps a listing of New Hampshire collaborative professionals. See the Resources for more information.

6.3 What is involved in the mediation process? What will I have to do, and how long will it take?

The mediation process will be explained to you in detail by the mediator at the start of the mediation session. Mediation involves one or more meetings with you, your spouse, and the mediator. In many cases, the attorneys will also be present.

Prior to meeting with you and your spouse for an initial mediation session, the mediator or his or her staff may conduct an individual initial screening session with each of you to assess your ability to communicate with each other and to determine whether there is domestic or intimate partner abuse or other forms of intimidation or coercion. After the mediator's initial screening, he or she will decide whether you and your spouse should mediate together, or whether your mediation should take place separately.

The mediator will outline ground rules designed to ensure you will each be treated respectfully and given an opportunity to be heard. In most cases, you and your spouse will each be given an opportunity to make some opening remarks about what is important to you in the outcome of your divorce.

How long the process of mediation continues depends upon many of the same factors that affect how long your divorce will take. These include how many issues you and your spouse disagree about, the complexity of these issues, and the willingness of each of you to work toward an agreement.

Your case could settle after just a couple of mediation sessions, or it might require a series of meetings. This occurs all the time because mediation is a process, not a magic wand. It is common for the mediator to clarify at the close of each session whether the parties are willing to continue with another session.

6.4 My lawyer said that mediation and negotiation can reduce delays in completing my divorce. How does this work?

When the issues in your divorce are decided by a judge instead of by you and your spouse, there are many opportunities for delay. These can include:

- Waiting for the trial date

- Having to return to court on a later, second date if your trial is not completed on the day it is scheduled

- Waiting for the judge's ruling on your case (which can take months)

- Needing additional court hearings after your trial to resolve disputes about the intention of the judge's rulings, issues that were overlooked, or disagreement regarding the language of the divorce decree

- Waiting for an appeal, which can take a year or more to decide in the courts

Each one of these events holds the possibility of delaying your divorce by days, weeks, or even months to years. Mediating or negotiating the terms of your divorce can eliminate these delays and save substantial emotional and economic costs.

6.5 How can mediation and negotiation lower the costs of my divorce?

If your case is not settled by agreement, you will be going to trial. If the issues in your case are many or complex, such as those relating to parenting or business valuations, the attorney fees and other costs of going to trial can be tremendous.

By settling your case without going to trial, you may be able to save thousands of dollars in legal fees. Ask your attorney for a litigation budget that sets forth the potential costs of going to trial, so that you have some idea of these costs when deciding whether to settle an issue or to take it to trial before the judge.

6.6 Are there other benefits to mediating or negotiating a settlement?

Yes. A divorce resolved by a mediated or negotiated agreement can have the following additional benefits:

Recognizing common goals. Mediation and negotiation allow for brainstorming between the parties and lawyers. Looking at creative solutions, even the impractical ones, invites collaborative solutions to common goals. For example, suppose you and your spouse both agree that you need to pay your spouse some amount of equity for the family home you will keep, but you have no cash to make the payment. Together, you might come up with a number of options for accomplishing your goal and then select the best one. Contrast this with the judge who simply orders you to pay the money without considering all of the possible options and with the risk of the sale of your home.

Addressing the unique circumstances of your situation. Many years ago a judge told parties that "they can do their divorce with a scalpel or I can do it with a hatchet." Even the best judges will never know as much about you or your family as you and your spouse do. Rather than using a one-size-fits-all approach, as a judge might do, a settlement reached by agreement allows you and your spouse to consider the unique circumstances of your situation in formulating a good outcome. For example, suppose you disagree about the parenting times for the Thanksgiving holiday. The judge might order you to alternate the holiday each year, even though you both would have preferred to have your child share the day between you.

Creating a safe place for communication. Alternative dispute resolution gives each party an opportunity to be heard. Perhaps you and your spouse have not yet had an opportunity to share directly any concerns about settlement. For example, you might be worried about how the temporary parenting time arrangement is impacting your children, but you have not yet talked to your spouse about it. A mediation session or settlement conference can be a safe place for you and your spouse to communicate your concerns about your children or your finances.

Fulfilling your children's needs. You may see and learn that your children would be better served by you and your spouse deciding their future together, rather than having it decided by a judge who does not know, love, and understand your children like the two of you do. Moreover, you can discuss these issues privately and without publicly embarrassing each other or your children in a trial. This also means that parents can retain the dignity and respect needed to co-parent in the future.

Eliminating the risk and uncertainty of a trial. If a judge decides the outcome of your divorce, you give up all control over the terms of the settlement. The decisions are left in the hands of the judge. If you and your spouse can reach an agreement, however, you have the power to eliminate the risk of an uncertain outcome and settle your differences privately.

Reducing the risk of harm to your children. If your case goes to trial, it is likely that you and your spouse will give testimony that will be upsetting to each other. As court conflict increases, the relationship between you and your spouse inevitably deteriorates. This is harmful to your children. Contrast this with mediation or settlement negotiations. It is not unusual for the relationship between parents to improve as the professionals create a safe environment for rebuilding communication and reaching agreements in the best interest of a child.

Having the support of professionals. Using trained professionals, such as mediators, can help you to reach a settlement that you might think is impossible. These professionals have the necessary skills to help you focus on what is most important to you, and shift your attention away from irrelevant facts or legal arguments that just are not possible to win in the court system in New Hampshire. They also understand the law and know the possible and probable range of outcomes if your case goes to trial.

Lowering stress. The process of preparing for and going to court is very stressful. Your energy is then not going toward caring for your children, looking at your finances, and coping with the emotions of divorce. You might decide that you would be better served by settling your case rather than proceeding to trial.

Achieving closure. When you are going through a divorce, the process can feel as though it is taking an eternity. By reaching an agreement, you and your spouse are better able to put the divorce behind you and move forward with your lives.

6.7   Is mediation mandatory?

When you have minor children, mediation is mandatory in New Hampshire. Although mediation is not mandatory prior to filing for divorce in New Hampshire, mediation is mandatory after a divorce filing unless there is domestic violence in the case or another compelling reason that makes mediation inappropriate. Talk to your attorney if you have concerns about mediation, as it may be possible to waive the mediation requirement.

Even in cases without children, a judge is likely to order a good-faith mediation or settlement conference to try to resolve the case. Any lawyer or judge knows the effects and costs of a trial, and that court time is often scarce, so you will probably have at least one attempt at settlement before trial.

6.8   My spouse abused me, and I am afraid to participate in mediation. Should I participate anyway?

If you have been a victim of domestic violence or abuse by your spouse, it is important that you discuss the appropriateness of such mediation with your attorney. In this case, mediation may not be a safe way for you to reach agreement.

Prior to allowing mediation to proceed, any mediator should ask you whether you have been a victim of domestic violence. This is critical for the mediator to both assess your safety and to ensure that the balance of power in the mediation process is maintained.

Talk with your attorney if you have experienced domestic violence or if you feel threatened or intimidated by your spouse. If so, your case may be referred to an approved specialized mediator for parties involved in high-conflict situations. It may be possible to mediate with you and your spouse in different rooms or during separate sessions.

If you do not have an attorney, this process still may not feel safe for you. If you feel threatened or intimidated by your spouse but still want to proceed with mediation, request to have the mediation occur at the courthouse where there are security officers, or in your own lawyer's office, where you may feel safer. You may also request that a domestic violence advocate attend mediation with you. If you do participate in mediation, insist that your mediator have an understanding of the dynamics of domestic abuse and how that may impact the mediation process as well as the outcome of the mediation.

6.9 What training and credentials do mediators have?

The background of mediators varies. Some are attorneys; many come from other backgrounds, such as teaching, business, or counseling. Some mediators have received their training through programs approved by the Family Mediation Certification Board (FMCB) of New Hampshire; others are trained out of state. Ask your attorney for help in finding a qualified mediator who has completed training in mediating family law cases. The availability of mediators varies depending upon where you live.

Mediators who work in the New Hampshire courts have to complete hours of training and be approved by the FMCB. Also called *certified family mediators (CFM),* these mediators also have continuing educational requirements. You and your lawyer should discuss whether private or court-sponsored mediation is the best course for you. Mediation in court is inexpensive, but it is scheduled on the court's time and only when the court is open. Private mediation is more flexible, but it also may cost more. In some cases, private mediation is preferable if you have a sophisticated economic or psychological issue that requires someone with specialized training in that area, like valuations or mental health.

6.10   What types of issues can be mediated or negotiated?

All of the issues in your case can be mediated or negotiated. However, in advance of any mediation or negotiation session, you should discuss with your lawyer which issues you actually want to be mediated or negotiated.

You may decide that certain issues are nonnegotiable for you. Discuss this with your attorney in advance of any mediation or negotiation sessions so that he or she can support you in focusing the discussion on the issues you are open to consider.

6.11   What is the role of my attorney in the mediation process?

The role of your attorney will vary significantly depending upon your situation. Your attorney can assist you in identifying which issues will be discussed in mediation and which are better left to negotiation between the lawyers or the decision of a judge. Effective lawyers are well prepared for mediation with a plan that you have approved and the boundaries of their authority as given by you.

Sometimes it may be possible to settle the parenting issues but not the economic issues. That is fine and not unusual at all. In other cases, the parties may settle the economic issues, but they may not be able to resolve their parenting plan.

In all cases it is important that your attorney review any agreements discussed in mediation before a final agreement is reached. Under New Hampshire law, once a mediated agreement is signed it is a binding contract between the parties and may not be revoked; after it is approved by the judge, it is as binding upon you as a court order, so be very careful and clear about what you are signing.

6.12   How do I prepare for mediation?

Prior to attending a mediation session with your spouse, discuss with your attorney the issues you intend to mediate.

In particular, be sure to discuss the impact of parenting time arrangements on child support.

Enlist your attorney's support in identifying your intentions for the mediation. Make a list of the issues most important to you. For example, when it comes to your child, you might consider whether it is your child's safety, the allocation of time in the parenting schedule, or the ability to attend your children's events that concerns you most.

Be forward-looking. Giving thought to your desired outcomes while approaching mediation with an open mind and heart is the best way to move closer to settlement. But always, *always* be prepared.

6.13 Should children attend the mediation sessions?

Not ever, if possible. Children may later participate in the case if a guardian *ad litem* is appointed. Aside from that, they should not be involved with any part of the process without agreement of all parties and counsel.

Do not ever take your child to court with you without advance notice to all parties or the permission of the judge. This can backfire badly on you in the eyes of a judge or other professionals involved in your case.

6.14 I want my attorney to look over the agreements my spouse and I discussed in mediation before I give my final approval. Is this possible?

Yes. Always. Even if you did not have your lawyer attend the mediation sessions, these are important legal documents with long-term consequences to you. In many cases, both clients missed something with the mediator that is mutually important. (Allocation of tax exemption or child-care tax credits come to mind as ones we often see.)

Before giving your written or final approval to any agreements reached in mediation, it is critical that your attorney review the agreements first. This is necessary to ensure that you understand the terms of the settlement and its implications. Your attorney should also review the agreement for compliance with New Hampshire law.

Always remember that divorce cases are different from other mediation cases because you may have relationships, both legal and economic, that require future dealings with your spouse. In a car accident case that settles, the insurer can write a $10,000 check for damages and the parties never see each other again. Not so much in divorce, especially if you have children together.

6.15   Who pays for mediation?

The cost of mediation must be paid for by you or your spouse. Often it is a shared expense. Expect the court or your mediator to address the matter of fees before or at your first session. If you are unable to pay the court for mediation, you may complete a request for a fee waiver for indigence from the clerk. However, only a judge can waive the court's mediation fee.

If you hire a private mediator you need to agree in advance as to who will pay the fee and from what source, like a marital bank account. Most mediators will want payment before the mediation starts or at the session so you and your spouse should be prepared to make that payment. Just make sure you know the cost before you schedule the appointment.

6.16   What if mediation fails?

If mediation is not successful, you still may be able to settle your case through negotiations between the attorneys. Also, you and your spouse can agree to preserve the partial settlement that was reached and to take only the remaining disputed issues to trial.

Be patient with this process. In many cases, parties need more information or are unprepared to approve the agreement without more details. Cases frequently settle a few weeks after mediation, once there has been a chance to reflect upon and measure the cost of settlement or trial. Always remain open-minded.

6.17   What is a *neutral case evaluation?*

A *neutral case evaluation (NCE)* is a meeting in which you, your spouse, and your lawyers, along with a judge, confer with the intention of negotiating the terms of your divorce. This judge cannot be the trial judge in your case because the judge is hearing settlement positions that may not be admissible in court. If you do not reach a settlement, the judge who presided over your NCE will not tell the trial judge what was said or occurred during the NCE. It is a confidential, voluntary process, much like mediation, and both parties do not have to take the advice given by the judge.

An NCE can be a powerful tool for the resolution of your case. This is also your chance to tell your story. An NCE does allow you to hear from a judge with many year's experience in hearing and deciding contested cases similar to yours. He or she can help you decide whether your position is realistic in court. No two judges think exactly alike, but judges do share common knowledge; a judge can help you understand how another judge may look at your case and the range of possible outcomes.

NCEs are most effective when both parties and their attorneys see the potential for a negotiated resolution and have the necessary information to accomplish that goal. If an NCE is successful, the parties may write up and sign agreements, counsel may prepare and sign agreements to be given to a judge to approve and enter as a divorce decree.

6.18 Why should I consider mediation or NCE when our attorneys can negotiate through letters and phone calls?

Either mediation or NCE can eliminate the delays that often occur when negotiation takes place through correspondence and calls between attorneys. Rather than waiting days or weeks for a response, you can receive a response on a proposal in a matter of minutes. Human nature often means that letters and e-mails can be misunderstood. In a settlement conference the mediator or judge can facilitate new ideas and communicate much more efficiently if spouses act in good faith and the lawyers are collaborative, working to a common goal of settlement.

A settlement conference also enables you and your spouse, if you choose, to use your own words to explain the reasoning behind your requests and to get immediate feedback as to whether your lawyer's arguments or your position is likely to prevail. For example, one party may feel strongly that an asset should be awarded to him or her; however, an NCE judge may

Divorce in New Hampshire

explain that although this position is understandable, another judge may rule differently, so you have a risk of losing. Or the NCE judge may help your spouse see that an argument is overreaching, and they may suggest a more reasonable and practical approach.

6.19 How do I prepare for any settlement conference in my case?

Being well prepared for the settlement conference can help you make the most of this opportunity to resolve your case without going to trial. Actions you should take include the following:

- *Provide in advance of the conference all necessary information.* If your attorney has asked you for a current pay stub, tax return, updated financial affidavit, debt amounts, asset values, or other documentation, make sure this is done in a timely manner.

- *Discuss your goals and priorities for the conference with your attorney.* Is it more important to address temporary issues, or can you jump to long-term issues? Be sure to come in with realistic expectations about what you hope to achieve.

- *Discuss your topics of concern with your attorney in advance.* Your lawyer can assist you with understanding your rights under the law so that you can have realistic expectations for the outcome of negotiations.

- *Bring a positive attitude, a listening ear, and an open mind.* Come with the attitude that your case will settle. Be willing to first listen to the opposing party, and then to share your position to encourage your spouse to listen to your position; in other words, listen to her or his opinion first. Resist the urge to interrupt.

Few cases settle without *each* side demonstrating flexibility and a willingness to compromise. Most cases settle when the parties bring these qualities to the process. You may feel spiteful and angry, but these emotions may not protect your rights in the divorce, nor help you achieve your goals for a settlement.

106

Mediation and Negotiation

6.20 What will happen at my mediation or neutral case evaluation?

Typically, a neutral case evaluation or mediation will be held at the office of one of the attorneys or mediator, with both parties and lawyers present. A neutral case evaluation will typically be held at the courthouse for the convenience of the NCE judge because the judge may have more than one case in a day. A written agenda may be used to keep the focus on relevant topics. From time to time throughout the conference, you and your attorney may meet alone to consult, as needed. Counsel and the judge may meet without the parties on occasion or frequently, depending on the style of the judge. If additional information is needed to reach an agreement, some issues may be set aside for later discussion.

The length of the conference depends upon the number of issues to be resolved, the complexity of the issues, and the willingness of the parties and lawyers to communicate effectively. An effort will be made to confirm which issues are resolved and which issues remain disputed. Then, one by one, the issues are addressed.

6.21 What is the role of my attorney in the neutral case evaluation?

Your attorney is your advocate during the neutral case evaluation. You can count on him or her to support you throughout the process, to see that important issues are addressed, and to counsel you privately outside of the presence of your spouse and his or her lawyer. But advocacy does not mean just agreeing with you. Your lawyer is there to provide objective advice consistent with the law. Discussing the legal challenges of your position with you directly is part of giving you good advice.

6.22 Why is my lawyer appearing so friendly with my spouse and her lawyer?

Successful negotiations rely upon building trust between the parties working toward agreement. Your lawyer may be respectful or pleasant toward your spouse or your spouse's lawyer in order to promote a good outcome for you.

6.23 What happens if my spouse and I settle some of our issues but not all of them?

You and your spouse can agree to maintain the agreements you have reached and let the judge decide those matters that you are unable to resolve.

6.24 If we do reach an agreement, how long will it take before it can be finalized?

If a settlement is reached through negotiation or mediation, one of the attorneys or the mediator will put the agreement in writing for approval by both you and your spouse. After the agreement is signed and filed, it will likely be a few weeks to a few months before you have the agreement signed and returned. Your divorce will then be finalized as the date the judge signs it.

7

Domestic or Interpersonal Violence

Suddenly you are in a panic. Maybe your spouse was serious when threatening to take your child and leave the state. What if you're kicked out of your own home? What if there are threats of aggression or violence? Suppose all of the bank accounts are emptied? Your fear heightens as your mind spins with every horror story you've ever heard about divorce.

Facing an emergency situation in a divorce can feel as though your entire life is at stake. You may not be able to concentrate on anything else. At the same time, you may be paralyzed with anxiety and have no idea how to begin to protect yourself. No doubt you have countless worries about what your future holds.

Remember that you have overcome many challenges in your life before this moment. There are people willing to help you. You have strength and wisdom you may not yet even realize. Step by step, you will make it through this time.

When facing an emergency, do your best to focus on what to do in the immediate moment. Set aside your worries about the future for another day. Right now it is time to stay in the present moment, let others support you, and start taking action right away.

7.1　My spouse has left the home, and I need to get divorced as quickly as possible. What is my first step?

Your first step should be to seek legal advice at your earliest opportunity. The earlier you get legal counsel to advise you about your rights, the better. The initial consultation will answer most of your questions and start you on an action plan for your divorce.

The filing of a divorce is not the same as getting a final divorce. Even if your spouse has left the home, you may have a significant wait for a hearing to be scheduled and your spouse may not cooperate without a trial.

7.2 I'm afraid my abusive spouse will try to hurt me and/or our children if I say I want a divorce. What can I do legally to protect myself and my children?

Always remember: Safety first! Developing a plan for your safety and that of your children must be your highest priority. You should contact your local domestic violence agency or call the hotline number to obtain the assistance of an advocate. Contact information for this agency may be found in the Resources at the back of this book. If you do not have the time or opportunity to contact those services, you should immediately contact your local police department for assistance.

Your risk of harm from an abusive spouse may actually increase when you leave the relationship. For this reason, all actions must be taken with safety as the first concern. Find a lawyer who understands domestic violence. Often your local domestic violence agency can help with a referral. Talk to your lawyer about your concerns about the safety of you and your children. Ask your lawyer about a *domestic violence petition* or *restraining order*. This is a court order that may offer a number of protective measures, including granting you temporary emergency custody of your children, as well as ordering your spouse to leave the family residence and have no contact with you or, in some cases, your children until there is a hearing, usually within thirty days, but sometimes as soon as five business days if your spouse requests.

7.3 I am afraid to meet with a lawyer because I am terrified my spouse will find out and become violent. What should I do?

Schedule an initial consultation with an attorney who is experienced in working with domestic violence victims. When you schedule the appointment, let the firm know your situation and instruct the law office not to place any calls to you that you think your spouse might discover. If possible, if there is a fee, pay for your consultation in cash.

Any consultations with your attorney are confidential. Your lawyer has an ethical duty to not disclose your meeting with anyone outside of the law firm. Let your attorney know of all your concerns so that extra precautions can be taken by the law office in handling your file.

7.4 I want to give my attorney all the information needed so my children and I are safe from my spouse. What does this include?

Provide your attorney with complete information about the history, background, and nature and evidence of your abuse, including:

- The types of abuse (for example: physical, sexual, verbal, financial, mental, or emotional)
- The dates, time frames, or occasions of the abuse
- The locations (for example: whether it took place at home or in public)
- Whether you were ever treated medically; if so, the accompanying medical records
- Any police reports made or filed or any police involvement
- Any e-mails, letters, notes, or journal entries documenting the abuse
- Any photographs taken
- Any witnesses to the abuse or evidence of the abuse
- Any statements made by your spouse admitting the abuse
- Any evidence of alcohol or drug abuse
- The presence of guns or other weapons

The more precise and detailed the information provided to your lawyer, the easier it will be for him or her to make a strong case for the protection of you and your children.

7.5   I'm not ready to hire a lawyer for a divorce, but I am afraid my spouse is going to become violent with me and my children in the meantime. What can I do?

It is possible to seek a *domestic violence restraining order* from the court without an attorney. You can obtain the forms at the courthouse in any county in New Hampshire or online. You should also consider contacting your local domestic violence agency because the advocates there can help you complete the necessary forms and even attend court with you in many cases.

7.6   What is the difference between a *domestic violence restraining order* and a *civil restraining order* in a divorce?

Domestic violence restraining orders are intended to protect a person who has been subject to abuse as described under the law. In order to obtain a domestic violence restraining order in New Hampshire, you must have a "qualifying relationship," which means you must be current or former spouses, share children, or be current or former romantic partners. The orders are reviewed and signed by a judge if granted and they direct the other person not to engage in certain behaviors.

This order is intended to protect a victim and children. Although any of these orders can initially be obtained without any notice to the other spouse, the receiving spouse always has a right to a hearing to determine whether a restraining order should remain in place. Domestic violence restraining orders are served upon the party by law enforcement officers, who are required to carefully explain the terms and consequences of the order. The person who is served with the domestic violence restraining order is required to surrender all firearms and weapons to law enforcement.

Talk to your attorney about obtaining a domestic violence restraining order if you are concerned about your safety or your children's safety, or if there has been a history of domestic abuse. If your spouse has attempted to cause you bodily injury, has caused you bodily injury, or has threatened to cause you bodily injury, you may qualify for a domestic violence restraining order. The violation of a domestic violence restraining order is a criminal offense, which often results in immediate arrest.

The judge can also order that firearms or other weapons be removed temporarily, and, in some case, permanently.

If you are concerned that your spouse will annoy, threaten, harass, or intimidate you after your divorce complaint is filed, ask your lawyer about a civil restraining order. A *civil restraining order* is issued by a judge, and it directs one or both parties to not engage in certain behaviors such as calling the other spouse at work or entering a spouse's residence without invitation.

A civil restraining order is less serious than a domestic violence restraining order because law enforcement is typically not involved in delivering these restraining orders. A person subject to this type of order is not required to surrender firearms or weapons, and it is not required for a crime to be alleged as it is with a domestic violence restraining order. If your spouse violates the civil restraining order, he or she may be brought before the court for *contempt*. But this type of civil order in a divorce may not mean arrest and a criminal charge like the domestic violence restraining order described above.

It is common practice in New Hampshire to negotiate a civil restraining order and its protections to limit contact of the parties if a domestic violence restraining order is not necessary for the parties to be able to continue to co-parent. Talk to your attorney about whether this might be appropriate in your case.

Your lawyer or an advocacy organization in your county will help select the order most applicable to you and your facts. Any of these orders can be in effect for months or years.

7.7 My spouse has never been violent, but I know that when the divorce papers are served, he will be very angry. Do I need a restraining order?

The facts of your case may not warrant a restraining order. This is always difficult advice for a lawyer to give because you are attempting to predict human behavior. In many cases, there will be anger but no physical aggression or violence as the law defines that behavior for the purposes of an emergency court order. Your lawyer may include a motion for interim or temporary relief with the petition.

You want to get good advice before you file for a restraining order. Under New Hampshire law, a court may consider (in very limited circumstances) the misuse or abuse of the restraining order process in deciding parenting orders. Just be careful and consult with a qualified lawyer or advocate before you file anything under oath about your spouse.

7.8 My spouse has been harassing me since I filed for divorce. What can I do?

It may be possible to seek a restraining order from the court depending on the specific facts of your case. In order to qualify, you must be able to prove good cause, especially if you need to continue to have a co-parenting relationship with your spouse moving forward. Talk with your lawyer about whether you should seek the court's protection from your spouse.

7.9 I'm afraid my spouse is going to take all of the money out of our bank accounts and leave me with nothing. What can I do?

Talk to your attorney immediately. If you are worried about your spouse emptying financial accounts or selling off marital assets, it is critical that you take action at once. Your attorney can advise you concerning your right to take possession of certain assets in order to protect them from being hidden or disposed of by your spouse.

Under New Hampshire law, once a divorce petition is filed and served, non-hypothecation orders are automatically entered against both parties. These orders forbid your spouse from selling, transferring, hiding, or otherwise disposing of marital property until the divorce is complete.

This does not mean, however, that a party will not violate the order. Sadly, this happens too often. But a judge can punish that behavior with a *contempt of court* charge or a court order to return funds or property. In extreme cases, the court may impose a receiver to oversee a business, especially in certain circumstances when there is a serious risk of the loss of business assets or income and one party controls all of that income. A receiver may be an accountant, a lawyer, or another professional who is appointed by the court to oversee and report on the business and its income during the case.

Domestic or Interpersonal Violence

7.10   My spouse says that I am crazy, that I am a liar, and that no judge will ever believe me if I tell the truth about the abusive behavior. What can I do if I don't have any proof except my word?

Most domestic violence is not witnessed by third parties or recorded on camera or tape. Often there is little physical evidence. Even without physical evidence, however, a judge can enter orders to protect you and your children if you give testimony about your abuse that the judge finds believable. Your own testimony of your abuse is considered to be evidence.

It is very common for persons who abuse others to claim that their victims are liars and to make statements intended to discourage disclosure of the abuse. This is yet another form of controlling behavior.

Your attorney's skills and experience will support you and enable you to give effective testimony in the courtroom to establish your case. Let your lawyer know all of your concerns so that a strong case can be presented based upon your statements of the truth of your experience.

7.11   My spouse told me that if I ever file for divorce, I'll never see my child again. Should I be worried about my child being abducted?

Your fear that your spouse will abduct your child is a common one. It can be helpful to look at some of the factors that appear to increase the risk that your child will actually be removed from the state by the other parent. Exit activities such as obtaining a new passport, getting financial matters in order, or contacting a moving company could be indicators.

Talk to your lawyer to assess the risks in your particular case. Together you can determine whether statements by your spouse are threats intended to control or intimidate you, or whether legal action is truly needed to protect your child.

7.12   What legal steps can be taken to prevent my spouse from removing our child from the state?

This a complex area of the law, so make sure you speak with a lawyer who is familiar with federal and state law as it relates to national or international child custody. If you are concerned about your child being removed from the state, ask your lawyer whether any of the following options might be available in your case:

- A court order giving you immediate parenting rights until a temporary hearing can be held
- A court order directing your spouse to turn over passports for the child and your spouse, to be held by a neutral third party or counsel
- Supervised visitation

Both state and federal laws are designed to provide protection from the removal of children from one state to another when a parental rights matter is under consideration, so as to protect children from parental kidnapping.

The *Uniform Child Custody Jurisdiction Enforcement Act (UCCJEA)* was passed specifically to encourage decisions regarding the custody of children to be made in the state where they have been living most recently and where they have the most ties. The *Parental Kidnapping Prevention Act (PKPA)* makes it a federal crime for a parent to kidnap a child in violation of a valid custody or parenting order.

If you are concerned about your child being abducted, talk with your lawyer about all options available to you for your child's protection.

7.13   If either my spouse or I file for divorce, will I and my children be ordered out of my home?

If you and your spouse cannot reach a temporary or final agreement regarding which of you will leave the residence during the divorce, a judge (or referee in some cases) will decide whether one of you should be granted exclusive possession of the home until the case is concluded.

Abusive behavior should be a critical factor for seeking temporary possession of the home or apartment. Other factors a judge may consider, along with abuse or violence, include the following:

- Whether one of you owned the home prior to the marriage
- Historical parenting arrangements, including children's attendance in the school district and who is available to daily monitor and supervise the children

116

- After provisions are made for payment of temporary support, who can afford to remain in the home or obtain other housing

- Who is most likely to be awarded the home in the divorce

- Options available to each of you for other temporary housing, including other homes or family members who live in the area

- Special needs that would make a move unduly burdensome, such as a health condition or accessibility of other housing in the area

- Self-employment from home that could not be readily moved out of the home, such as a child care or other business

If staying in the home is important to you for the safety or security of you and your child, talk to your attorney about your reasons so that a strong case can be made for you at the temporary hearing in the divorce or a domestic violence hearing in an emergency.

8

Parental Rights and Responsibilities

Ever since you and your spouse began talking about divorce, chances are your children have been your greatest concern. You or your spouse might have even postponed the decision to seek divorce because of your concern about the impact on your children. Now that the time has come, you may still have doubts about whether your children will be all right after the divorce.

Remember that you have been making wise and loving decisions for your children since they were born. You've always done your best to see that they had everything they really needed. You loved them and protected them. This won't change because you are going through a divorce. You were a good parent before the divorce, and you will be a good parent after the divorce.

It can be difficult not to worry about how the sharing of parenting time with your spouse will affect your children. You may also have fears about being cut out of your child's life. Try to remember that regardless of who maintains the primary residence and how parenting time is allocated, it is likely that a court order will award you significant time with your children, as well as the right to be involved in their day-to-day lives.

With the help of your lawyer, you can make sound decisions regarding the parenting time arrangement that is in the best interest of your children.

8.1 What types of parental rights and responsibilities are awarded in New Hampshire?

Under New Hampshire law, there are two aspects to a parenting determination. In the traditional language you will see on the Internet or in various books about divorce, these are rights to *legal custody* and rights to *physical custody,* though in New Hampshire, we call those *decision-making responsibility and residential responsibility* and *parenting time.*

Decision-making resposibility refers to the power to make fundamental decisions regarding your children, such as which school they attend, what religious practices they will follow, and the identity and selection of health-care providers, for example. Residental responsiblity refers to the physical location of the children, that is, where they spend their time. Like decision-making responsibility, residential responsibility may be awarded to either parent or to both parents jointly. New Hampshire has eliminated the designation of a *primary parent* in a parenting plan. Instead, the schedule of *parenting time* is laid out, and the court determines and interprets the schedule as necessary. The intention of the legislature was to reduce the conflict surrounding the primary parent designation.

Regardless of which parent has which rights, the parent who is physically with the children may make day-to-day or nonmajor decisions unless a court order clearly states otherwise.

Shared decision-making responsibility means that you must first consult with the other parent as to major decisions concerning the best interest of a child and that major nonemergency decisions require the consent of both parents. For example, school placement or a change of schools, the choice of a physician, the selection of a therapist, or orthodontic treatment fall within the definition of major decisions.

Sole decision-making responsibility means that a parent can make the major decisions described above without the consent of or consultation with the other parent. Judges may require that a notice of the decision be given to the other parent. This power is not unlimited, as the other parent may still ask a judge to review the decision in the context of the best interest of the child. The burden on the parent without authority is, however, very high.

On rare occasions, the court may determine some hybrid between sole and shared decision-making responsibility is in your children's best interest. This may mean that there are some types of issues you must decide together, but others that one parent may decide in absence of agreement. You likely would need a significant and compelling reason for why this is appropriate and supporting testimony or evidence for a judge. As a matter of tradition and practice in New Hampshire, parents usually have shared decision-making unless one parent is unavailable (for example, due to a prison sentence, a trip out of the country, or domestic violence). There is a presumption in the law for shared decision-making. Shared decision-making is encouraged so as to facilitate the following forms of healthy parenting involvement:

- Effective and open communication between parents concerning the child
- A strong desire on the part of both parents to continue to co-parent
- A history of active involvement of both parents in the child's life
- Similar parenting values held by both parents
- A willingness on the part of both parents to place the child's needs before their own
- A collaborative willingness to be flexible and to compromise when making decisions concerning the child

Regardless of which form of decision-making you may agree upon, what a court may order, or who maintains the primary residence, specific parenting time may be awarded to each parent. Some parents require substantial details, and other parents have a broadly stated parenting schedule that is only a default for when they cannot agree.

Provisions for days of the week and school breaks such as the summer break, holidays, and other vacations are typically made in detail. If one of your children will primarily reside with you and another child will primarily reside with the other parent, the arrangement is referred to as *split residence*. A split residence more often occurs when you have an older adolescent child who may have different needs or school preference than the younger child. It is often preferable to keep siblings on the same or similar schedule.

Whatever schedule you are considering, be sure to discuss with your attorney not only the best interest of your children, but also the possible ramifications for child support. Under New Hampshire law, *substantially equal parenting time* can affect the amount of child support required or ordered under certain situations.

8.2   What is a *parenting plan?*

A *parenting plan* is a document detailing how you and your spouse will parent your child in good faith after the divorce. Among the issues addressed in a parenting plan are:

- Parental rights and responsibilities and decision-making
- Parenting time, including specific times for:
  - The regular school year
  - Holidays
  - Birthdays
  - Mother's Day and Father's Day
  - Summer vacation
  - School breaks
- Phone access to the child
- Communication regarding the child
- Access to records regarding the child
- Notice regarding parenting time
- Attendance at the child's activities
- Decision-making regarding the child
- Timely exchange of information, such as addresses, phone numbers, and care providers
- Alternative dispute resolution methods, such as mediation

Sufficiently detailed parenting plans are good for children and parents. They increase clarity for the parents, provide security for the child in knowing what to expect, reduce conflict, and lower the risk of needing to return to court for a modification. The New Hampshire court form Parenting Plan is a great starting point for discussion of all of these points.

8.3 What factors may a judge use to award a parenting schedule if we cannot settle on a parenting plan ourselves?

A judge may consider many factors when determining primary residence. The law requires the court to apply the *best interest of the child standard,* which, in New Hampshire, includes thirteen factors as outlined in the statute. To determine the best interest of a child, the judge may look at the following factors:

- *The relationship of the child with each parent and the ability of each parent to provide the child with nurture, love, affection, and guidance.* The judge may take into consideration the emotional bond between each parent and the child.

- *The ability of each parent to assure that the child receives adequate food, clothing, shelter, medical care, and a safe environment.* The court may consider factors such as the safety, stability, and quality of nurturing appropriate to the age of a child as found in each home.

- *The child's developmental needs and the ability of each parent to meet them, both in the present and in the future.* The judge may look at any special health needs of a child and each parent's ability to meet those needs.

- *The quality of the child's adjustment to the child's school and community and the potential effect of any change.* The judge will consider if making a determination about parenting or a parent's possible decision to move will cause a change of school or community, and may consider this in determining whether a change is in a child's best interests.

- *The ability and disposition of each parent to cooperate with the other parent, including whether contact is likely to result in harm to the child or to a parent.*

The court may consider your ability and willingness to be cooperative with the other parent. This is sometimes referred to as the *friendly parent factor.* Chronic interference, domestic violence, or subtle or overt coercion of a child may all be considered by a court when deciding guidelines for a parenting plan. In extreme cases, such behaviors may result in a parent having supervised visitations or mental health intervention as a prerequisite to parenting time.

- *The support of each parent for the child's relationship with the other parent, as shown by allowing and promoting frequent and continuing physical, written, and telephone contact with the other parent, including whether contact is likely to result in harm to the child or to a parent.* Whether a parent is supportive of the child's relationship with the other parent is very important. The judge will expect parties to be supportive of the child's relationship with the other parent unless that relationship is objectively harmful or dangerous to a child. Parents who prevent a child from calling the other parent or consistently interfere with contact for their own purposes are not likely to be seen as acting in their child's best interest. Exceptions to this include if a parent is abusive to a child or a parent, in which case, protecting a child from the other parent may be necessary to avoid harm.

- *The relationship of the child with any other person who may significantly affect the child.* This may include stepparent and grandparent relationships that are important to a child, and how those relationships may be affected by a judge's determination.

- *The ability of the parents to communicate, cooperate with each other, and make joint decisions concerning the children, including whether contact is likely to result in harm to the child or to a parent.* It is important for the parents to be able to effectively communicate about the children, and if they cannot, the judge will consider those factors in making best-interest decisions.

- *Any evidence of abuse and the impact of the abuse on the child and on the relationship between the child and the abusing parent.* Domestic violence is a crucial factor when determining parental rights and responsibilities, including the structure of parenting time. A restraining order or a criminal charge or conviction may require much more serious consideration of parenting arrangements, like supervised contact or safe places for transfers. Whenever domestic violence is a concern, you should discuss that in detail with your attorney during the initial consultation so that every measure can be taken to protect the safety of you and your children.

- *If a parent is incarcerated, the reason for and the length of the incarceration, and any unique issues that arise as a result of incarceration.* The more serious the crime and time, the more likely this will affect a court's determination of best interest of a child. Unless a child is older, or both parents are supportive, it is unlikely a judge will order visits to occur in a prison setting. These decisions are, however, on a case-by-case basis.

- *The policy of the state regarding the determination of parental rights and responsibilities. New Hampshire's policy is that children do best with active involvement from both parents and frequent and continuing contact with both parents.* Therefore, the policy of the state is for both parents to have significant roles, so long as the other factors are present.

- *Any other additional factors the court deems relevant.* This catchall phrase allows the judge to use any other evidence it feels relevant to make final determinations about what is best for your child or children.

8.4 What is the difference between visitation and parenting time?

Historically, time spent with the non-primary residential parent was referred to as *visitation*. Today, the term *parenting time* is used to refer to the time a child spends with each parent. This change in language reflects the intention that the child spend time with both parents and have two homes, as opposed to their living with one parent and just visiting the other. The exception to this is if parenting time is subject to restrictions, such as being at a supervised visitation center or subject to the supervision of a third party.

It is important to state your goals for your child very clearly and carefully from the beginning of your case regarding the development and design of a parenting plan. Take the time to design a parenting plan that is practical and meets the needs of your child for the foreseeable future. Sometimes these parenting plans will last for many years without modification. Being flexible and recognizing that both parents will go through changes during the divorce and thereafter may feel uncomfortable at various times, but like those of your child, your life circumstances will change during this process.

Remember that most parenting plans may be good only for a few years because your child's developmental age, school demands, and activities, as well as your own personal and work life, are fluid events that will change. Patience, flexibility, and reflection are helpful to maintain a parenting plan that works best for you and your family.

8.5 How can I best protect my children's interests during the divorce?

The best way to make sure your child's interests are protected is to provide clarity about living arrangements and respective parenting time in writing or to obtain a temporary order. Informal or vague agreements between parties cannot always be trusted.

Additionally, informal agreements with your spouse lack the capacity to be enforced by a court. If a judge does not approve an agreement, it is not a court order but merely a contract and it may or may not be determined to be binding. Even if you and your spouse have agreed to temporary arrangements, talk with your attorney about whether this agreement should be formalized in a court order.

This can be a tough call because parents may cooperate more if they believe the power rests with them rather than feeling forced to do something by court order. Human nature can be unpredictable, so try to do the best you can to keep stability in place.

Obtaining a temporary order can provide not only important protection for your children, but also address other issues such as support, possession of the marital home, protection from your spouse, or attorney fees.

Finally, until a temporary order or written agreement is entered, it is best that you continue to reside with your children. If you are considering leaving your home, talk with your attorney before making any significant changes to your living situation. If you must leave your home, you may be able to take your children with you, but absent agreement with your spouse, this will likely escalate conflict and lead to restraining orders or other emergency motions, as well as possible police involvement, so undertake these decisions with great care and only after you get clear advice from your lawyer.

8.6   Must I let my spouse see the children before we are actually divorced?

Unless your children are at risk for being harmed by your spouse, your children should maintain regular contact with the other parent during the divorce.

It is important for children to experience the presence of both parents in their lives, regardless of your separation. Even if there is no temporary order for parenting time, cooperate with your spouse in making reasonable arrangements.

If safety is not an issue and you deny contact with the other parent prior to a trial, a judge is likely to question whether you have the best interest of your child at heart. Talk to your spouse or your lawyer about what parenting time schedule would be best for your children on a temporary basis. More parental rights determinations turn on interference by one parent toward another than you may think.

8.7   Can my attorney speak with my children?

With very rare exceptions, your attorney should never speak with your children. A lawyer could be accused of planting the seeds of preference for a parent (his or her client, of course), and this may make the lawyer an actual witness in the case. If a guardian *ad litem* (GAL) is appointed by the court, a lawyer should never interview a child without the prior consent of the GAL or the court.

If your lawyer asks to interview your child, you should carefully discuss the legal and ethical consequences of such a decision. This can backfire in a parenting case.

8.8 What is a *guardian ad litem,* or *GAL?* Why is one appointed?

A *guardian ad litem (GAL)* is a state-certified professional, such as a lawyer, psychologist, or social worker, who has attended and completed court-mandated training and appears on a court-approved roster.

When a child needs to be interviewed, or the court wants a factual investigation and there is a need for an independent voice or advocate, a GAL may be appointed by a judge to represent the best interest of the child.

A GAL must be directed by the judge to conduct an investigation on specific issues that must be explicitly contained in the *order of appointment.* This order must also include the time frame for the investigation and a report, as well as the amount and means for paying the GAL fees.

A GAL has the responsibility to represent and advocate for the child's best interest in the proceeding. This is required because, under the ethical code governing judges, they cannot leave the bench and visit your home or talk to you, your child, or witnesses except at the courthouse with both parents and their lawyers present.

In New Hampshire, court-appointed GALs granted at state expense for children are only available in child protection proceedings brought by the State of New Hampshire against parent(s). There are constitutional reasons that do not yet apply in private parenting cases brought by one parent against another parent in a divorce. Therefore, any fees for a GAL in your divorce must be paid for by you or your spouse from your respective incomes or assets. The court may find a GAL willing to accept the appointment for a reduced fee if parents are truly indigent, but that is the exception not the rule.

8.9   What is a *family systems evaluation (FSE)* or *child custody evaluation (CCE)* expert? Why is one appointed?

If parenting time is disputed, the court may order an expert to be appointed as a neutral evaluator, who is usually a licensed clinical psychologist with extensive forensic or court experience in testing and evaluation of parents and children in a parenting case. The precise role of the evaluator may be to conduct *family systems evaluation (FSE)* or *child custody evaluations (CCEs)* and/or *psychological or parenting capacity evaluations* of the parents, including an assessment of the child, so as to make recommendations to the court concerning residence, parenting time, or the need for a specific therapeutic intervention if one or both parent(s) have a diagnosable mental health or substance abuse problem. The scope of the evaluation will depend upon the precise questions proposed by the GAL, the court, or the attorneys to the expert.

The expert will conduct a complete evaluation of the parties, including psychological testing, interviews of the parents and children, and evaluations of the interaction between the children and both parents. The expert is also authorized to review and receive information, records, and reports concerning all parties involved. The expert will then submit a report to the court, the GAL, and the attorneys with his or her recommendations and may also testify at trial.

Under the ethical rules of the American Psychological Association, which govern the behavior of psychologists, an evaluator cannot act in that role and also serve as a GAL in the same case. Therefore, the evaluator is not a GAL. And the same is true in the other direction: a GAL cannot conduct psychological testing of the parents, but they can rely on a report written by a qualified expert. The purpose for using the evaluator is to gain insight into the personality and functional parenting capacities of both parents and the needs of the children. These evaluations will be used to design a parenting plan that reduces conflict as well as engages therapeutic strategies that may help the family move beyond the divorce conflict. In cases in which one or both parents suffer from psychological issues, significant and ongoing mental health counseling may be necessary or required by the judge.

8.10 How old do children have to be before they can speak to a judge?

Judges make every effort to protect minor children from the conflict of their parents. For this reason, most judges will not allow children to be present in the courtroom to hear testimony or to testify themselves.

Under New Hampshire law, a child of any age can testify as a witness if a judge finds the child competent to tell the truth. However, this does not mean that testifying in court is a good idea for a child. Some judges may actually consider a parent's request for a child to testify as a negative factor for determining parenting time. You need to be very careful when asking the judge to let your child testify.

The decision about whether a child testifies will also depend upon the judge. There is no set age at which children are allowed to speak to the judge about their preferences. Some judges do not mind allowing that in certain cases involving teenagers, but other judges will be very uncomfortable with the idea. The law gives a judge broad discretion to decide if, when, and how a child may testify.

If either you or your spouse wants the judge to listen to what your child has to say, such a request is ordinarily made to have the child speak to the judge in the judge's office, or chambers, rather than from the witness stand. Depending upon the judge's decision, the attorneys for you and your spouse, or the GAL, may also be present.

It is possible that the judge may allow the attorneys to question the child; however, the types of questions can be limited. If you have concerns about the other parent learning what your child says to the judge, talk to your lawyer about the possibility of obtaining a court order to keep this information confidential.

No matter the circumstances, in all cases in New Hampshire, a judge must record the interview of your children for the record. This is done so that the testimony can be transcribed later in the event of an appeal by either parent.

8.11   How much weight does a child's preference carry in a parenting rights case?

The preference of your child is only one of many factors a judge may consider. However, the judge may not consider the child's preference at all. The age and maturity of your child and his or her ability to express the underlying reasons for their preference to live with either parent will determine the amount of weight a judge may give to your child's preference. Although there is no set age under New Hampshire law at which your child's preference carries weight, most judges give more weight to the wishes of an older adolescent child. A child's maturity level is weighed more heavily than the age of a child.

The reasoning underlying your child's preference is also a factor to consider. Consider the fifteen-year-old girl who wants to live with her mother because "Mom lets me stay out past curfew, I get a bigger allowance, and I don't have to do chores." Greater weight might be given to the preference of a fourteen-year-old boy who wants to live with his mother because "she helps me with my homework and doesn't call me names like Dad does."

If you see that your child's preference may be a factor, discuss it with your lawyer so that this consideration is an early part of assessing your case. Their advice may include other interventions, including a guardian *ad litem* to protect the child's interest or prevent the child from having to testify in court.

8.12   How can I prove that I was the primary care provider?

One tool to assist you and your attorney is a chart indicating the care you and your spouse have each provided for your child. The clearer you are about the history of your parenting, the better job your attorney can do presenting your case to the judge.

The old admonition that "a picture is worth a thousand words" applies with particularity here. A judge may have a difficult time taking notes or trying to follow oral testimony about your life as you explain it with words alone. So *draw* that picture in a parental roles chart and make it accurate and clear. Do not exaggerate here because, just as a picture can illuminate truth, it can also illuminate, or quite painfully bring to light, exaggerations or falsehoods on cross-examination.

A parental roles chart is not just useful for trial, but it can be used in mediation and neutral case evaluation. Look at the activities in the following chart to help you review the roles of both you and your spouse as care providers for your child:

Parental Roles Chart

Activity	Parent 1	Parent 2
Attended prenatal medical visits		
Attended prenatal classes		
Took time off work after child was born		
Got up with child for feedings		
Got up with child when sick at night		
Bathed child		
Put child to sleep		
Potty-trained child		
Prepared and fed meals to child		
Helped child learn numbers, letters, colors		
Helped child with practice for music, dance, sports		
Took time off work for child's appointments		
Stayed home from work with sick child		
Took child to doctor visits		
Picked up child's medication		
Took child to therapy		
Took child to optometrist		
Took child to dentist		
Took child to get haircuts		
Bought clothing for child		
Bought school supplies for child		
Transported child to school		

Parental Roles Chart (Continued)

Activity	Parent 1	Parent 2
Picked up child after school		
Drove carpool for child's school		
Attended child's school activities		
Helped child with homework and projects		
Attended parent-teacher conferences		
Helped in child's classroom		
Chaperoned child's school trips and activities		
Transported child to day care		
Attended day-care activities		
Signed child up for music, sports, dance		
Attended music, sports, dance activities		
Coached child's sports		
Transported child from music, sports, dance		
Knows child's friends and friends' families		
Took child to religious education		
Participated in child's religious education		
Obtained information and training about special needs		
Comforted child during times of emotional upset		

8.13 How might photographs or a video of my child help my parental rights case?

Photographs or a video depicting your child's day-to-day life can help the judge learn more about your child's needs. It may demonstrate how your child interacts with you, siblings, and other important people in your family's life. The photographs or video can portray your child's room, home, and neighborhood, as well as show your child participating in various activities.

Talk to your lawyer about whether photographs or a video would be helpful in your case. Although photographs are more commonly used and are typically sufficient evidence, ask your lawyer if he or she recommends making a video, and if so, what scenes to include, the length of the video, whether or not to keep the original media used, and what editing process should be used.

8.14   I am seeing a therapist. Will that hurt my chances for being granted parenting time?

If you are seeing a therapist, it demonstrates a positive acknowledgment that your well-being is important to you and that you are seeking to be the best parent you can be after the pain of separation. Your therapist should understand that you are there to engage in positive change and assure that the stress of the divorce does not harm you or your children over the long run.

Not every therapist, however, is comfortable with the legal system, so it is crucial that you ask your therapist how he or she will share information about your case if asked to do so by a guardian *ad litem*, lawyer, or judge. It is particularly important that you ask your therapist whether you will receive any diagnosis or recommendations for medication. Unfortunately, a diagnosis can be misconstrued or abused in the legal system, so you need to know at the outset of treatment whether you believe a contested parenting case may be on the horizon for you. This is very unfair to good parents who are seeking treatment, but it is no less important to protect yourself from the misuse of your treatment plan or records.

Your mental health records may be subpoenaed by the other parent's lawyer depending on the grounds for the divorce case you have filed, or the court may require you to release those records to a GAL. For this reason, it is important to discuss with your attorney an action plan for responding to a request to obtain the records in your therapist's file. Ask your attorney to contact your therapist to alert him or her regarding any potential requests for your mental health records.

If your therapist is uncomfortable with the legal system and parenting matters, then you need to know at the beginning of treatment. It is not fair to you or your therapist for there to be conflict later if your therapist is unequipped to deal with potential litigation. This is not a criticism, but a necessary warning.

Discuss with your therapist and your lawyer the implications of your being treated by a therapist. It may be that the condition for which you are being treated would in no way be seen by the court as affecting your child or your ability to be a loving and supportive parent.

8.15   I am taking prescription medication to treat my depression. Will this hurt my chances of getting parental rights of my children?

It should not. Feelings of depression and anxiety, as well as difficulty sleeping, are common during a divorce. If you do have any significant mental health concerns, seek help from a professional. Following through with the recommendations made by your health-care provider will be looked upon favorably by the court, including the proper and prescribed use of prescription medication.

With that said, there is still, rather sadly, a bias in our society concerning mental health diagnosis and treatment, and there are many myths that can be distorted or contorted. Americans will immediately rally around a parent or child with cancer, but they still frequently act as if seeking mental health treatment itself is a weakness or a barrier to parenting. This prejudice is something your lawyer needs to be prepared to manage in court with you and your therapist.

8.16   Should I hire a private detective?

It is rare to hire a private detective just to prove poor behavior by your spouse. However, if parenting is in dispute and your spouse is involved with someone with a criminal record or if drug abuse or other illegal activities are involved, discuss with your attorney how a private investigator might help you gather evidence to support your case. Discuss the following considerations with your attorney:

- How is the activity affecting your children?
- How much will a private investigator cost?
- Will the evidence gathered actually help your case?

- Will a judge really care about this, or will it backfire on you?

Your attorney can help you determine whether hiring a private investigator is a good idea in your particular case.

8.17 Will the fact that I had a relationship with someone other than my spouse during the marriage, or that I have such a relationship during the divorce, hurt my chances of obtaining parenting time with my children?

Whether any relationship during your marriage or during the divorce process will have an impact on your time with your children will depend upon many factors, including:

- Whether the children were or are exposed to the relationship

- Whether the relationship had any impact on the children's emotional stability or their trust of a parent

- Whether the relationship is currently active or strictly in the past

- Whether the relationship has distracted your parenting or influenced the quality of your parenting

- Whether the relationship has added another source of conflict for your children because the person has injected him or herself in your divorce

In determining primary residence or access, a court may consider a parent's moral fitness, which includes his or her relationships with other people. However, these considerations may only be taken into account if the children were adversely affected by exposure to the relationship. If you had or still have a relationship, discuss it with your attorney at the outset so that you can assess its impact, if any, on parental rights. Secrets rarely remain secrets, and surprises rarely help a lawyer protect your interests.

A final point based upon years of observation: If you decide to get involved with someone during your divorce, it may have little or no legal effect on your case, but it may prolong it and add substantial expense. Just remember that a divorce is rarely just about the law or the lawyers or the judge. It is about your relationship with the other parent and how the history of that relationship is seen by the lawyers and the courts.

8.18 During the time it takes to get a divorce, will dating other people hurt my case?

If parenting arrangements are in dispute, talk with your attorney about your plan to date. Your dating other people may be legally irrelevant if the children are unaware of it, but often judges will frown upon exposing your children to a new relationship when they are still adjusting to the separation of their parents.

You have the right to maintain a personal relationship with another person, but you should be very careful about continuing that relationship if:

- The relationship involves someone with a criminal record
- That person has a substance abuse problem or a prior loss of child custody
- That person is or was involved in a child protective case which alleged abuse or neglect
- There has been a finding of domestic violence or abuse against them
- There are other kinds of civil or criminal findings concerning that person in which a judge or jury determined there was abuse or a crime

If your spouse is contesting parenting arrangements, it may be best to focus your energy on your children, the litigation, and taking care of yourself at this time. Exposing your children to a new dating relationship can seriously harm your case and may even harm your children for years to come.

8.19 Can having a live-in partner hurt my chances of getting parenting time?

If you are contemplating having a new dating partner live with you, discuss your decision with your attorney first. If you are already living with such a partner, let your attorney know right away so that the potential impact on any parenting ruling can be assessed, because living with someone who is not your spouse may significantly impact your case in a negative way.

Judges' opinions of the significance of this factor can vary greatly. Talk promptly and frankly with your lawyer. It will be important for you to look together at many aspects of your living arrangement, including the following:

- How the judge assigned to your case views these situations. You may not like that opinion and consider it unfair, but the judge has the power over the final decision.

- Whether your living arrangement is likely to prompt a parenting dispute that would not otherwise arise

- How long you have been separated from the other parent

- How long you have been in a relationship with your new partner

- The history and nature of the children's relationship with your new partner or the new partner's own children

- Any existing parenting cases or court-ordered parenting plans or orders involving your new partner and his or her children

- Your future plans with your partner (such as marriage)

Consider such a decision thoughtfully, taking into account the advice of your lawyer and the impact of your decision on the emotional and financial costs of your divorce.

8.20 What impact will my sexual orientation have on my case for primary residence or parenting time?

There are no laws in New Hampshire that limit your rights as a parent based upon your sexual orientation. In fact, New Hampshire law prohibits any such form of discrimination, just as New Hampshire law forbids an award of residence or limits on parenting time based upon presumptions about gender alone.

Exposing your child to relationships of any kind or sexual activity that harms your child are relevant factors in any parenting dispute. *Sexual orientation* is not the same as *sexual activity*.

Be sure to choose a lawyer whom you are confident will fully support your goals as a parent. Understand that in order to dispel certain myths, you may need to further educate your spouse, opposing counsel, and the judge. The law may be clear, but that does not mean that prejudice is nonexistent.

8.21 What defines *abandonment,* and is it a factor in a parenting case?

Abandonment is rarely an issue in parenting litigation unless one parent has been absent from the child's life for an extended period of time without a rational explanation. Under New Hampshire law, the relevance of abandonment is determined by the facts and circumstances of each case. The intentional absence of a parent's presence, care, protection, and financial and personal support are all carefully weighed and considered.

For example, a parent convicted of a crime who is imprisoned may have his or her right to parent limited by that absence. Conversely, a parent serving on active duty in the military service of the country may not be considered to have abandoned his or her child, but the absence may require careful consideration of reunification or access depending upon many factors, including the age of the child and the past parenting role.

In very specific circumstances, a court may consider terminating parental rights for abandonment, but only if doing so would be in the best interest of the child.

8.22 Can I have witnesses speak on my behalf in my parenting dispute?

Witnesses are critical in many parenting cases. At a temporary hearing, a witness is more likely to provide testimony by affidavit, which is a written, sworn statement, or in some other summary form because of time limits. However, at a trial for the final determination of parental rights and responsibilities, you will each have an opportunity to have witnesses provide live testimony under oath, including that of:

- Family members
- Family friends

- Child-care providers
- Neighbors
- Teachers
- Health-care providers
- Clergy members
- Mental health providers

In considering which witnesses may best support your case, your attorney may consider the following questions:

- What has been this witness's opportunity to observe you or the other parent, especially in relationship with your child?
- How frequent were these observations? How recently?
- How long has the witness known you or the other parent?
- What is the relationship of the witness to the child and the parents?
- How valuable and relevant is the knowledge that this witness has?
- Do these witnesses have knowledge different from other witnesses, or is it just cumulative and could possibly tax the judge's patience?
- Is the witness available and willing to voluntarily testify?
- Is the witness clear or vague when conveying information?
- Is the witness credible; that is, will the judge believe this witness?
- Does the witness have any biases or prejudices that could impact their testimony?
- What could go wrong if this witness takes the stand?
- Will the testimony harm an existing therapeutic, medical, or educational relationship that is more important to the parent or child than the value of the testimony?

- Is there an alternative way to document the evidence that still protects those important relationships?

You and your attorney should work together to determine which witnesses are most important and will best support your case. Provide a list of potential witnesses together with your opinion regarding the answers to the above questions. Be honest about the strengths and weaknesses of those whom you want as witnesses, including what they may know about you that could hurt the case. Once again, surprises are usually not helpful.

Give your attorney the phone numbers, addresses, and workplaces of each of your potential witnesses. This information can be critical to the role that the attorney has in interviewing the witnesses, contacting them regarding testifying, or issuing subpoenas to compel their court attendance if needed. Keep in mind that out-of-state witnesses who are unwilling to appear in court are more difficult to subpoena.

When parents give conflicting testimony during a parenting trial (and they often do), the testimony of witnesses can be a key to determining the outcome. But it is always important to carefully consider whether witnesses could hurt your case. Even family members with the best of intentions are not professional witnesses, and on cross-examination they can say things that may be damaging.

In addition, you may want to avoid snatching defeat from the jaws of victory if you have a favorable GAL report and the judge is experienced. Sometimes in parenting cases, less really is more, so you and your lawyer need to work to gain an understanding of the most effective strategy.

And finally, sometimes a good case simply goes bad. When all the witnesses negatively attack the other parent in a way the judge does not find credible, especially given observations of that parent and his or her witnesses, or the data provided by the GAL to the court is more reliable, a judge can actually find against you.

8.23   I don't think it's safe for my children to have any contact with my spouse. How can I prove this to a judge?

Keeping your children safe is so important that this discussion with your attorney requires immediate attention.

Options might include a domestic violence restraining order, supervised visitation, or certain restrictions on your spouse's parenting time, such as no overnight visitation. Unless any of these outcomes are voluntarily agreed to by your spouse and his or her lawyer, however, you will have to file a petition or motion so that a judge can hear the facts and apply the law.

However, it is very rare in New Hampshire for the court, in a private parenting case, to enter a *no-contact order* with respect to children. And it is important to remember that there is a difference between what you *believe* is true and what a lawyer may be able to prove in court. This is the reason that judges appoint a guardian *ad litem* to investigate the facts and try to gather more evidence than a judge might get from you in a short hearing in court.

Make sure you have an attorney who understands your legitimate concerns for the safety of your children. If your attorney is not taking your concerns seriously, you may want to consider a second opinion by a qualified lawyer.

Give your attorney a complete history of the facts upon which you base your belief that your children are not safe with the other parent. Although the most recent facts are often the most relevant, it is important that your attorney have a clear picture of the background facts as well.

Your attorney also needs information about your spouse, such as whether your spouse is or has been:

- Using or abusing alcohol or drugs
- Treated for alcohol or drug abuse
- Arrested, charged, or convicted of crimes of violence or sexual crimes
- In possession of firearms that are not legal or not safely secured
- Treated for serious mental health issues
- Subject to a protection order for harassment or violence
- Found to have abused or neglected children by a state entity or court

8.24 How can I get my spouse's parenting time to be supervised?

If you are concerned about the safety of your children when they are with your spouse, talk to your lawyer. Ask your attorney whether, under the specific and provable facts of your case, the judge would consider any of the following court orders:

- Supervised visits
- Exchanges of the children in a public place or police station
- Parenting education or training classes for the other parent
- Anger management or other educational or rehabilitative programs for the other parent
- A prohibition against drinking or substance use by the other parent when with the children

Judges have differing approaches to cases when children are at risk. Recognize that there are also often practical considerations, such as cost or the availability of qualified professional services or objective available family or third persons to supervise visits. Urge your attorney to advocate fairly and appropriately for court orders to protect your children from harm by the other parent.

8.25 My spouse keeps saying he'll get parental rights because there were no witnesses to his abuse and I can't prove it. Is he right?

The situation is not as clear-cut as that, but these cases are always harder to decide because there is often little evidence beyond what each spouse says happened. Most domestic violence is not witnessed by others, and judges know this is frequently the case. Unlike decades ago, however, judges are much better trained to assess interpersonal violence.

Be sure to tell your attorney about anyone who may have either seen your spouse's behavior or spoken to you or your children right after an abusive incident. They may be important witnesses.

If you have been a victim of abusive behavior by your spouse, or if you have witnessed your children as victims, your testimony is likely to be the most compelling evidence. Moreover, you should seek the assistance of your local domestic violence organization and try to obtain the assistance of their advocates, who are trained to understand and assist victims.

8.26 I am concerned about protecting my child from abuse by my spouse. Which types of past abuse by my spouse are important to tell my attorney?

Keeping your child safe must always be your top priority. So that your attorney can help you protect your child, a full history of the following is helpful:

- Hitting, kicking, pushing, shoving, or slapping you or your child
- Sexual abuse
- Threats to harm you or your child
- Threats to abduct your child
- Destruction of property
- Torture of pets or other harm to them
- Requiring your child to keep secrets

The process of writing down past events may help you to remember other incidents of abuse that you had forgotten. Be as complete as possible. If the process of telling the narrative or writing it down has a negative effect on you, speak immediately with a therapist or an advocate who can assist you with the documentation of your history.

8.27 What documents or items should I give my attorney to help prove a history of domestic violence by my spouse?

The following may be useful exhibits if your case goes to court:

- Photographs of injuries
- Photographs of damaged property
- Abusive or threatening notes, letters, or e-mails
- Abusive or threatening voice messages
- Your journal entries about abuse

143

- Police reports
- Medical records
- Court records
- Criminal and traffic records
- Actual damaged property, such as torn clothing or photos of holes punched in walls
- Electronic or social media material

Tell your attorney which of these you have or will be able to obtain. Ask your lawyer whether others can be acquired through a subpoena or other means.

8.28 After the trial is completed, why might I not be awarded the majority of parenting time?

In determining parenting time, the court considers the best interest of the child, which includes many factors but often emphasizes the following considerations:

- The relationship of the child to each parent prior to the divorce
- The wishes of the minor child, if he or she is of sufficient maturity to state a preference
- The general health, welfare, and social behavior of the minor child
- Credible evidence of abuse inflicted on any family or household member
- An ongoing pattern of negative thinking and lack of cooperation with the other parent
- Whether a parent may engage in good faith alternative dispute resolution after the divorce to resolve disputes or whether they plan to keep the other parent in court

Some cases are simply close calls, and you may have been awarded the majority of parenting time before a different judge. Even if the judge determines that you and your spouse are both fit to parent, he or she may nevertheless decide that it is in the best interest of your child to declare the majority of time to one parent because the judge must pick one when a parent elects a trial rather than a settlement. A decision by the judge that your spouse should have the majority of parenting time does not necessarily require the conclusion that you are an unfit parent. It remains about the best interest of the child, which can be a subjective determination.

8.29 What does it mean if a judge finds me to be an *unfit parent*?

Parental unfitness means that you have an emotional or psychological deficiency or other incapacity that likely prevents you from functionally performing essential parental obligations or is likely to result in a reasonably foreseeable detriment or risk to your child's future well-being or there is current jeopardy to a child in your care. Some reasons why a parent might be found to be unfit include a history of interpersonal abuse, chronic alcohol or drug abuse, or mental health problems that affect the ability to safely or consistently parent.

8.30 Does a *shared schedule* always mean equal time at each house?

No. A *shared schedule* means that each parent has continuous blocks of parenting time with the child for substantial lengths of time. However, this outcome does not require that each parent have precisely equal amounts of parenting time. A judge can award a *substantially equal* amount of time in the parenting plan when parents live in the same school district or relatively near each other.

8.31 If my spouse is awarded most of the parenting time, how much time will our child spend with me?

Parenting time schedules vary from case to case. However, historically, a standard parenting time schedule appropriate in some cases where an equal or approximately equal schedule is not appropriate is alternating weekends and one evening during the week. Additionally, holidays are often alternated between the parents and Mother's Day and Father's Day are spent with the appropriate parent. Holiday parenting time and vacation time supersedes the regular weekly schedule for parenting time.

The best interest of the child is what a court considers in determining the parenting time schedule. Among the factors that can impact a parenting time schedule are the past history of parenting time, the age and needs of the child, the distance the parents reside from one another and the child's school, and the parents' work schedules.

If you and your spouse are willing to reach your own agreement about the parenting time schedule, you are likely to be more satisfied with it than with one imposed by a judge. Because the two of you know your child's needs, your family traditions, and your personal preferences, you can design a plan uniquely suited to your child's best interest.

If you and your spouse are unable to reach agreement on a parenting time schedule on your own or with the assistance of your lawyers or a mediator, the judge will decide the schedule—and that can have consequences to your family for years to come.

8.32 If we are awarded equal or approximately equal parenting time, or we agree to do so, what are some examples of how this can work?

Some parents follow a 2-2-3 schedule, or a variation thereof, in which one parent has the child for two weekdays, the other parent has the child for the following two weekdays, and then the child goes back to the first parent for a three-day weekend. Below is a sample parenting chart to demonstrate that form of schedule.

2-2-3 Parenting Time Schedule

	Monday	Tuesday	Wednesday	Thursday	Friday	Saturday	Sunday
Week 1	Parent 1 at 8 A.M.	Parent 1	Parent 2 beginning at 5 P.M.	Parent 2	Parent 1 beginning at 5 P.M.	Parent 1	Parent 1
Week 2	Parent 2 at 8 A.M.	Parent 2	Parent 1 beginning at 5 P.M.	Parent 1	Parent 2 beginning at 5 P.M.	Parent 2	Parent 2

A popular variation to this schedule is the 2-2-5, which provides that the same parent will have time each weekday of the week, alternating the Friday through Sunday nights. In other words, Parent 1 will have Monday and Tuesday nights each week, Parent 2 will have Wednesday and Thursday nights each week, and the weekends will alternate. Neither parent will be away from the children for more than five nights, and the children have predictability of knowing, if it's a Monday I'm always at Mom's house, and if it's a Thursday I'm always at Dad's house.

Some parents prefer to have a one-week-on, one-week-off parenting schedule. However, this is not preferred by the courts because the child is away from the other parent for such an extended period of time. Think about the age of your child and how you can make such a schedule work. Week-on, week-off schedules work well in the summer and allow each parent significant time to vacation with the children and also permits working parents to plan for summer camps for the children. They also work better for high school-aged children.

Judges think about the following questions during a trial as well:

- Can your child pick up things like homework or sports or dance equipment at either home without stress or conflict?

- Can you and the other parent behave civilly at pickups and drop-offs?

- Is there flexibility when changes need to be made to the schedule for family emergencies or trips or work?

- Does either parent calculate time using a metaphorical stopwatch to assure an exact 50/50 certainty, or do both parents realize that over the course of the year, it all works out for the children fairly and seamlessly?

8.33 How is the parental right to make important decisions decided by a judge?

An award of *shared decision-making* means a parent has the responsibility and authority to make fundamental, major life decisions regarding their child's welfare. Examples of fundamental decisions include religious training, public or private education, and nonemergency medical treatment.

If you are awarded *sole decision-making,* you have the exclusive authority to make fundamental decisions for your child, such as what school your child will attend, who your child's treating physician will be, and whether your child should undergo elective treatments or surgeries. However, even if you are awarded these sole rights, your spouse may still have the responsibility to make the day-to-day decisions for your child when the child is in your spouse's care.

If you are awarded shared decision-making, this necessitates that you and your spouse communicate and reach agreement about fundamental decisions regarding your children. You and your spouse might be good candidates for this if you share a mutual respect for each other, communicate effectively, and can cooperate in a respectful relationship even when, just like in marriage, there are disagreements.

If you share decision-making but are unable to reach agreement on a major decision, such as a child's school or child-care provider, you and your former spouse may be required to return to mediation to resolve your dispute before a judge will hear your case. This can lead to delays in decision-making for matters important to your child, increased conflict, and further substantial legal fees.

A court is less likely to award shared decision-making if you and your spouse continually disagree about fundamental decisions regarding your child's welfare, or if you are unable to be consistent and support each other regarding your children. Additionally, if domestic violence has been present in the marriage, it is less likely that the court will award shared decision-making over all decisions.

8.34 What does it mean to have *split parenting time?*

Split parenting time refers to an arrangement in which each parent has one or more of the children living with that parent most of the time. Courts generally disfavor this arrangement because it separates the children from each other. However, split parenting time may be a preference in families with a disabled child, or a child who needs additional health services, or when there may be risk of physical or emotional harm by one sibling to another.

8.35 I want to talk to my spouse about our child, but all the other spouse wants to do is argue. How can I communicate without it always turning into a fight?

Sometimes what appears to be an argument is a discussion that has escalated because parents are tired or have too little time to discuss an issue. Sometimes, lingering emotions from the divorce are unresolved and interfere with communication. Other times, new partners or spouses may intentionally or unintentionally interfere with these discussions.

First, make sure you have time for the discussion so that you won't feel stressed about time. Avoid having discussions with the children present. Before filing to modify your parenting plan, you may want to consider going to a mediator or a parenting counselor, so a third-party professional can help guide the conversation and develop creative solutions. Also consider the following options:

- Asking your lawyer to help you obtain a court order for parenting time that is specific and detailed. This lowers the amount of necessary communication between you and your spouse.
- Putting as much information in writing as possible
- Using e-mail or a parenting journal, especially for less urgent communication
- Avoiding criticisms of your spouse's parenting
- Avoiding telling your spouse how to parent
- Being factual and businesslike
- Acknowledging to your spouse the good parental qualities he or she displays, such as their concern, attentiveness, or generosity
- Keeping your child out of any conflicts
- Talking to your attorney about developing a communication protocol to follow with your spouse

By focusing on your own behavior, conflict with your spouse has the potential to decrease over the long run to the benefit of your family.

8.36 What if my child is not returned from parenting time with my spouse at the agreed-upon time? Should I call the police?

Calling the police should be done only as a last resort if you genuinely believe that your child is at risk for abuse or neglect, or if you have been first advised by your attorney that such a call is warranted. The involvement of law enforcement officials can result in greater trauma to a child than a late return at the end of a parenting time.

The appropriate response to a child not being returned according to a court order depends upon the circumstances. If the problem is a recurring one, talk to your attorney regarding your options. It may be that a change in the schedule would be in the best interest of your child. Every violation of a court order, even if technically wrong, is not a reason to involve law enforcement. Regardless of the behavior of the other parent, make every effort to keep your child out of any conflicts between the adults whenever possible.

8.37 If I have sole parental rights, may I move out of state without the permission of my former spouse or the court?

If your court-ordered parenting plan does not provide explicit permission for you to exercise that power, you cannot do so. A parent must provide thirty days' written notice to the other parent of any relocation unless there is an exception made for specific circumstances. This exception is usually very narrowly available to you, so you should consult with a lawyer or trained domestic violence advocate or agency before making such a decision.

Ordinarily you must obtain the permission of the court prior to moving out of state or far enough away to change school districts or substantially change the parenting time schedule with a child. If your former spouse agrees to your move, contact your attorney for preparing and submitting the necessary documents to your former spouse and the court for approval.

If your former spouse objects to your move, you must apply to the court for permission, give your spouse notice of the application, and participate in a court hearing for the judge to decide. The temporary removal of a child in such cases is unlikely to be granted. It may be important to expedite your case so you can have a final court ruling determining whether you may move out of state with your child.

8.38   I have shared parental rights. What must I do if I want to move from New Hampshire to another state?

Under New Hampshire law, all court orders require notice of the intended relocation of a child by a parent awarded shared parental rights and responsibilities. This notice must be given at least thirty days before the relocation. If the relocation must occur in fewer than thirty days, the parent who is relocating needs to provide notice as soon as possible to the other parents.

However, if the parent who is relocating believes that notifying the other parent will cause danger to the relocating parent or child, this requirement may be waived by a judge. A judge may take into considerations such things as military deployment or a situation in which someone was fleeing domestic violence.

Still, giving notice does not automatically mean you can move. You may need to file a motion with the court to get permission to move your children. Judges take these events seriously, but it may take weeks or months before you get to move.

If you are contemplating relocation to another state, you should consult with a qualified lawyer in that state concerning the *Uniform Child Custody Jurisdiction and Enforcement Act (UCCJEA)*. You will need to make new arrangements for parenting time and the collection or payment of support in that state, so do not wait until the last moment.

8.39   After the divorce, can my spouse legally take our children out of the state during his or her parenting time? Out of the country?

The answer to this question depends upon the terms of the parenting plan from your divorce decree or any later court orders that may have modified your decree.

If you are concerned about your children being out of New Hampshire with the other parent, you may want some of these provisions entered in your decree regarding out-of-state travel with your child:

- Limits on the duration or distance for out-of-state travel with the child
- Notice requirements

- Information on phone numbers
- Information on physical addresses
- E-mail address contact information
- Possession of the child's passport to be kept with the concerned parent or with a neutral third party
- Requiring a court order for travel outside of the country

Although judges are not ordinarily concerned about short trips across state lines, you should let your attorney know if you are concerned that your child may be abducted by the other parent so that reasonable safeguards may be put in place.

Out-of-the-country visits are different, requiring the approval of both parents. *The Hague Convention* governs international travel, but it is a complex law that requires a very experienced lawyer. If you think that such travel may occur, however, it is better to deal with it before an emergency arises.

8.40 What rights do I have regarding medical or educational records for my child?

Regardless of which parent has the children most of the time, standard language in the parenting plan allows both parents to have access to the records of their children unless a judge specifically orders otherwise in rare circumstances.

8.41 If I'm not the primary caregiver, how will I know what's going on at my child's school?

Regardless of your custodial status, you have a right to access your child's school records and to attend school events or important appointments for your child. If you have a restraining order or other court order against you, you may need special permission from a judge to attend school events when the other parent is present or to review your child's records.

Develop a relationship with your child's teachers and the school staff. Request to be put on the school's mailing list for all notices. Find out what is required in order for you to receive copies of important school information and report cards.

Communicate with the other parent to both share and receive information about your child's progress in school. This will enable you both to support your child and one another through any challenging periods of your child's education. It also enables you to share a mutual pride in your child's successes.

Regardless of which parent has the child most of the time, your child will benefit by your involvement in his or her education through your participation in parent-teacher conferences, your attendance at school events, your help with school homework, and your positive communication with the other parent.

8.42 If I have shared decision-making, can I still take my child to church during my parenting time?

Yes. The decision about religion is a fundamental decision that is made by both parents. As long as your spouse does not object to you taking your child to church during your parenting time, this should not be an issue. However, if there is a dispute, a judge may have to decide what is in the best interest of the child. Judges typically try to respect the religious decisions of the parents and encourage respect and dignity between parents.

8.43 What if my child does not want to participate in his or her parenting time with my spouse? Can my former spouse force my child to do something he or she does not want to do?

If your child is resisting going with the other parent, it can first be helpful to determine the underlying reason. Consider these questions:

- What is your child's stated reason for not wanting to go?

- Does your child appear afraid, anxious, or sad?

- Do you have legitimate concerns regarding your child's safety while with the other parent?

- Have you prepared your child for being with the other parent, speaking about the experience with enthusiasm and encouragement?

- Is it possible your child perceives your anxiety about the situation and is consequently having the same reaction?

- Have you provided support for your child's transition to the other home, such as completing fun activities in your home well in advance of the other parent's starting time for parenting?

- Have you spoken to the other parent about your child's behavior?

- Can you provide anything that will make your child's time with the other parent more comfortable, such as a favorite toy or blanket?

- Have you established clear routines that support your child being ready to go with the other parent with ease, such as packing a backpack or saying good-bye to a family pet?

The reason for a child's reluctance to go with the other parent may be as simple as being sad about leaving you or as serious as being a victim of abuse in the other parent's home. It is important to look at this closely to determine the best response.

Judges treat compliance with court orders for parenting time seriously. If one parent believes that the other is intentionally interfering with parenting time or the parent-child relationship, it can result in further litigation. At the same time, you still want to know that your child is safe. Talk with your attorney about the best approach in your situation.

8.44 What steps can I take to prevent my spouse from becoming the children's guardian in the event of my death?

Unless the other parent is not fit to have parenting rights, he or she will have first priority as the guardian of your children in the event of your death.

All parents should have a will naming a guardian for their children. In the event you do not intend to name the other parent as a guardian in your will, talk with your attorney. Seek counsel about how to best document and preserve the evidence that will be needed to prove that the other parent is unfit to have parenting rights in the event of your death.

9

Child Support and Medical Care

Whether you will be paying or receiving child support is often the subject of much anxiety. Will you receive enough support to take care of your children? Will you have enough money to live on after you pay child support? How will you make ends meet?

Most parents want to adequately provide for their children. Today, child support laws make it possible for parents to have a better understanding of their financial obligations to their children. The mechanisms for both payment and receipt of child support are more clearly defined, and help is available for collecting support if it is not paid.

Under federal law, all states must adopt child support guidelines that make the amount and calculation the same in your state. The New Hampshire Child Support Guidelines and the New Hampshire Bureau of Child Support Services (BCSS) help to simplify the child support system. As you learn more about them, matters regarding child support that appeared complex may eventually become routine for you and the other parent.

9.1   What determines whether I will receive child support?

Whether you will receive child support depends upon a number of factors. These include how much time your child is living with you in your household, which parent earns more, and each parent's ability to pay support.

If you receive government assistance benefits, often known by its acronym under federal law as *TANF* or *Temporary*

Assistance for Needy Families, child support may be paid to the BCSS. This is the Bureau of Child Support Services for New Hampshire, which is responsible for payment and collection of those benefits. Because laws can change annually, speak with your case manager about whether there are any fees or delays associated with your receiving support.

If your spouse is not the biological or adoptive parent of your child, it is possible you will not receive child support. If paying child support will cause your spouse to reduce his or her net income below the federal poverty guideline, the support you receive may be as little as $50 per month.

9.2 Can I request child support even if I do not meet the residency requirement for a divorce in New Hampshire?

Yes. There are specific laws that require states to cooperate with each other concerning the calculation and collection of child support. Even though you may not have met the requirements to obtain a divorce, you still have a right to seek support for your children. Contact your attorney or BCSS for information and to apply for child support services.

9.3 Can I get temporary child support while waiting for parenting time to be decided?

A judge or referee has the authority to enter a temporary order for residence and child support. This order usually remains in place until a final divorce decree is entered.

In most cases, a hearing for temporary issues (including child support) will be held within a few months of the filing of the petition for divorce. How long it will take to schedule a hearing will depend upon the facts of your case and the availability of court time. Your lawyer can ask for a child support order or a hearing in the petition.

The court requires you to go to mediation before holding a hearing on temporary issues. It is usually better economically and emotionally for parents to reach an agreement rather than have a judge order financial support after a contested hearing.

9.4   What is *temporary support* and how soon can I get it?

Temporary support is paid for the support of a spouse or a child until a final order is mandated. It is paid sometime after the divorce petition is filed, and it continues until your final divorce is entered by the court or your case is dismissed.

If you are in need of temporary support, talk to your attorney at your first opportunity. If you and your spouse are unable to agree upon an amount of temporary support, it is likely that you will need to get support ordered at a temporary hearing, asking the judge to decide how much the support should be and when it can start.

Child support in a divorce may not be ordered for any period prior to the service of the petition upon your spouse. The following are common steps in the process:

- You attend mediation in an attempt to settle issues of temporary support.

- A temporary hearing is held, which typically occurs by offers of proof (your lawyer offering testimony to the judge on your behalf while you are under oath).

- The temporary order is signed by the judge, including the *uniform support order* that addresses child support.

- If necessary, your spouse's employer is notified by you or your attorney in order to begin withholding your support from your spouse's paychecks.

- Your spouse's employer sends the support to you or to the New Hampshire BCSS.

- BCSS sends the money to you (depending upon whether you receive any TANF or government assistance benefits).

If your spouse is not paying you support voluntarily, time is of the essence so this should be one of the first issues you discuss with your lawyer.

9.5   How soon does my spouse have to start paying support for the children?

Your spouse may begin paying you or BCSS support voluntarily at any time. A temporary order for support will give you the right to collect the support if your spouse stops paying. Talk to your lawyer about court hearings for temporary support in your county.

You may have to wait a few weeks, months, or longer before your temporary hearing can be held. It is also possible that the judge will not order child support to start until the first of the following month or in installments consistent with the pay periods of the parent ordered to pay (such as weekly or biweekly). This can depend upon how much your spouse has helped with other expenses, like the rent, mortgage, or utilities, for example.

9.6　How is the amount of child support calculated?

The New Hampshire Legislature has adopted a child support law that establishes guidelines for how judges should calculate child support. The guidelines are set forth in tables that determine how your child support is calculated.

According to New Hampshire guidelines, both parents have a duty to contribute to the support of their children in proportion to their respective gross incomes. As a result, both your income and the income of your spouse will factor into the child support calculation. Under New Hampshire law, a court must consider various other factors in the calculation as well. These may include additional cost of health and dental insurance for children, court-ordered child support paid for other children, self-employment taxes paid, any mandatory retirement benefits paid by either spouse, any state income taxes paid by either parent, and child-care costs.

A court may also increase or decrease child support from the guidelines when, for example, a child has extraordinary medical costs or is disabled or has special needs. If a judge finds that the application of the guidelines in an individual case would be unjust or inappropriate, a court may grant a deviation.

Due to the complexity of calculations under the guidelines, many attorneys use computer software to calculate child support. You can review guidelines and calculations at www.dhhs.nh.gov/dcss/calculator.htm.

9.7 What if a parent receives Social Security or Social Security Disability Income?

Under federal law, your child may receive a benefit paid directly to the residential (custodial) parent. If the benefit is because the nonresidential parent is disabled (SSDI), then the amount will offset any child support obligation and may actually exceed the child support obligation under the guidelines. The residential parent could receive that entire amount as child support, and no other support may be ordered.

If the residential parent is disabled and there is a benefit paid for a child, a judge may consider that payment when calculating child support under the guidelines, but this allows the judge some discretion depending upon household income, the nature of the disability, and the needs of the children.

If a parent qualifies for Social Security because of age, then you should contact the Social Security office near you to discuss whether any additional benefit is available for your child.

9.8 Does the type of parenting arrangement or the amount of parenting time impact the amount of child support?

It can. In New Hampshire, "equal or approximately equal parenting residential responsibilities" in and of itself does not eliminate the need for child support and does not by itself constitute ground for an adjustment to the presumption of the guidelines. However, the court can make an adjustment if the spouses have agreed to the specific apportionment of variable expenses for the children, including but not limited to education; school supplies; day care; after school, vacation, and summer care; extracurricular activities; clothing; health-care coverage costs and uninsured health-care costs; and other child-related expenses.

Further, the court will consider whether the higher-earning parent has established that the equal or approximately equal residential responsibility will result in a reduction of any of the fixed costs of child rearing incurred by the parent receiving support, and finally, whether the income of the parent who is earning lower wages enables that parent to meet the costs of child rearing in a similar or approximately equal style to that of the other parent. Practically speaking, this can occur when the parents make substantially similar incomes, but not if one parent makes double the other, for example. For this reason, it is essential that you discuss child support with your attorney prior to reaching any agreements.

If you intend to mediate parenting time, be sure to talk with your attorney in advance and calculate the effect on child support. With that said, however, lawyers and judges prefer that child support not be linked to parenting time as a negotiating tool. Be careful and act in good faith. The appearance that either parent is trying to leverage the children for money can backfire.

9.9   Is overtime pay considered in the calculation of child support?

Yes, if overtime is a routine or historically common part of your employment that you can actually expect to earn regularly, then it will be considered. The judge must consider your work history, the degree of control you have over your overtime, and the nature of the field in which you work.

9.10   Will rental income be factored into my child support, or just my salary?

Yes, income from other sources may be considered in determining the amount of child support as a means to calculate gross income. But you are also entitled to adjust for legitimate expenses, like a mortgage or maintenance costs. Depreciation and other paper losses may be added back in by a judge or child support referee.

You may find that your accountant needs to help explain your tax return to a judge or referee by providing an affidavit or testifying at a hearing if there is a dispute about income or expenses. If both parties and lawyers cooperate, a qualified accountant should be able to explain any concerns so that the cost of any accounting fees is minimized. Do not wait until the day of your trial to acquire this information and attempt to make it clear. A judge may use a higher or lower number if your evidence is disorganized or incomplete.

9.11 My spouse has a college degree but refuses to get a job. Will the court consider this in determining the amount of child support?

The earning capacity of your spouse may be considered instead of actual current income. The court can look at your spouse's work history, education, skills, health, and job opportunities. Further, the court will look at your spouse's historical earnings as an indication about what he or she may be capable of earning in the future. A New Hampshire court may also apply incomes for various professions by using federal or state employment tables for calculating earning capacity for specific jobs in your geographical area.

If you believe your spouse is earning substantially less than the income she or he is capable of earning, provide your attorney with details. Judges can consider a former spouse as being underemployed when considering child support. Ask about making a case for child support based on earning capacity of your spouse. You can also use a reasonable estimate of what your spouse is capable of making or has made in the past based upon tax returns or lifestyle—personal expenses on travel, vehicles, and credit cards. Talk to your lawyer about how to build such a case with information that you may have access to or that you can get from other sources such as past employers, banks, or credit unions.

9.12 Will I get the child support directly from my spouse or from the state?

There are muliple ways child support can be paid. New Hampshire law requires that child support can be withheld from the income of the payer of child support, unless there is a good reason not to have the support automatically withheld. Employers routinely withhold child support from employee wages just as they withhold taxes or retirement savings. BCSS sends the child support to you, either by direct deposit or by mail. Payments can also be made directly from one spouse to the other by mail. Another method of payment is by automatic electronic withdrawals as a way of reducing conflict and confusion.

Do not ever use your children to deliver or receive child support. Also, do not write unpleasant notes on the checks or in the memo line.

If you receive government assistance benefits, like TANF, you may not have a choice as to how to pay child support, as the state collects the child support and may choose wage garnishment whether you approve or not. You may arrange for your payments through BCSS and their child support services.

9.13 Is there any reason not to pay or receive payments directly to or from my spouse once the court has entered a child support order?

Yes. Once a child support order is entered by the court, the BCSS Payment Center keeps a record of all support paid. If the payment is not made, the state's records will show that you are behind in your child support.

Direct payments of child support can result in misunderstandings between parents. The payer may have intended the money to fulfill a child support payment, but the parent receiving the support may have thought it was extra money to help with expenses. The payment of support through BCSS protects both parents.

If you decide to pay directly, using cash or money orders can be unwise because you need a record that is clean and easily proves the payments. If no receipt is available for a direct payment, it may later be considered a gift or payment for some other purpose.

9.14 Can I go to the courthouse to pick up my child support payment?

No. Child support payments in New Hampshire that are withheld from wages are processed through a central location at the BCSS and paid by direct deposit or by mail to the spouse or former spouse.

9.15 How soon can I expect my child support payments to start arriving from BCSS?

A number of factors may impact the date on which you begin receiving your child support payments. Here are the usual steps in the process:

- By agreement or through a court order after hearing evidence, a child support amount and start date is decided and entered in court.

- The judge, your attorney, or your spouse's attorney prepares the court order.

- The attorney who did not write the court order reviews and approves it.

- The court order is taken to the judge for signature.

- You or BCSS may deliver the wage-withholding order to your spouse's employer, asking that child support be withheld from future paychecks.

- Your spouse's employer withholds the support from the paycheck.

- The child support is transferred by the employer to BCSS.

- BCSS sends the child support to you, either by direct deposit or by mail (with the amount depending upon whether you are receiving TANF benefits).

As you can see, there are many steps in this process. Plan your budget ahead of time, knowing that the initial payment of child support might be delayed for weeks.

9.16 Will some amount of child support be withheld from every paycheck?

The answer to this question depends upon the employer's policy and how the employee is paid. If support is due on the first of the month, the employer has the full month to withhold the amount ordered to be paid. If an employer issues paychecks twice a month, it is possible that half of the support will be withheld from each check and paid to BCSS at the end of the month.

If an employer issues checks every other week, which is twenty-six pay periods per year, there will be some months in which a third paycheck is issued. Consequently, it is possible that no child support will be withheld from the wages paid in that third check of the month, or that some checks will be for less than 50 percent of the monthly amount due.

For example, suppose the child support payment is to be $650 per month. The payer is paid every other Friday, or twenty-six times per year. The employer may withhold $300 per paycheck for child support. Although most months the support received will be $600, for a few months it will be $900. By the end of the year, however, the payer will have paid the same amount as if $650 had been paid each month.

Over time, child support payments typically fall into a routine schedule, which makes it easier for both the payer and the recipient of support to plan budgets.

9.17 If my spouse has income other than from an employer, is it still possible to get a court order to withhold my child support from his income?

Yes. Child support can be automatically withheld from most sources of income. These may include unemployment, workers' compensation, retirement plans, or investment income. But this is harder to enforce than W-2 income, so you may need to consult with a lawyer if your spouse has income that is not derived from his or her employment alone.

9.18 The person I am divorcing is not the biological parent of my child. Can I still collect child support from my spouse for my child?

Only in very rare circumstances can this occur, and that usually requires a judge to find a *de facto* parenting arrangement, which means that your spouse has established and maintained a very significant relationship with your child over a sustained period of time. There are consequences to such a strategy in that your spouse may also have rights to decision-making and parenting under a court order that will be legally enforceable.

Discuss the facts of your case in detail with your lawyer. When you are clear about what will be in the best interest of your child, your attorney can support you in developing a strategy that takes into consideration not only child support, but also the future relationship of your spouse with your child.

Child Support and Medical Care

9.19 Can I collect child support from both the biological parent and the adoptive parent of my child?

When your child was adopted, the biological parent's duty to support your child ended. However, it may be possible for you to collect past-due child support from the period of time before the adoption.

9.20 What happens with child support when our children go to the other parent's home for summer vacation? Is child support still due?

It depends. Whether child support is adjusted during extended parenting times with the other parent depends upon the specific court order in your case.

In most cases, child support is seen as being an average of payments spread over time. This means that the cost of housing, for example, remains constant whether the child is with you or not. A judge may reduce or abate (temporarily suspend) child support during extended periods of parenting time when there may be the cost of airline travel paid for by the other parent. There is no clear-cut guideline; it is determined on a case-by-case basis.

What is important is that this be clear in the original order for both parents because wage withholding will not stop without a court order.

9.21 Will my child support be decided by a judge if we do not agree?

If you attempt to resolve child support at mediation and are unsuccessful, the next step will be for the judge to decide for you at a temporary hearing. If you do not agree with a temporary order, there are a few limited reasons you may ask the judge to reconsider (change his or her mind), but there is a very short time frame allotted for this type of request, so you should consult with your lawyer. Sometimes you must simply wait for the final hearing on your divorce to make that argument to the judge.

A judge may set the final child support amount to be different from the support ordered at the temporary hearing after hearing testimony and reviewing evidence at the trial, deciding parenting, property division, debts, and income.

9.22   After the divorce, if I choose to live with my new partner rather than marry, can I still collect child support?

Yes. Although spousal support may terminate if you cohabitate in a married-like state with your new partner, child support does not terminate for this reason.

9.23   Can I still collect child support if I move to another state?

Yes. A move out of state will not end your right to receive child support. However, the amount of child support could be changed if other circumstances change, such as your income or costs for exercising parenting time.

If you are contemplating relocation to another state, you should consult with a qualified lawyer in that state concerning the *Uniform Interstate Family Support Act (UIFSA)*. You will need to make arrangements for the collection or payment of support in that state, so do not wait until the last moment.

9.24   Can I expect to continue to receive child support if I remarry?

Yes. Your child support will continue even if you remarry.

9.25   How long can I expect to receive child support for each child?

Under New Hampshire law, child support terminates when a child turns eighteen years of age or graduates from high school, whichever occurs later. If a child marries or joins the armed services prior to that date, child support ceases. Alternatively, the parents may agree to support a child beyond these dates. If your child has a mental or physical disability and is declared to be legally dependent, support may continue until the child is age twenty-two.

Even when the court loses jurisdiction to order child support at that time, a judge may still enforce any support owed in the past, including past-due medical expenses.

9.26   Can interest accrue on past-due child support or unpaid expenses?

Yes, interest can accrue on past-due child support, and a judge can order the payment of interest or penalties. The interest rate is established under New Hampshire law, so you would need to get that information from the court clerk or your lawyer.

9.27 What can I do if my former spouse refuses to pay child support?

If your former spouse is not paying child support, you may take action to enforce the court order, either with the help of your lawyer or with the assistance of a child support attorney from BCSS. Unlike a private attorney, you do not have to pay for the services of a child support attorney. For child support questions and contact information, you may visit the BCSS website or call (800) 852-3345.

In an enforcement or contempt case, a judge may order payment of both the current amount of support and an additional amount to be paid each month until the past-due child support (referred to as *arrearages*) is paid in full. In cases of significant noncompliance, a judge may order civil incarceration, or jail time, until some or all of the support is paid.

Civil incarceration means that the offending person may go to jail if the judge finds there was a violation of the child support order and, by clear and convincing evidence, that the person has the current capacity to pay from their income or assets. Bail is often set at the amount that is unpaid or overdue; friends or family of the payer may need to pay the child support owed in order to get the payer released from jail.

You may request that your former spouse's state and federal tax refunds be sent directly to BCSS. It may also be possible to garnish a checking or savings account, or request a sheriff's sale if there are assets in the payer's name, such as trucks or equipment. The proceeds of the sale can be used to satisfy some or all of the unpaid amounts.

A driver's license or professional license may also be suspended if a parent falls too far behind in child support payments. However, if there is a payment plan for arrearages, then the license(s) may not be suspended.

Finally, a judge may also order your spouse to pay your attorney fees as part of the enforcement or contempt proceeding. Your lawyer will need to submit an affidavit to the court to get those fees ordered.

9.28 At what point will the state help me collect back child support? What methods do they use?

The answer to this question typically depends on the amount of back child support that is owed and whether there are any state benefits used by your family. However, if a spouse is not paying, and children are relying on state benefits, the state will likely aggressively pursue that individual to pay.

A spouse who is not paying may have his or her driver's license, recreational, and professional licenses suspended. If more than $500 in back support is due, state or federal income tax refunds can be intercepted. When more than $2,500 is owed, a passport can be denied or revoked by federal authorities. In some cases, failure to pay child support can even result in a jail sentence.

It is important to follow up with the state if you need assistance in collecting child support, because the state will likely not take steps to intervene if it is not paying state assistance for the benefit of a child. You will likely need the help of a state or a private attorney if you want help collecting your child support.

9.29 I live outside of New Hampshire. Will the money I spend on airline tickets to see my children impact my child support?

It might. If you expect to spend large sums of money for transportation in order to have parenting time with your children, talk to your attorney about how this might be taken into consideration when determining the amount of child support.

A judge may deviate from guidelines support for legitimate travel expenses, not just plane rides. This is a complex issue so you want to be very clear in your court order so there is no argument or confusion later that may prevent parenting time or cause more litigation between you and your former spouse.

Therefore, travel costs such as plane or train tickets or driving should be clearly defined as to who pays and whether there are any caps on the cost of any reimbursement, the location of airports, who may pick up and drop off, how old a child may be before they may travel or fly alone (if at all), and what type of notice is required in terms of travel dates and costs before any trips are to occur.

9.30 After the divorce, can my former spouse substitute buying sprees with the child for child support payments?

No. Purchases of gifts and clothing for a child do not relieve your former spouse from an obligation to pay you child support under a court order. Many parenting plans require both parents to provide clothing for the children at his or her residence.

9.31 Are expenses such as child care supposed to be taken out of my child support?

No. Child-care expenses are separate from child support, because the New Hampshire Child Support Guidelines recognize that child care for young children is often a tremendous expense. Therefore, the guidelines often provide that each parent pay a percentage of work- or school-related day-care expenses in addition to the basic child support amount. The spouses may also agree to share child-care expenses differently, such as each parent pays child-care costs for his or her parenting time.

9.32 How does providing health insurance for my child affect my child support?

If you pay the health insurance premium for your child, the amount you pay will be taken into account when calculating child support. You will then receive a credit for the amount you pay per month for your child's health insurance premium. Note that depending on each party's income, it may not be a dollar-for-dollar credit.

9.33 How do we pay for uninsured medical or dental expenses for our child?

Unless you agree differently, a child support order will typically allocate uninsured expenses equally between parties.

Both parents should make sure that they promptly provide the other parent with a copy of any bills and receipts if payment was made by one parent. You should also be careful to make sure that any treatment for your child is with a provider in a network under your insurance plan.

For many parents, payment or reimbursement for uninsured medical expenses is a great source of conflict. For that reason, it is often helpful to have an agreement that requires exchange of information and receipts made within a specific time period. This helps set expectations between the parents and reduces questions and conflict in the future. Speak to your attorney about the best provisions to include in your child support order to ensure timely payment of uninsured medical expenses.

9.34 Am I required to pay everyday expenses from the child support I receive?

Yes, if you are receiving child support, you are responsible for expenses such as housing, clothing, school lunches, and the cost of activities when your child is with you, and the other parent pays those expenses when the child is in his or her care.

You will need to coordinate with the other parent for purchases of major expenses related to your child, or create an agreement in your court order as to how to divide those costs and when you will share those costs. This frequently includes travel for school, sports, recreation, camps, dance, or other events that benefit your child but which one parent alone may be not be able to afford. In New Hampshire, if extracurricular expenses are not agreed upon to be shared, the burden will fall on the parent receiving support, so be sure to speak with your lawyer about how these expenses will be handled moving forward if your child is involved in expensive sports or activities. In many families, parents spend more on extracurricular activities than the child support obligation may be.

9.35 What about the tax exemption for our child?

Unless otherwise ordered by a judge, the default for claiming the dependency exemption is the parent who has the child most of the time. After a hearing or by agreement of the parents, a judge may grant a deviation and order the exemption to go to the other parent. For example, if the parent with the most parenting time is not working at that time, the exemption may have no value to her but may benefit the other parent.

If you have more than one child, each parent may receive an exemption by agreement or court order. Tax exemptions, however, may have other value under the federal and state tax code, so you should consult with a lawyer or accountant before you waive or release the tax exemption. If you have substantially equal parenting time, and only have one child, the judge may order you to alternate claiming the dependent each year.

If you are ordered to give the exemption to the other parent, you may need a Form 8332 to be signed each year to attach to your tax return. You may also want a provision in your order that requires you to sign the form only if all child support and uninsured expenses were paid for the preceding year.

If both parents claim the exemption for the same child in the same year, you will likely receive a letter from the IRS expressing concern over this matter. If a parent wrongfully claims an exemption, that parent can be forced to file an amended return and may have to pay back any refund plus penalties and interest.

9.36 Can my spouse be required by court order to pay for our child's private elementary and high school education?

If your child is already enrolled in private school and you both agree that the child will continue to go to that school, or you reach an agreement for that to take place, it is likely the court will order that to continue. The New Hampshire Child Support Guidelines make no specific provision for private education tuition except as a deviation from guidelines support. However, some parents agree to include a provision in the decree for payment of such tuition because both of them believe it is important for their child.

If you want your spouse to share this expense for your child, talk it over with your lawyer. Be sure to provide your attorney with information regarding tuition, fees, and other expenses related to your child's private education as well as the history of your child's attendance at the private school.

9.37   When can a *motion to modify child support* be filed?

Until your child is emancipated, a motion to modify can be filed at any time. You must show a substantial change in circumstances to obtain a downward or upward change in support. The court, however, does not have to grant your motion if it is filed earlier than three years from the last support order, and if the court does not believe that a substantial change in circumstances has occurred since the last support order.

9.38   How far back can the court retroactively modify child support?

Typically, the court cannot modify child support at any time before a former spouse is served with the motion to modify. Every support payment is otherwise vested and owed as due. This means that if you do not file a motion to modify, you are still obligated to comply with the current court order. You cannot receive an adjustment in child support obligation until you file and your former spouse is served with the motion. Never fail to pay or change your support without a court order; an agreement between you and your former spouse may not be considered binding by a judge if it is informal.

9.39   On a motion to modify child support, can my new spouse's income be considered for a child support calculation?

Possibly. If you and your new spouse operate a business together, such as rental properties, an automotive garage, or Internet sales, a judge can look at the total income from your business in determining whether your spouse is earning much more of the income than you. Sometimes this is because one of you is working more hours in the business or one of you has special skills such as those of a mechanic or plumber while the other spouse is doing the books and billings. If there is a good-faith reason why you are earning less than your spouse, that may be acceptable to a judge. But if a judge decides that you are being paid less to avoid paying child support or getting more child support from your former spouse, then the judge can adjust your income to a higher amount based upon the gross earnings of the business.

A judge may order you to disclose financial information on joint tax returns whether personal or business and consider that income when determining your household's gross income or your available resources for guideline support. It is important that your accountant be able to explain any differences in earnings as reasonable for your hours and duties depending upon the kind of business you operate.

Alternatively, if your income has decreased as a result of your being partially supported by your new spouse so that you are working less, this may make you *voluntary underemployed*. Your new spouse's income will likely be credited to you (treated as if you earned it) up to your prior income level. For example, assume you have left your prior job after having a baby with a new spouse, and you were earning $60,000 annually at your prior job when child support was calculated in your divorce decree. You and your new spouse have agreed that you stay home or leave your job entirely for the baby. The court may still keep your income level at its previous amount from the divorce because having a new child and voluntarily leaving your job may not be valid reason to reduce child support that you were obligated to pay under your divorce decree.

Having children in a new marriage is an extremely sensitive subject. There is no one-size-fits-all advice for this situation but it is important to know that you may have to disclose financial information from your new spouse if you seek to modify a prior child support order.

You may also have to share any joint tax returns or information related to joint assets if that information is relevant to a child support calculation in the future. If you believe your spouse is earning substantially less than the income she or he is capable of earning, provide your attorney with details. A person's earnings history is reflected in their Social Security earnings statement, Form SSA-7050 Request For Social Security Earnings Information, or past individual or joint personal or business tax returns.

9.40   Can my spouse be required by court order to contribute financially to our child's college or post–high school education?

Not in New Hampshire, unless you agree upon this in your original court order. The legal duty of a parent to support a child ends upon his or her graduation from high school and does not include payment for a college education. However, if your spouse agrees in a court order to pay or share this expense, it will then be enforceable, so long as it is specific in nature as required under the law.

If your divorce decree is to include a provision for payment of college education expenses, be sure it is specific, answering such questions as:

- What expenses are included (for example: tuition, room and board, books, fees, or travel)?
- Is there a cost limit (for example: up to the level of the cost of tuition and room and board at the University of New Hampshire, or a certain dollar amount)?
- When is the payment due?
- For what period of time does it continue (for example: until age twenty-one, age twenty-two, four completed years of college, or some other term)?
- Are there any limits on the type of education that will be paid for?
- What grade point average must the child maintain? Consider whether your child is failing each semester; if so, should your obligation to pay continue?
- Does the child have to contribute any funds from loans or work?

Do not leave this type of provision in your divorce decree too vague. Clarity lowers the risk for a misunderstanding or conflict years later.

10

Spousal Support

The mere mention of the words *alimony* or *spousal support* might stir up emotions for both of you. If your spouse has filed for divorce and is seeking alimony, you might see it as a double injustice—your marriage is ending and you feel like you have to pay for it, too. If you are the one seeking alimony, you might feel hurt and confused that your spouse is resistant to helping support you, even though you may have interrupted your career to stay home and care for your children, or you earn substantially less income.

Learning more about New Hampshire's laws on this matter can help you move from an emotional reaction to an understanding of the possible or probable outcomes in your case. Uncertainty about the precise amount that may be awarded or the number of years it might be paid is not unusual.

Work closely with your lawyer. Be open to possibilities. Try looking at it from your spouse's perspective. And remember that unlike child support, there is less predictability in alimony. The law now provides a framework and a basic formula, but there are many variations to it provided in the law.

These decisions are very fact-bound. With the help of your lawyer, you can learn the most likely and feasible approach when you are the person who may have to pay or the person who needs to be paid spousal support.

10.1 Which gets calculated first, child support or alimony?

Child support is usually calculated first, because child support uses gross income. You need to know that guideline child support amount before you can determine whether and how much alimony is realistic or feasible.

Just to be clear: Any alimony payment to your current spouse is not deducted from your gross income for the child support calculation. If you have an alimony order owed to another spouse, then that amount may be deducted first.

10.2 What is the difference between *alimony* and *spousal support?*

In New Hampshire, alimony and spousal support have the same meaning. Our statute now describes alimony, though judges and attorneys sometimes use the terms interchangeably.

10.3 Are there different types of alimony allowed by New Hampshire law?

Yes, and knowing the type of alimony you are eligible for or may have to pay is critical to understanding your case, protecting yourself, and reaching an agreement.

Term alimony may be ordered if the parties agree or if the judge orders it. The purpose of term alimony is to allow both parties to maintain a reasonable standard of living following the divorce. To receive an award of alimony, the judge must find that the party in need lacks sufficient income, property, or both to provide for his or her own reasonable needs considering the lifestyle of the marriage and the changes both parties must make to their finances considering the need for two households in place of one.

Further, if one party is unable to be self-supporting for reasonable needs through employment, or has parenting time of a child of the parties and the circumstances therefore make employment outside the home inappropriate (such as with an infant or disabled child), and the payer parent is still able to meet his or her own reasonable needs, term alimony would be appropriate.

The amount of term alimony is calculated according to a formula where the alimony will be the lesser of the receiver's reasonable need or 23 percent of the difference between the parties' gross incomes at the time of the order (or agreement).

Gross income will first adjust child support by taking it from the person paying it and adding it to the recipient's side.

An alimony payer may also deduct health insurance paid for a spouse and add it to the recipient's side. If the judge determines another amount of support is appropriate, he or she has the authority to modify this calculation. (*See* question 10.7 for an example of how the amount of term alimony is calculated.) Speak to your attorney to determine whether any factors may be appropriate to deviate from this formula in your case.

As for duration, there is now a presumption in the law that the maximum duration of alimony is 50 percent of the length of the marriage unless the parties agree otherwise or the judge finds justice requires otherwise. The length of the marriage is measured by the date of the marriage up to the date of service of the petition for divorce. By agreement, you and your spouse can agree on specific terminating events, such as cohabitation or either party's death.

Alimony also terminates upon remarriage of the recipient unless the parties agree otherwise. The judge does have authority to either extend or shorten the duration if justice requires. There are a number of factors for the court to consider, such as the property received by the parties, either party's health or disability, Social Security benefits of the parties, and others. Speak with your attorney about analyzing the factors in your case to determine if varying from the duration set out in the statute is appropriate in your case.

The other type of alimony is *reimbursement alimony,* which may be awarded to compensate the payee for economic or noneconomic contributions to the financial resources of the payer, or if the property subject to division is inappropriate or inadequate to provide compensation. This contribution may include support in the form of education or job training, or an investment of time or money. Reimbursement alimony is only ordered if the parties agree or if a judge determines it is equitable. The duration is no more than five years from decree, and it is not modifiable unless by agreement.

10.4 How will I know if I am eligible to receive or likely to pay spousal support?

Under New Hampshire law, there is a list of factors a judge may consider. A judge need not consider all of these factors, or they may give more weight to one than another.

The opinions of New Hampshire judges vary greatly as to the reasons for awarding alimony. Among the factors that may affect your eligibility or obligation to pay are:

- The length of the marriage
- The ability of each party to pay
- The age of each party
- The employment history and employment potential of each party
- The income history and income potential of each party
- The education and training of each party
- The provisions for retirement and health insurance benefits of each party
- The tax consequences of the division of marital property, including the tax consequences of the sale of the marital home, if applicable
- The health and disabilities of each party
- The tax consequences of an alimony award
- The contributions of either party as homemaker
- The contributions of either party to the education or earning potential of the other party
- Economic misconduct by either party resulting in the diminution of marital property or income
- The fault of either party in the breakdown of the marriage
- The standard of living of the parties during the marriage
- The ability of the party seeking support to become self-supporting within a reasonable period of time
- The effect of actual or potential income from marital property on a party's need for alimony or a party's ability to pay alimony
- Any other factors the court considers appropriate

Providing your lawyer with clear and detailed information about the facts of your marriage and your current financial and personal situation will allow him or her to make a more accurate assessment of your case.

10.5 What information should I provide to my attorney if I want alimony?

If your attorney advises you that you may be a candidate to receive alimony, be sure to provide complete facts about your situation, including:

- A history of interruptions in your education or career, including transfers or moves, due to a spouse's employment
- A history of interruptions in your education or career for raising children, including periods during which you worked part-time
- Your complete educational background, including the dates of your schooling or training and degrees earned
- Your work history, including the names of your employers, the dates of your employment, your duties, your pay, and the reasons you left
- Any pensions or other benefits lost or accrued during the marriage
- Your health history, including any current diagnoses, treatments, limitations, and medications
- Your monthly living expenses, including anticipated future expenses such as health insurance and taxes
- A complete list of the debts for you and your spouse
- Income for you and your spouse, including all sources

If there has been any economic misconduct, then you may need the services of a forensic accountant, or your lawyer may have to undertake discovery early in the case to gather documentation. If you have any documents or electronic records, you should provide those to your lawyer as soon as possible.

No two alimony cases are alike. The more accurate and complete the information provided to your lawyer, the more effectively your lawyer can assess your case and advocate for you.

10.6 My spouse told me that because I had an affair during the marriage, I have no chance to get alimony, even though I quit my job and have cared for our children for many years. Is it true that I have no case?

Your right to support will be based upon many factors, but having an affair is not an absolute bar to paying or receiving alimony. If your extramarital relationship had a financial impact on the marital estate or if it reduced income or increased expenses, this may be taken into consideration when determining the duration and amount of support given or received. The judge in your case can consider fault as one of a number of factors in determining an appropriate alimony award.

Many adultery cases do not have a significant financial impact on the marital estate and, therefore, the judge may not weigh this as heavily as some spouses may wish. On other occasions, significant gifts or money may have been spent on an affair and that may be economic misconduct, which a judge can consider for spousal support. Speak with your attorney about the specific facts in your case and how much he or she believes the adultery will be considered in determining an alimony award.

10.7 How is the amount of alimony calculated?

The State of New Hampshire has a formula to help calculate how much alimony is appropriate in a given case. A judge will look at the expenses and income of both you and your spouse, after giving consideration to the payment and receipt of child support, if any. Thereafter, the alimony will be the lesser of the receiver's reasonable need or 23 percent of the difference between the parties' gross incomes at the time of the order (or agreement).

For example, imagine Ed earns $38,000 per year. Sarah earns $100,000. They have one child and Sarah will pay Ed child support of $1,241 monthly. They have been married ten years. Using the state's formula, Sarah's monthly income is $8,333 less the $1,241 child support paid, which leaves her with a monthly income of $7,092.

Ed's monthly income is $2,833 plus $1,241 child support received, which comes to $4,074. The difference between

$7,092 less $4,074 is $3,018 multiplied by 23 percent, equals: $694.14. This is the presumed per month alimony for five years.

However, suppose reviewing the parties' monthly expenses, Ed's reasonable need for expenses is only $3,500 per month, then the alimony would only be $3,500 minus $3,018, which comes to $482 per month.

Judges are given great discretion to analyze whether expenses are reasonable in a given case. Therefore, it is incumbent upon you to work with your lawyer under the law to try to minimize the risk of an unpredictable outcome.

10.8   My spouse makes significantly more money than he reports on our tax return, but he hides it. How can I prove my spouse's real income?

This is a complex issue that frequently occurs in divorce. More than likely you and your spouse filed a joint federal and state tax return, which you signed under oath. The personal tax returns may be derived from a corporate or partnership return over which you had no control. Therefore, you may have what is called an *innocent spouse defense* if you did not have knowledge or control over the finances for your spouse's business affairs.

However, you should consult with your lawyer and a qualified tax accountant before you proceed to challenge the accuracy of income and expenses. You have a duty to tell the truth in court, so if you pursue such a strategy your divorce may expose you and your spouse to IRS penalties and interest, and, in very unusual circumstances, criminal prosecution.

With that warning said, one of the ways of proving income is to use the "Al Capone" approach used by the IRS. You take monthly expenses (mortgage, credit card payments, car and boat payments, cost of living, taxes, travel expenses, retirement and savings contributions, and the like, which have documentation), add them all together, and compare them to the reported monthly income on your financial statements, bank loan applications, and tax returns over a three-to five-year period. You need this time frame to account for stability or fluctuations in income.

Your lawyer can also take a number of actions to determine your spouse's income with greater accuracy, including discovery to obtain the information mentioned above. By partnering with your lawyer, and a qualified forensic accountant if necessary, you may be able to build a case to establish your spouse's actual income as being greater than reported.

10.9   I want to be sure the records of my alimony payments are accurate. What's the best way to ensure this?

If you are paying child support in addition to alimony, your alimony payments can be made to BCSS and automatically withheld from your pay, just like your child support. If you pay alimony but no child support, you should arrange for electronic direct deposit. Do not use cash or money orders to pay alimony because you may need a record for the court.

Note that the tax laws have recently changed with regard to the deductibility of alimony on your federal income taxes. Alimony payments are now treated without tax implication. For more information, *see* the following question and consult with your tax professional or attorney about the tax implications of alimony.

If you are paying both child support and alimony and pay your spouse directly by check, try to avoid paying with one check as you are better off (despite the inconvenience) issuing two separate checks. One should be clearly marked for child support and the other for alimony.

10.10   What effect does alimony have on my taxes?

Before 2019, if you were required to pay alimony, your payments were tax deductible. Likewise, if you received alimony prior to 2019, you were required to pay income tax on the amount received. However, the law on the taxable nature of alimony has since changed, and alimony payments are now treated without tax implication, like child support. For more information, consult with your tax professional or attorney about the tax implications of alimony.

10.11   What types of payments are considered alimony?

Payments to a third party on behalf of your spouse under the terms of your divorce decree may be treated as alimony. These may include payments for your spouse's medical expenses, housing costs, taxes, and tuition. These payments are treated as if they were received by your spouse and then paid to the third party.

Additionally, if you pay the premiums on a life insurance policy that is owned by your spouse, those payments are also considered alimony. Finally, if you are ordered to pay for expenses for a house owned by both you and your spouse, some of your payments may be considered alimony.

Be careful to make sure that designated third-party payments equaling alimony is made clear in your divorce decree. Later disputes can have very expensive tax consequences, including penalties and interests for the losing side.

10.12 How is the purpose of alimony different from the payment of my property settlement?

Alimony and the division of property serve two distinct purposes, though many of the equitable and legal factors are the same. The purpose of alimony is to provide future support and a revenue stream through which a party can support him- or herself. In contrast, the purpose of a property division is to distribute the marital assets equitably between you and your spouse. Although some of the assets may be income producing, and may affect a party's need for support, the alimony is a key to resolving cases where the parties have substantially different incomes and one party will need support following the divorce.

The idea is not that the lower-income spouse can immediately liquidate assets they are awarded in the divorce and live on savings while the other spouse continues to save for the future. The idea is that the spouses, as a result of alimony, are on a more level playing field so they may both have some security moving forward. When one spouse has been out of the workforce and raising children for twenty years and the other spouse has been supporting the family comfortably and improving his or her earning potential during that time period, the spouse who has been out of the workforce typically cannot simply jump back into employment at a similar level to his or her spouse. This takes time and often may never happen, depending on the parties' ages, education levels, and work history.

10.13 My spouse makes much more money than I do. Will I be awarded alimony to make up the difference in our incomes?

Although the purpose of alimony is to provide periodic support, awards are not typically used to equalize the incomes of the parties. Instead, alimony may be awarded to assist the economically disadvantaged spouse for the transitional period during and after the divorce, until he or she becomes economically self-sufficient.

However, a difference in income may be one factor the judge contemplates when considering an award of alimony. A judge must, however, also consider other factors, such as the length of the marriage, your respective ages, the property distribution and debts, and whether there are minor children involved.

Although unlikely, a judge may equalize incomes, depending on whether the judge believes it a fair decision; the judge will also consider all other assets and debts or earning capacities under New Hampshire law. The judge must explain the reasons for doing so in an order.

10.14 How long can I expect to receive or have to pay alimony?

Like your right to receive alimony, how long you will receive alimony (or how long you may have to pay) will depend upon the legal presumptions that apply to your case based upon the length of the marriage. (*See* question 10.3.) In general, the longer your marriage, and the greater the earning differential, the stronger the case is for a long-term spousal support award.

You may receive only temporary alimony if the marriage was short or there was not much of an earnings differential. You may also receive a lump sum alimony award if you and your spouse can agree. Talk to your attorney about the risks and benefits of agreeing to a lump sum alimony award.

Some spouses prefer a lump sum in cash or retirement accounts because then they never have to return to court to enforce the order nor have to file or defend a motion to modify. This is more of a "clean break" if sufficient assets are available to make it work fairly for both of you.

Talk to your attorney about the facts of your case to get a clearer picture of possible outcomes. You may want to consider meeting with a licensed and reputable financial planner before making any decision that impacts your financial future.

10.15 Will remarriage affect my alimony?

Almost universally, yes. Under New Hampshire law, unless your divorce decree provides otherwise (or the parties agreed otherwise), alimony automatically terminates upon the remarriage of the recipient. If your decree does not provide for the termination of alimony upon remarriage of the recipient, you may file a motion to modify when a spouse remarries and it is likely to be granted.

You should read any documents carefully before signing to make sure that this point is clear to you and your spouse.

10.16 Does the death of my former spouse affect my alimony?

Yes, it can. If your divorce decree did not provide for life insurance to be paid to you in the event of your spouse's death, or if the decree stated that alimony terminated forever upon the death of your spouse, then alimony ends. You should consult with a lawyer immediately because you may have a claim or "charge" against your former spouse's estate for future spousal support—if you did not give up that right. This is why it is so important at the time of your divorce, if you are receiving alimony, to make sure that you have rights after the death of your spouse to life insurance or to a claim on the estate.

Be sure to review your divorce decree and consult with your lawyer with any questions about the impact of death on alimony payments before the judge grants the divorce, and make sure all the paperwork for life insurance is drawn up properly. Under federal law, if your former spouse changes the life insurance beneficiary in the future, without you knowing or having the right to know, then the new beneficiary may inherit the whole death benefit regardless of what it says in the divorce decree.

10.17 Must I keep paying alimony if my former spouse is now living with a new significant other?

If your divorce decree is silent on the issue of cohabitation, yes, keep paying alimony. Do *not* unilaterally stop making your alimony payments. Instead, contact your attorney to seek a modification of the alimony award. Alimony may be reduced or terminated with a new court order if your former spouse is cohabitating in a "marriage-like state." New Hampshire law provides a number of factors for the court to consider, including evidence of shared expenses, an intimate relationship, presenting themselves to be a couple, and owning shared assets, including real estate. If the judge considers this evidence and determines it would be unjust for alimony to continue, it may be terminated. Use caution, however, because if your former spouse ends the cohabitation, he or she may request that the prior alimony order be resumed, and a judge may agree.

10.18 Can I continue to collect alimony if I move to a different state?

Yes. The duty of your former spouse to follow a court order to pay alimony does not end simply because you move to another state, unless this is a specific provision in your divorce degree. You should always contact a lawyer in that other state, however, because the law may be different and you want to make sure you are not giving up rights that are yours in New Hampshire by going to another state.

10.19 What can I do if my spouse stops paying alimony before the end of the alimony term?

If your spouse stops paying alimony, see your attorney about your options for enforcing the court order. The judge may order the support be taken directly from a source of your spouse's income or from a financial account belonging to your spouse.

If your spouse is intentionally refusing to pay alimony, talk to your attorney about whether pursuing a contempt of court action would be effective. In a *contempt action,* your spouse may be ordered to appear in court and provide evidence explaining why support has not been paid. Possible

Spousal Support

consequences for contempt of court include a jail sentence or a fine.

The court can also award reasonable attorney fees if a party is found in contempt. Your lawyer will need to file an affidavit asking for such fees.

10.20 Can I return to court to modify alimony?

Yes. Either party may request a modification of alimony. At any point you may agree to modify an alimony order with your former spouse. If you do not have an agreement, you may file a petition requesting that the judge modify your alimony. When you go to court, you will have to prove to the judge that there's been a "substantial and unforeseeable change in circumstances" since the alimony order. You will also have to explain that this change will not prove a hardship on either party, and that a change to the order is justified in the current circumstances. As the party making the request, you will have the burden of proving to the judge that the change is necessary. In New Hampshire, you may not agree to a non-modifiable alimony award.

Examples of cases where a modification would likely be successful include a serious illness or disability, the loss of a job or obtaining of a new job with substantially increased or decreased income. If you think you have a basis to modify your alimony, contact your attorney at once to be sure a timely modification request is filed with the court.

10.21 Can a spouse request a retroactive change in alimony payments

Alimony arrangements can be changed retroactively, but retroactive only to the date a spouse filed papers with the court, seeking the change. If you are paying or receiving spousal support, and you want to have it modified, you must file such a request with the court as soon as possible.

A judge must approve the change. Keep in mind that it may take weeks or months to get in front of the judge and to get a decision.

11

Division of Property

You never imagined that you would face losing the house you and your spouse so happily moved into—the house where you celebrated family traditions and spent countless hours making it "home." But both you and your spouse want it, and to be fair, your lawyer says it might have to be sold.

During a divorce, you must decide whether you or your spouse will take ownership of everything—from bathroom towels to the stock portfolio. Suddenly you find yourself with a strong attachment to that lamp in the family room or the painting in the hallway. Why does a collection of coins or baseball cards suddenly take on new meaning?

Do your best to reach an agreement regarding the division of household or personal goods. Enlist the support of your attorney in deciding which assets should be valued by an expert, such as the family business or real estate. From tax consequences to replacement values, there are many factors to consider when deciding if you should fight to keep an asset, give it to your spouse, sell it, or compromise in the global context of settlement.

Moreover, all of your property is to be valued as of the date of divorce. You may have had a house or retirement plan worth $500,000 only a few years ago, but in a divorce it is only worth what a willing arm's-length buyer will pay or how the stock market values the stock in a mutual fund. New Hampshire's courts cannot consider possible future commissions or tax consequences unless there is an immediate sale at the time of divorce.

You need to remember that this is the law, because judges cannot speculate as to future market forces or values. You may have a legitimate dispute about fair market value, but it is what it is worth on the date of divorce and not three years earlier or three years later.

Like all aspects of your divorce, take one step at a time in this process. By starting with the items that are most easily divided, you and your spouse can avoid paying lawyers to litigate value, which is often not the issue as much as control and emotion.

11.1 What system of law does New Hampshire use for dividing property after a trial or in divorce settlements?

The state's law provides for an equitable, but not necessarily equal, division of property and debts acquired during your marriage. In a long-term marriage, an equal division of property is considered equitable. Things look different in a short-term marriage, in which the goal is to attempt to put the parties back where they were before the marriage, financially. In other words, if a wife entered the marriage with a house and retirement, and the husband with a car and a boat, the goal would be for the wife to leave with her house and retirement and the husband to leave with his car and boat.

Regardless of how the asset is held legally (jointly or individually), the court can use its discretion to divide marital assets and debts. In many cases, this may mean an equal division, but there are cases where an unequal division is what the court believes is equitable.

The court may also consider a number of other factors when deciding what is equitable. This can mean considering dividing up your debts, and the current and future economic circumstances of both you and your spouse. Also considered is the history of your respective economic, household, and parenting contributions to the marriage.

11.2 What does *community property* mean?

Community property is a term used in several states that have a community property system for dividing assets in a divorce. In states with community property laws, each spouse holds a one-half interest in most property acquired during

---

the marriage. Because New Hampshire is not a community property state, however, such laws do not apply.

11.3   When is property considered to be *marital property,* and are there any exceptions under the law?

This is a critically important concept for you to understand. New Hampshire's equitable distribution law means that all property acquired during the marriage, and some property that was acquired prior to the marriage as well, is *marital property*. A judge has the power to divide that property. For example, if you own a house jointly and you have a mortgage, the judge may consider both the value of the home and the amount of the mortgage to determine if there is *equity* (value) in the home that can be divided between spouses.

The term *property* refers to assets such as real estate, pensions and retirement accounts, bank accounts, personal property, cars, antiques, jewelry, and other *tangible* items.

Property can also include *intangible* things such as the goodwill of a business or the value of patents and trademarks, or a personal injury or workers' compensation case that is not yet finalized. You need to make sure that your lawyer knows about any assets or debts that may have been acquired during your marriage. Such assets may be difficult to value, but you need to make sure you know whether you have any rights to the property.

Although many states have laws that protect assets acquired before a marriage from being divided by a judge, New Hampshire does not have such a law. In New Hampshire, all property, regardless of whose name is on the deed when you file for divorce, is maritial property and potentially subject to valuation and division by the judge. This means, for example, that your current interest in an irrevocable trust created by your parents may be marital property and possibly subject to division in the divorce.

The court has discretion to consider these factors in dividing the assets, and there are very specific analyses involved in determining how these types of assets will be divided in a divorce. Speak with your attorney about your specific case if you have questions about how a judge might decide a specific asset.

11.4 What is a *prenuptial agreement,* and how might it affect the property settlement phase of the divorce?

A *prenuptial agreement,* sometimes referred to as an *antenuptial agreement,* is a contract entered into between two people prior to their marriage. It can include provisions for how assets and debts will be divided in the event the marriage is terminated, as well as provisions regarding alimony. For example, if a couple marries later in life, and they want to ensure that certain assets are set aside for their children in the event of divorce or death, they could make their wishes known in part with a prenuptial agreement. In other words, if a couple marries, and each spouse has assets that they want left to their children from a previous marriage, a prenuptial agreement means that the spouse's children, not the new spouse, will be the recipient of their assets upon their death.

Your property settlement is likely to be impacted by the terms of your prenuptial agreement if the agreement is upheld as valid by the court.

11.5 Can a prenuptial agreement be contested during the divorce?

Yes. A judge may consider many factors in determining whether to uphold a prenuptial agreement as valid, including the following:

- Whether your agreement was entered into voluntarily
- Whether your agreement was fair and reasonable at the time it was signed
- Whether you and your spouse gave a complete disclosure of your material assets and debts
- Whether you and your spouse each had your own lawyer or the chance to obtain a lawyer before signing
- Whether you and your spouse each had enough time before the wedding to carefully consider the agreement
- Whether the agreement legally complied with the requirements of the law

If you have a prenuptial agreement, bring a copy of it to the initial consultation with your attorney. Be sure to provide your lawyer with a detailed history of the facts and circumstances surrounding this agreement.

11.6 Are all of the assets—such as property, bank accounts, and inheritances—that I had prior to my marriage still going to be mine after the divorce?

The answer to this question depends on many factors. In many cases the court may allow a party to retain an asset brought into the marriage, but the following are questions a judge will consider when making a determination at the final trial:

- How long was the marriage? If the marriage was a long one, the judge is more likely to equitably divide the property than if the marriage is less than ten years.
- Can the premarital asset be clearly traced?
- Did you keep the property separate and titled in your name, or did you commingle it with marital assets? Did the other spouse contribute to the increase in the value of the premarital asset, and can the value of that increase be proven?

The above factors may be considered in determining whether and how a judge may consider premarital or inherited assets. One of the most significant factors in determining what the court will do is likely the duration of the marriage. These assets will be considered much differently if you had a five-year marriage than if you had a thirty-year marriage.

11.7 What does it mean to *commingle* property?

Commingling occurs when one spouse's property is mixed, or combined, with the marital property, such that the property can no longer be distinguished from the marital property.

11.8 Can I keep any gifts and inheritances I received during the marriage?

Gifts that you and your spouse gave to one another may be treated as any other marital asset. For other gifts received during the marriage from a third party, such as a gift from a parent, these gifts are considered marital property and possibly subject to division at the time of divorce, depending on the specific circumstances in your case. Again, the duration of the marriage will likely play a significant role. Whether you will be entitled to keep assets you inherited will depend upon the unique circumstances of your case.

11.9 Is the property to be equitably divided if my spouse put my name on the deed in joint tenancy or on our bank account during the marriage?

If your spouse added your name on the deed to real estate in joint ownership then that real estate that was previously separately titled is presumptively marital property and subject to equitable division. The same holds true for bank accounts or investments.

11.10 What if my name is not on the property deed, but I am listed on the mortgage with my spouse?

In New Hampshire, the title is essentially irrelevant to how it will be divided by the judge. Certainly, it is more likely that an asset will be equitably divided if both parties assisted in financing the asset.

Just remember that the divorce court cannot rewrite your loan with the bank or mortgage holder. That contract is still binding on you and/or your spouse until the bank releases you or your spouse.

11.11 How is it determined which spouse gets the house?

The first issue regarding the family home is the determination of who will retain possession of it while the divorce is pending on a temporary basis. Later, it must be decided whether the house will be sold or whether it will be awarded to you or your spouse.

Several factors to consider when determining the disposition of the home include:

- Which spouse can afford the mortgage and expenses associated with the home? Whether a spouse can refinance or otherwise remove the other spouse from the mortgage in a reasonable length of time, or whether spouses will remain jointly responsible for the mortgage and if so, for how long?

- Who has the children most of the time and where will the children go to school?

- Whether the house was owned by one party or the other prior to the marriage, and if so, for how long?

- Whether there are other assets, such as a pension or savings account in the marital estate, which can be transferred to a spouse to offset the equity value in the marital home without having to increase the mortgage

Talk with your lawyer about your options. If you and your spouse are unable to reach an agreement regarding the house, the judge will decide who keeps it or whether it will be sold. Most of the time it is better to reach an agreement than to have a judge force a sale in which both of you may lose money. If you sell the house, expect closing costs you both would pay that can be avoided or reduced if one party keeps the home.

11.12   Should I sell the house during the divorce proceedings?

Selling your home is a very big decision. To help you decide what is right for you, ask yourself the following questions:

- What will be the impact on my children if the home is sold?

- Can I afford to stay in the house after the divorce?

- After the divorce, will I be willing to give the house and yard the time, money, and physical energy required for its maintenance?

- Is it necessary for me to sell the house to pay a share of the equity to my spouse, or are there other options?

- Would my life be easier if I were in a smaller home or apartment?

- Would I prefer to move closer to the support of friends and family?

- What is the state of the housing market in my community?

- What are the benefits of remaining in this house?

- Can I retain the existing mortgage, or will I have to refinance?

- Will I have a higher or lower interest rate if I sell this house and buy a new one?
- Can I see myself living in a different home?
- Will I have the means to acquire another home?
- If I don't retain the home and my spouse asks for it, what effect will this have on my parenting case?
- Will my spouse agree to the sale of the house?
- What will be the net profit after commissions, expenses, and debts are paid?
- What will be the cost of properly preparing the house for sale?

Selling a home is more than just a legal or financial decision. Consider what is important to you in creating your life after your divorce.

11.13 How can I determine how much our house is worth?

In a divorce, the value of your home can be determined a number of ways. You and your spouse can agree or stipulate to the value of your home. There are a number of online resources that can help you get a rough idea of the value of your home; however, a more reliable resource is a real estate agent, who can perform a market analysis.

Some agents do a market analysis for no cost; others charge for their analysis. Market analyses are frequently done with a range of *listing prices* which may differ from sale price, depending on the market. Be sure to speak with a realtor so that you have a clear understanding of the likely asking price for your home. This price is the best estimate of *market value* of your home.

Or, for a more authoritative valuation, you can hire a professional real estate appraiser to determine the value of your home. Talk to your attorney to determine the best method to value your particular home in your divorce.

11.14 My house is worth less than what is owed on the mortgage. What are my options?

First, it is important to get an accurate assessment of the fair market value of your house. Second, consider working with a professional, such as an appraiser or realtor, to obtain a realistic estimate of sale value, including how long your house may be on the market and whether it can sell at all.

If your house is *underwater,* meaning you owe more on the mortgage than your house is worth, you may decide to list your house for sale and keep it on the market while continuing to make your mortgage payments. Another option to consider is a short sale, in which the lender accepts less money for your house than you owe. Be aware that there may be tax liabilities associated with a short sale.

Seek advice from your lawyer and other financial experts to determine which option is best for you. Just remember that you and your spouse must cooperate to prevent both of you from losing even more money.

If you are underwater and facing other financial stressors, you may want to consult with a bankruptcy lawyer earlier rather than later. Even if you are not going to file for bankruptcy, you need to know what rights and responsibilities you may have after a divorce.

11.15   What is meant by *equity* in our home?

Equity is the difference between the value of the home and the amount owed on the mortgage or liens against the property. For example, if the mortgage owed against the house is $60,000 and your home is valued at $200,000, the equity is $140,000.

If one spouse remains in the home, the issue of how and when to give the other spouse his or her share of the equity must be considered at the time of divorce. Because the residence is often among the most valuable assets considered in a divorce, it is important that you and your attorney discuss the details of its disposition. These include:

- Valuation of the property
- Refinancing to remove a party from liability for the mortgage
- The dates on which certain actions should be taken, such as listing the home for sale
- The real estate agent

- Costs for preparing the home for sale
- Who is to make the mortgage payments?
- Who remains in the home and for how long?
- Who pays for any needed repairs?

Regardless of who is awarded your house, the court will consider whether the spouse not receiving the house should be compensated for the equity in the house.

11.16 How will the equity in our house be divided?

If your home is going to be sold, the equity in the home will most likely be divided at the time of the sale, after the costs of the sale have been paid.

If either you or your spouse will be awarded the house or agree that one of you will keep the house, there are a number of options for paying the other spouse his or her share of the equity, including the following:

- The spouse who does not receive the house may receive other types of assets (for example, retirement funds or savings) to compensate for his or her share of the equity.

- The person who wants to keep the home may agree to refinance the home immediately or at some future date and then pay the other party his or her share of the equity.

- The former spouses may agree that the property will be sold at a future date, or upon an event (such as the youngest child completing high school or the remarriage of the spouse); then, the net equity is divided by some agreed-upon percentage formula.

Always keep in mind, however, that the type, value, or nature of all belongings are not the same. If you trade off other assets such as retirement accounts or pension for the home's equity, or cash, the spouse who receives the home equity or cash is receiving assets which are posttax, meaning you have already paid taxes on them. With assets such as a retirement account or pension, these are savings which occur pretax, meaning the person who receives these assets has not yet paid taxes on them, but will have to pay tax when they collect the assets. It is important to keep in mind the pretax or posttax nature of assets in a divorce.

If you take the retirement assets and cash those in early, you may pay a 10 percent penalty as well as federal and state taxes on any gain or profit (which can be 20 percent or more of the amount you withdraw). This is fine if you need the money right away or in the foreseeable future, but you also need to be prudent. If you spend all of your retirement assets, you will not have them when you need them in your retirement years.

11.17 If either my spouse or I sign a *quitclaim deed* to the other spouse, does that automatically remove our joint obligation to pay the mortgage?

No, never. A *quitclaim deed,* by itself, is a legal document that transfers one person's interest in property to another person. However, removing a name from the title of the property does not automatically remove the joint obligation to repay the mortgage. You and your spouse signed a contract with the lender to repay the debt you borrowed to purchase your home. The divorce judge cannot change that contract, and you both remain responsible for the mortgage.

In order to remove one of your names from the mortgage debt, you must refinance your current mortgage or convince the lender to give the other spouse a complete release.

11.18 What does *date of valuation* mean?

Because the value of assets can go up or down while a divorce is pending, it can become necessary to determine a set date for valuing the marital assets. This is referred to as the *date of valuation.* You and your spouse should agree on the date the assets should be valued. If you cannot agree, the judge will decide the date of valuation.

Among the most common dates used are the date of separation, the date of the filing of the divorce petition, or the date of the divorce trial or decree.

11.19 How are the values of property determined?

The value of some assets, like bank accounts, is usually not disputed. The value of other assets, however, such as homes or personal property, is more likely to be disputed.

If your case proceeds to trial, you may give your opinion of the value of the property you own. You or your spouse may also have certain property appraised by an expert. In such cases it may be necessary to have the appraiser appear at trial to give testimony regarding the appraisal and the value of the asset.

If you own substantial assets for which value is likely to be disputed, talk to your attorney early in your case about the benefits and costs of securing expert witnesses, such as forensic accountants, commercial and residential appraisals, and business valuations.

11.20 How is the fair value or *fair market value* of a sole proprietorship, corporation, partnership, subchapter C or S corporation, limited liability company, or other business entity determined?

This is a complex question that is very different from valuing a house or car. There are three fundamental ways to measure what a business is worth: asset, market, and/or income approaches. A valuator may use more than one of these methods depending upon the type and ownership interest of the business.

This process requires an expert who can review tax returns, profit and loss statements, checking accounts, cash flow, bank statements, depreciation schedules, reasonable business expenses, owner salaries, and other pieces of the income, assets, and debts of the business entity. From this data, a valuator may compare your business to other similar businesses in your geographical area or even nationally.

Of particular importance is: Does the spouse own the entire business, or are there other owners? This is relevant because, in most circumstances, the court can only value what the spouse owns on the date of divorce. There are different "pieces" of a business. For example, suppose a plumbing business owns a building, tools, and inventory. Those pieces of the business all have separate value. Additionally, the business has a good reputation, and the husband has contracts with multiple other businesses to do their plumbing work. This is called the *goodwill* of the business. The goodwill also has value, but it is often difficult to put a figure on it. Speak with your attorney about options to value a business if that's an issue in your divorce.

There is no single method by which a business valuator may establish a fair value of a business. There are standard valuation methods that a business appraiser will use, but this matter is too complicated to give an answer here that will apply to all businesses. It is important to make sure that if you own a business, you find a professional familiar with your type of business who will objectively help with evaluating the business.

11.21 What factors determine whether I can obtain a share of my spouse's business?

Many factors determine whether you will obtain a share of the value of your spouse's business and in what form you might receive it. Among the factors the court will look at are:

- Whether your spouse owned the business prior to your marriage
- Your role, if any, in operating the business or increasing its value
- The overall division of the property and debts

If you or your spouse own a business, it is important that you work with your attorney early in your case to develop a strategy for valuing the business and making your case for how it should be treated in the division of property and debts.

11.22 My spouse and I have owned and run our own business together for many years. Can I be forced out of it?

Deciding what should happen with a family business when divorce occurs can be a challenge. New Hampshire courts typically prefer a "clean break" between spouses. This means that one spouse will continue to own the business and the other spouse will be bought out or "forced" to sell to the other spouse. Unless the parties agree, continued management of a business by former spouses is rarely a good idea.

When discussing your options with your lawyer, consider the following questions:

- If one spouse retains ownership of the business, are there enough other assets left over for the other spouse to receive a fair share of the total marital assets?

- Which spouse has the skills and experience to continue running the business successfully?
- What would each spouse do if he or she was not working in the business?
- What is the actual value of the business?
- What is the market for the business if it were to be sold to a third party?
- Could either spouse remain an employee of the business for some period of time even if he or she was not an owner?
- Are there tax consequences or risks associated with the business?
- Are there assets in the business or divorce to secure the buyout?
- Is the business insolvent or operating at a loss?
- Can you and your spouse cooperate on a creative solution if no bank will lend a lump sum for the buyout and there are insufficient assets to do so?

You and your spouse are the ones who know your business best. With the help of your lawyers, you may create a settlement that can satisfy you both. If you cannot, however, the judge will make the decision for you at trial, and that can cause substantial loss to one or both spouses.

11.23 Who gets the interest from certificates of deposit, dividends from stock holdings, during the divorce proceedings?

Whether you or your spouse receives interest from these assets is decided as a part of the overall division of your property and debts.

11.24 Does each one of our financial accounts have to be divided in half if we agree to an equal division of our assets?

No. Rather than incurring the administrative challenges and expense of dividing each asset in half, you and your spouse can decide that one of you will take certain assets equal to the value of assets taken by the spouse. If necessary, one of you can agree to make a cash payment to the other to make an equitable division.

11.25 Who keeps all the household goods until the decree is signed?

The court will ordinarily not make any decisions about who keeps the household goods on a temporary basis. Most couples attempt to resolve these issues on their own or by using a mediator rather than incur legal fees to dispute the possession of household goods. It is always better if spouses are sensitive to leaving the house in good working order, particularly if children still live there. Try to cooperate to make sure each of you has the basic necessities. Dignity and respect in this area can make the divorce much less expensive.

However, the court may enter an order restraining the parties from transferring, selling, or destroying household goods during the divorce process, so that the goods remain intact and are still available to be divided by the final decree.

11.26 How can I reduce the risk that assets will be hidden, transferred, or destroyed by my spouse before the final divorce?

This question becomes especially important if your spouse has a history of destroying or selling property, incurring substantial debt, or transferring money without your knowledge. Under laws of the state, when a divorce is filed or served, *non-hypothecation orders* are issued by the court. These orders forbid the parties from selling property, incurring substantial debt, or cashing in retirement accounts.

There is an exception that can be made for the necessities of life like the need for a car after an accident, but that is not usually where problems occur.

Consulting with an attorney before the filing of your divorce can reduce the risk that assets will be hidden, transferred, or destroyed, or benefits like health insurance canceled. These are among the possible actions you and your attorney can consider together:

- Placing your family heirlooms or other valuables in a safe location

Division of Property

- Transferring some portion of your financial accounts prior to filing for divorce
- Preparing an inventory of your personal property
- Taking photographs or video recordings of the property
- Obtaining copies of important records or statements
- Obtaining a supplemental court order

Plans to leave the marital home should also be discussed in detail with your attorney so that any actions taken early in your case are consistent with your ultimate goals.

Speak candidly with your lawyer about your concerns so that a plan can be developed that provides a level of protection appropriate to your circumstances.

11.27 When and how are assets such as cars, ATVs, motorcycles, and boats divided?

In most cases, spouses are able to reach their own agreements about how to divide personal property such as boats and vehicles. If you disagree about how to divide certain items, a court will have to do that for you.

Most times, the disagreement has to do with value, which may be determined by accepted websites that regularly publish the fair market value of cars and boats. Always check to see whether it is a good use of your attorney fees to argue over items like this.

You should also pay careful attention to whether any debt is secured by the car, boat, or other vehicles. If the debt is listed in your joint names, you are still liable to the lender even if the title of the vehicle is transferred. It is better if a loan is paid in full or refinanced into one party's name at the time of a divorce.

However, if that is not possible, you should discuss this situation with your lawyer. He or she may want to add language to your divorce decree that makes your spouse solely responsible for the obligation and protects you if he or she files for bankruptcy or defaults on the debt. It is usually better to have a "clean break" when possible so there are no joint debts after divorce.

11.28 How can I value our personal property?

In a divorce, your personal property will be valued at its fair market value on the date of the divorce. The fair market value is simply the price a buyer would be willing to pay for the item at a garage sale or on an online auction website.

For example, if you bought a sofa for $3,000 five years ago, the fair market value of the couch is what you could sell it for at a garage sale today. The fair market value is not how much the couch was worth when you bought it or how much it will cost to replace the couch. Instead, the value of your personal property is what you could reasonably sell it for in its current used condition.

11.29 My wife and I own a coin collection. How will our collection be valued and divided in our divorce?

If you own a unique collection, such as a gun, art, or coin collection, talk with your attorney about how to value the collection in your divorce. It may be that you will need to have the collection appraised by an expert who has the specialized training and knowledge necessary to determine its value.

If you and your spouse cannot agree on who will keep the collection, it is possible the judge will order the collection to be sold. Or the judge may order you to divide the collection between you and your spouse one piece at a time.

11.30 What is meant by a *property inventory,* and how detailed should mine be?

A *property inventory* is a listing of the property and debts (debts secured against the property or unsecured debts like credit cards) that you own. It may also include a brief description of the property. Discuss with your attorney the level of inventory detail needed to benefit your case. Factors to consider when creating your property inventory may include:

- The extent to which you anticipate you and your spouse will disagree regarding the division of your property

- Whether you anticipate a dispute regarding the value of the property either you or your spouse is retaining

Division of Property

- Whether you will have continued access to the property if a later inventory is needed, or whether your spouse will retain control of the property
- Whether you and your spouse are likely to disagree about which items are premarital, inherited, or gifts from someone other than your spouse

In addition to creating an inventory, your attorney may request that you prepare a list of the property that you and your spouse have already divided or a list of the items you want to keep but which your spouse has not agreed to give to you.

If you do not have continued access to your property, talk to your attorney about taking photographs or obtaining access to the property in order to complete your inventory.

11.31 What happens to our individual checking and savings accounts during and after the divorce?

Regardless of whose name is on the account, bank accounts are considered marital assets and may be divided by the court. Discuss with your attorney how to retain access or obtain an accounting of these accounts, how to use these accounts while the case is pending, and the date on which financial accounts should be valued.

11.32 How and when are liquid assets such as bank accounts and stocks divided?

In many cases, couples will agree to divide bank account balances equally at the outset of the case. However, this may not be advisable in your case if, for example, you have limited cash assets and you may need to find new housing or pay marital debts, such as a car loan or a joint credit card. You should always keep an accounting of how you spend any money used from a bank account while your divorce is in progress.

Stocks are ordinarily a part of the final agreement for the division of property and debts. If you and your spouse cannot agree on how your investments should be divided, the judge will have to make the decision at trial as a part of the division of all property and debts.

205

11.33 Will debts be considered when determining the division of the property?

Yes. The court will consider any debts incurred during the course of the marriage when dividing the property. For example, if you are awarded a car valued at $12,000, but you owe a $10,000 debt on the same vehicle, the court will take that debt into consideration in the overall division of the assets. Similarly, if one spouse agrees to pay substantial marital credit card debt, this obligation may also be considered in the final determination of the division of property and debts. The court may also consider premarital debts, though in most cases, those debts will be allocated to the party who incurred them.

If your spouse incurred debts that you believe should be his or her sole responsibility, tell your attorney as soon as possible. Some debts may be considered and treated differently from other debts incurred during the marriage. For example, if your spouse spent large sums of money on gambling or illegal drugs without your knowledge, you may be able to argue that those debts should be the sole responsibility of your spouse.

11.34 Will I get to keep my engagement ring?

If your engagement ring was given to you prior to your marriage, it will be considered a gift in contemplation of marriage that you can keep. However, the value of the ring may be considered in the overall property settlement.

11.35 How is pet custody determined?

This is an emotional issue that occurs more often than people would like to admit. Pet custody is determined on a case-by-case basis, but pets are considered property and can be awarded to one spouse or the other. Factors that courts have considered include the following:

- Who held title to the pet?
- Who provided care for the pet?
- Who will best be able to meet the pet's needs?

Some courts have awarded the pet to one party and given the other party certain rights, such as:

- Specific periods of time to spend with the pet

- The right to care for the pet when the other person is unable
- The right to be informed of the pet's health condition
- Ordering shared expenses for pets

If it is important to you to be awarded one of your family pets, discuss the matter with your attorney. It may be possible to reach a pet care agreement with your spouse that will allow you to share possession of and responsibility for your pets.

11.36 How will our property in another state be divided?

For the purposes of dividing your assets, out-of-state property is treated the same as property in New Hampshire. Although a New Hampshire court cannot order a change in the title to property located in another state, a judge can order your spouse either to turn the property over to you or to sign a deed or other document to transfer this title to you

Sometimes this gets complicated if there is a need to value an asset like a time-share or land in another country or state. If possible, you should try to reach an agreement with your spouse because those kinds of disputes can get very expensive and legally complicated.

11.37 If my spouse and I can't decide division of property, who decides? Can that person's decision be contested?

If you and your spouse cannot agree on the division of your property, a judge will make the determination after considering the evidence presented at your trial.

If either party is dissatisfied with the decision reached by the judge, an appeal to the New Hampshire Supreme Court is possible. However, it is difficult to win on the Supreme Court level in divorce cases because the Supreme Court often defers to the judgment of the trial judges. The Supreme Court considers a lower court judge the person best able to determine credibility of witnesses and review the evidence.

Such appeals can also delay a final divorce by a year or more, so any appeal requires careful consideration with the help of your lawyer.

11.38 Is my *health savings account* an asset that can be divided in the divorce?

Yes. A *health savings account (HSA)* is a tax-advantaged medical savings account to which contributions may be made by employees, employers, or both. Your HSA is an asset to be included in the property distribution and may be divided according to your divorce decree and transferred to another HSA. A division according to a decree does not constitute a distribution and is therefore a tax-free transfer.

11.39 I worked very hard for years to support my family while my spouse completed an advanced degree. Do I have a right to any of my spouse's future earnings?

Your contribution during the marriage is a factor to be considered in both the division of the property and debts, as well as any award of alimony. Be sure to give your attorney a complete history of your contribution to the marriage and ask about their impact on the outcome of your case.

11.40 I suspect my spouse is hiding assets, but I can't prove it. How can I protect myself if I discover later that I was right?

Ask your lawyer to include language in your divorce decree to address your concerns. Insist that it include an acknowledgment by your spouse that the agreement you arrive at is based upon a full and complete disclosure of your spouse's financial condition. Discuss with your lawyer a provision that allows for setting aside the agreement if it is later discovered that assets were hidden.

11.41 My spouse says I'm not entitled to a share of his stock options because he gets to keep them only if he stays employed with his company. What are my rights?

Stock options are often a very valuable asset. They are also one of the most complex issues when dividing assets during a divorce for these, among other, reasons:

- Each company has its own rules about awarding or exercising stock options.
- Complete information is needed from the employer.

- There are different methods for calculating the value of stock options.

- The reasons the options were given can impact the valuation and division. For example, certain types of stock options are given for future performance and may be not be considered marital property.

- There are cost and tax considerations when options are exercised.

Rather than being awarded a portion of the stock options themselves, you are likely to receive a share of the proceeds when the stock options are exercised.

If either you or your spouse owns stock options, begin discussing this asset with your attorney early in your case to allow sufficient time to settle the issues or to be well prepared for trial.

11.42 I'm Jewish and want my husband to cooperate with obtaining a *get*, which is a divorce document under my religion. Can I get a court order for this?

Talk to your lawyer about obtaining a *get cooperation clause* in your divorce decree, including a provision regarding who should pay for it. At this time, the law regarding this has not yet been established in New Hampshire. But the law in other jurisdictions does permit a judge to order cooperation with a get.

11.43 Who will get the frozen embryo of my egg and my spouse's sperm that we have stored at the clinic?

The law on this issue is not yet well established in New Hampshire and is in a complex state of flux all over the country. The terms of your contract with the clinic may impact the rights you and your spouse may have to the embryo, so provide a copy of the contract to your attorney for review. Keep in mind that with the broad definition of marital property in New Hampshire, it is likely that the embryos could be awarded to one party or the other. There are significant considerations to the possibility that one party may create a child with the other parent's genetic material without his or her permission, so speak with an attorney about this important issue.

11.44   What is a *permanent stipulation* or *agreement?*

A *permanent stipulation* or *agreement* is a written document that includes all of the financial agreements you and your spouse have reached in your divorce. This may include the division of property, debts, child support, spousal support, insurance, and attorney fees.

The permanent stipulations, upon being signed by the judge, becomes a final court order or decree dissolving your marriage.

11.45   What happens after my spouse and I approve the final decree or permanent stipulations? Do we still have to go to court?

No. New Hampshire law allows the spouses, by agreement, to waive an uncontested testimonial hearing about irreconcilable differences. After you and your spouse approve and sign the final decree or permanent stipulations, it must still be approved by your judge. Waiver of an uncontested hearing may only occur if you and your spouse have resolved all matters pertaining to your divorce and minor children.

11.46   If my spouse and I think our agreement is fair, why does the judge still have to approve it?

The judge has a duty to ensure that all agreements are reasonable and equitable under New Hampshire law. For this reason, your judge must review your agreement. The judge may consider the facts and circumstances of your case when reviewing the agreement. The judge also reviews the agreement to make sure all of the paperwork is filled out completely and that nothing is left ambiguous. If the judge has questions about the agreement, he or she will either notify the parties in writing of the issues needing to be addressed, or may call the parties in for a final hearing, even if the parties requested to waive it. It may be that the judge needs more information in order to determine if it is equitable, or to ensure the parties understand the agreement. This happens more often when the parties are not represented by counsel.

Not every case will result in an equal division of the assets and debts from the marriage, although this is very common in longer-term marriages. The court will also examine the child support and alimony provisions as part of the property settlement, because it is the totality of the allocation of income and property and debts that matters.

11.47 What happens to the property distribution if one of us dies before the divorce proceedings are completed?

If your spouse dies prior to your divorce decree being entered, but there is a signed agreement, the court may enforce the agreement and enter a divorce decree. If you are legally divorced at the time of your spouse's death, you will be treated as if you predeceased him in his will or have no right to claim any of his estate in the probate court. You may, however, have rights to make a claim against the estate for any parts of the decree not yet paid, such as transfers of property, or alimony,

If there is no agreement signed by both spouses, you will likely be considered still married and treated as a surviving spouse under probate law. This means that even if your spouse disinherited you, you have the right to claim some of his or her assets in probate court.

11.48 After our divorce is final, can the property agreement be modified?

Generally, provisions in your property agreement or decree dealing with the distribution of your assets and debts are not modifiable. Absent very specific instances of fraud, duress, or newly discovered evidence, the agreement or order cannot be modified.

Alimony, child support, and parenting are all modifiable under specific circumstances permitted under the law.

11.49 What if property was omitted or not included in our settlement or divorce decree?

Under New Hampshire law, if property, such as a pension or bank account, is left out of the agreement or decree, the court may still treat the property as subject to division. In fact, if it was determined that the property was intentionally left out or hidden by one party, the party who hid the asset may have to pay the innocent spouse a penalty of up to 100 percent of the hidden asset. You will have to consult a lawyer concerning the merits of your case and file a motion if appropriate.

12

Benefits: Insurance, Retirement, and Pensions

During your marriage, you might have taken certain employment benefits for granted. You might not have given much thought each month to having health insurance provided through your spouse's work. When you find yourself in the middle of a divorce, however, suddenly these benefits come to the forefront of your mind.

You might also, even unconsciously, have seen your own employment retirement benefits as belonging to you and not to your spouse, and you may have referred to "my 401(k)" or "my pension." After all, you are the one who went to work every day to earn it, right?

When you divorce, some benefits arising from your spouse's employment will end, some may continue for a period of time, and others may be divided between you. Retirement funds, in particular, are often one of the most valuable marital assets to be divided in a divorce.

Whether the benefits are from your own employer or from your spouse, with your attorney's help you will develop a better understanding of which benefits the law considers to be "yours," "mine," and "ours" for continuing or dividing.

Generally, the same rules described in question 11.3 in chapter 11 apply to the division of pension and retirement benefits at the time of divorce.

12.1 Will my children continue to have health coverage through my spouse's work even after the divorce?

If either you or your spouse currently provides health insurance for your children, it is likely that the court will order the insurance to remain in place until your child reaches the age of majority and for so long as child support is being paid for your child.

The cost of insurance for the children will be taken into consideration in determining the amount of child support to be paid under the guidelines. The general rule is that the cost of health insurance must be less than 4 percent of a party's gross income in order for the court to require a party to pay for it. If the party chooses to continue to insure the children on his or her health insurance plan, despite the fact that it is more than 4 percent of the party's gross income, the judge may sign off on the agreement; however, the agreement cannot force an unwilling party to insure their children at more than the 4 percent cost.

Changes in federal and state law concerning health insurance may influence the availability of coverage after divorce for spouses or children. You need to be very careful and consult a lawyer to avoid gaps in coverage or loss of coverage.

12.2 Will I continue to have health insurance through my spouse's employer after the divorce?

It depends. If your spouse currently provides health insurance for you, you may be treated as a spouse for health insurance purposes. However, some insurance companies refuse to treat a person as a spouse after the entry of the divorce decree. It also depends on the location of your spouse's employer. Some states have very generous laws regarding continuing coverage for a former spouse on health insurance; some employers will not allow continuing coverage. In New Hampshire, the law requires employers to continue health insurance coverage for a former spouse for up to three years, unless the employers are *self-insured*. This is a serious problem because most New Hampshire employers are now self-insured, which means that most employers based out of New Hampshire do not provide continuing coverage for a former spouse at the same cost as when the couple was married. Health insurance is complicated, so you should make sure you and your lawyer investigate your spouse's' insurance coverage to determine whether you have rights under a policy that the company may not voluntarily share. Get a copy of your insurance plan booklets and consider consulting with a health insurance specialist. This is especially true if you have a preexisting condition.

Investigate the cost of continuing on your spouse's employer-provided plans under a federal law known as *COBRA* after the expiration of your previous coverage. This coverage can be maintained for up to three years. However, the cost of *COBRA* can be high, so you will want to determine whether it is a realistic option for you.

If you have no other health insurance and it is permitted by your spouse's insurance company, talk to your attorney about including a provision in your decree to keep you on your spouse's health insurance policy for the maximum period allowed under the plan.

It is critically important to begin early to investigate your eligibility for coverage and your options for your future health insurance. The cost of your health care is an important factor when pursuing alimony and planning your postdivorce budget.

12.3   What is a *qualified medical support order?*

A *qualified medical support order (QMSO)* is a court order providing continued group health insurance coverage for a minor child. A QMSO may also enable a parent to obtain other information about the plan, without having to go through the parent who has the coverage. Rather than allowing only the parent with the insurance to be reimbursed for a claim, under a QMSO, a health insurance plan is required to reimburse directly whoever actually paid the child's medical expense.

12.4   What is a *qualified domestic relations order?*

A *qualified domestic relations order (QDRO)* is a court order that requires a retirement or pension plan administrator to pay you the share of your former spouse's retirement that was awarded to you in the decree. In the case of federal retirement plans, this order is called a *court order acceptable for processing (COAP)*.

These orders ensure that a nonemployee spouse actually receives his or her share directly from the employee spouse's plan.

Obtaining a QDRO or COAP is a critical step in the postdivorce process. These are complex documents, and various steps are required to reduce future concerns about enforcement so as to fully protect your rights. These court orders must comply with numerous technical rules and be approved by the plan administrator, which is often located outside of New Hampshire.

Whenever possible, court orders dividing retirement plans should be entered at the same time as the divorce or shortly thereafter.

12.5 How many years must I have been married before I'm eligible to receive a part of my spouse's retirement fund or pension?

This is a complicated question because there are many different plans with different requirements and policies. Some plans, such as those of the military and federal government, are governed by specific federal departments with strict rules and forms. Other plans are run by states or municipalities and may not be under federal law. It is very important early in your divorce case to get a description of the plan from the plan administrator or human resources office for your spouse's employer, and to review any forms long before agreeing to a final divorce decree. Most retirement plans do not have requirements about the years of marriage before you can collect any portion of your spouse's retirement; however, the longer the marriage, the more likely you will receive some portion of a former spouse's retirement plan.

As mentioned, this area of law is very complicated so you should make sure you and your lawyer investigate your rights and, if needed, hire an expert on pensions to help. Do not wait for trial to do this. Get the information early so you can protect yourself and have court orders drafted that will be accepted by the judge and a plan administrator to divide the pension at the time of divorce.

12.6 I contributed to my pension plan for ten years before I got married. Will my spouse get half of my entire pension?

Probably not. It is more likely the court will award your spouse only a portion of your retirement funds—a portion of the portion that was acquired during the marriage.

If either you or your spouse made premarital contributions to a pension or retirement plan, be sure to let your attorney know. This information is essential to determine which portion of the retirement plan should be treated as premarital and is unlikely to be shared except in a very long-term marriage.

12.7 I plan to keep the same job after my divorce. Will my former spouse get half of the money I contribute to my retirement plan after my divorce?

No. Your former spouse should be entitled to a portion of your retirement accumulated only during the marriage.

Talk with your attorney so that the language of the court order ensures protection of your postdivorce retirement contributions.

12.8 Am I still entitled to a share of my spouse's retirement fund even though I never contributed to my own during our marriage?

Probably. Retirement accounts are often the most valuable asset (other than a home) accumulated during a marriage. Consequently, a judge will consider the retirement fund along with all of the other marital assets and debts when determining an equitable division.

12.9 My lawyer says I'm entitled to a share of my spouse's retirement fund. How can I find out how much I will get and when I'm eligible to receive it?

More than one factor will determine your right to collect from your spouse's retirement fund. One factor will be the terms of the court order dividing the retirement fund. The court order will tell you whether you are entitled to a set dollar amount, a percentage, or a fraction to be determined based upon the length of your marriage and how long your spouse has worked or will continue working.

For a *defined benefit plan,* such as a pension that pays monthly, for example, the fraction used by the court will be the number of years you were married while your spouse was employed at that company *(the numerator),* divided by the total number of years your spouse is employed with the company *(the denominator).*

Another factor will be the terms of the retirement plan itself. For a *defined contribution plan,* some provide for lump sum withdrawals, while others issue payments in monthly installments. Review the terms of your court order and immediately contact the plan administrator before the settlement conference and trial to obtain the most precise understanding of your rights and benefits. Don't forget to consider tax implications on these assets, as well as penalties if you are under fifty-nine and one-half years old if you plan to access these assets prior to retirement.

12.10 If I am eligible to receive part of my spouse's retirement benefits, when am I eligible to begin collecting them? Must I be sixty-five to collect them?

It very much depends upon the terms of your spouse's retirement plan. In some cases it is possible to begin receiving your share at the earliest date your spouse is eligible to receive them, regardless of whether he or she elects to do so. Under other plans, you may not be eligible to receive them until your spouse actually begins to receive them, or until you are eligible to receive them. Check the specific terms of your spouse's plan to learn your options.

In many cases, it is prudent to hire an expert on pensions to research and protect your rights.

12.11 What happens if my former spouse is old enough to qualify for benefits, but I am not

Often you will be eligible to begin receiving your share of the benefits when your former spouse begins receiving his or hers. Depending upon the plan, you may even be eligible to receive them sooner. Therefore, it is important to be clear about your rights under the QDRO when the divorce decree is signed.

12.12 Am I entitled to cost-of-living increases on my share of the retirement funds?

It depends. If your spouse has a retirement plan that includes a provision for a *cost-of-living allowance (COLA),* this may be included in the court order dividing the retirement benefit. What matters is that if you have a right to a COLA, it should be a part of the original QDRO.

12.13 What circumstances might prevent me from receiving part of my spouse's retirement benefits?

Some government pension plans, if they are in lieu of a Social Security benefit or connected to disability, may not be subject to division as a matter of federal law. If you or your spouse is employed by a government agency, talk with your lawyer or an expert in pensions about whether you are entitled to any other retirement benefits and how this may affect the property settlement.

12.14 Does the death of my spouse affect the payout of retirement benefits to me or to our children?

It depends on the nature of your spouse's retirement plan and the terms of the court order dividing the retirement. If you want to be eligible for survivorship benefits, discuss the issue with your attorney *before* your case is settled or goes to trial. Keep in mind that if your former spouse remarries and names a subsequent spouse as his or her beneficiary, you may lose your own interest in the retirement account upon your former spouse's death. Be sure to review the terms of the plan and consult with an expert if you are unsure about your options.

Some plans allow only a surviving spouse or former spouse to be a beneficiary. Other plans may allow for the naming of an alternate beneficiary, such as your children.

12.15 Can I still collect on my former spouse's Social Security benefits if he or she passes on before I do?

It depends. You may be eligible to receive benefits if:

- You were married to your spouse for ten or more years
- You are not remarried

Benefits: Insurance, Retirement, and Pensions

- You are at least sixty-two years old
- The benefit you would receive based on your own earning record is less than the benefit you would receive from your former spouse

For more information, contact your local Social Security Administration office or visit the SSA website at www.ssa.gov.

12.16 What orders might the court enter regarding life insurance?

The judge may order you or your spouse to maintain a life insurance policy to ensure that future support payments, such as child support and spousal support, are made. In most cases, you will be required to pay for your own life insurance after your divorce, and you should include this as an expense in your monthly budget.

You may want a provision included that requires annual proof from your spouse that the insurance is in effect and the beneficiary status remains unchanged.

12.17 Because we share children, should I leave my spouse as a beneficiary on my life insurance?

It depends on your intentions. If your intention is to give the money to your former spouse, by all means name the other parent as a beneficiary.

However, if you intend the life insurance proceeds to be used only for the benefit of your children, talk with your attorney about your options. You may consider naming a trustee to manage the life insurance proceeds on behalf of your children, and there may be reasons to choose someone other than your former spouse.

You should always create a new estate plan after a divorce to be sure you meet your court-ordered obligations under the divorce decree and continue to protect your children.

12.18 Can the court require that I be the beneficiary of my spouse's insurance policy, for so long as the children are minors or indefinitely?

When a court order is entered for life insurance, it is ordinarily for the purposes of ensuring payment of future support and it will terminate when the support obligation has ended. Naming you as the beneficiary on your spouse's insurance policy for purposes of ensuring payment of future child support is one option. The court may also name the children directly as beneficiaries, or require that a trust be established to receive the life insurance proceeds on behalf of your children.

12.19 My spouse is in the military. What are my rights to benefits after the divorce?

As the former spouse of a military member, the types of benefits to which you may be entitled are typically determined by the number of years you were married, the number of years your spouse was in the military while you were married, and whether or not you have remarried. Be sure you obtain accurate information about these dates.

Among the benefits for which you may be eligible are:

- A portion of your spouse's military retirement pay
- A survivor benefit in the event of your spouse's death
- Health care or participation in a temporary, transitional health-care program
- The ability to keep your military identification card
- The continued use of certain military facilities, such as the commissary

Although your divorce may be pending, educate yourself about your right to future military benefits so that you can plan for your future with clarity. While your divorce is still pending, contact your base's legal office or, for more information, visit the website for the branch of the military of which your spouse was a member.

13

Division of Debts

Throughout a marriage, most couples have disagreements about money from time to time. You might think extra money should be spent on a family vacation, but your spouse might insist it should be saved for retirement. You might think it's time to finally buy a new car, but your spouse thinks your driving the ten-year-old van for two more years is a better idea.

If you and your spouse had different philosophies about saving and spending during your marriage, chances are you will have some differing opinions when dividing your debts in divorce. What you can count on is that New Hampshire law provides that payment of debts must also be taken into consideration when dividing the assets from your marriage. It is the net worth (value of assets minus debts) that a judge will consider in a final equitable distribution.

There are steps you can take to ensure the best outcome possible when it comes to dividing your marital debt. These include providing accurate and complete debt information to your lawyer and asking your lawyer to include provisions in your divorce decree to protect you in the future if your spouse refuses to pay his or her share.

Regardless of how the debts from your marriage are divided, know that you will gradually be able to build your independent financial success when making a fresh start after your divorce is final.

13.1 Who is responsible for paying credit card bills and making house payments during the divorce proceedings?

Unless you and your spouse can agree, the court will make decisions regarding the payment of credit card debt on a temporary basis after receiving each party's proposals prior to the temporary hearing. It is much better to work with your attorney and your spouse to reach a temporary agreement. Discuss the importance of making at least minimum payments on time to avoid substantial finance charges, late fees, and credit-reporting harm that may affect you for years to come.

Typically, the spouse who remains in the home is responsible for the mortgage payments, taxes, utilities, and other ordinary household expenses, but that depends upon available income or other resources like savings.

If you are concerned that you cannot afford to stay in the marital home on a temporary basis, talk with your attorney about your options prior to your temporary hearing.

13.2 What, if anything, should I be doing with the credit card companies as we go through the divorce?

If possible, it is best to obtain some separate credit prior to the divorce. This will help you establish credit in your own name and aid you with necessary purchases in the interim period.

Begin by obtaining a copy of your credit report from at least two of the three nationwide consumer reporting companies: Experian, Equifax, or TransUnion. The *Fair Credit Reporting Act* entitles you to a free copy of your credit report from each of these three companies every twelve months. To order your free annual report online, go to www.annualcreditreport.com, call toll-free to (877) 322-8228, or complete an Annual Credit Report Request Form and mail it to: Annual Credit Report Request Service, P.O. Box 105281, Atlanta, Georgia 30348-5281. You can print the form from the Federal Trade Commission website at www.ftc.gov/credit.

Your spouse may have incurred debt using your name. This information is important to relay to your attorney. If you and your spouse have joint credit card accounts, contact each credit card company to close the account. Do the same if your spouse is an authorized user on any of your own accounts.

If you want to maintain credit with a particular company, ask for a new account in your own name. Be sure to let your spouse know before you close an account.

13.3 How is credit card debt divided?

Credit card debt will be divided as part of the overall division of the marital property and debts. Just as in the division of property, the court considers what is equitable, or rational, given the specific facts of your case.

If your spouse has exclusively used a credit card for purposes that did not benefit the family, such as gambling or drug use, talk with your attorney. In most cases, the court will not review a lengthy history of how you and your spouse used the credit cards, but there can be exceptions.

As in property division, debts need not be divided equally. The court may consider debt secured by a home you want to keep different from a debt used to take a vacation or a school loan. Practically speaking, it does not often make sense for the lower-income earner to take on half of the debts if they are significant. The result would be that the higher-income earner would have to pay more support to the lower-income earner to enable him or her to pay the debts. That makes little sense so, more often than not, the higher-income earner may wind up with more of the debt. However, there is no formula that remains the same in every case.

13.4 Am I responsible for the repayment of my spouse's student loans?

The answer to this question depends on several factors. If your spouse incurred student loans prior to the marriage, it is most likely that he or she will be ordered to pay that debt.

If the debt was incurred during the marriage, however, how the funds were used may have an impact on who is ordered to pay them. For example, if your spouse borrowed $3,000 during the marriage for tuition, it is likely your spouse will be ordered to pay that debt. However, if a $3,000 student loan was taken out by your spouse, but $1,000 of it was used for a family vacation, then the court would be more likely to order the debt to be shared.

If you were a joint borrower on your spouse's student loan and your spouse fails to pay the loan, the lender may attempt to collect from you even if your spouse has been ordered by the court to pay the debt. You will need special protection in the event of a default.

If either you or your spouse has student loan debt, be sure to give your attorney the complete history and ask about the most likely outcome under the facts of your case.

13.5 During the divorce proceedings, am I still responsible for debt my spouse continues to accrue?

It depends. The court may order each of the parties to be responsible for his or her own post-separation debts. In many cases, the date for dividing debt is when the parties separated households; in others, it is the date the petition for divorce was filed.

In cases of economic misconduct in which there is actual evidence such as paper trails or other documentation—not just a "feeling"—the court may allocate debts disproportionately or consider a date for allocating the debt that is years earlier than the divorce filing.

13.6 During the marriage my spouse applied for and received several credit cards without my knowledge. Am I responsible for them?

It depends. The court will consider the overall fairness of the property and debt division when deciding who should pay this debt. If your spouse bought items with the cards and intends to keep those items, it is likely that she or he will be ordered to pay the debt incurred for the purchases.

The credit card companies are unlikely to be able to pursue collection from you for the debt unless you actually used the card or signed the loan application.

13.7 During our marriage, we paid off thousands of dollars of debt incurred by my spouse before we were married. Will the court take this into consideration when dividing our property and debt?

It might. Just as premarital assets can have an impact on the overall division of property and debts, so can premarital debt. Depending upon the length of the marriage, the evidence and reason for the debt, and the amount paid, it may be a factor for the judge to consider.

Be sure to let your attorney know if either you or your spouse brought substantial debt into the marriage. This information needs to be clear early on in the divorce process and not brought up later.

13.8 Regarding debts, what is a *hold-harmless* or *indemnity provision,* and why should it be included in the divorce decree?

A *hold-harmless* or *indemnity provision* is intended to protect you in the event that your spouse fails to follow a court order to pay a debt after the divorce is granted. The language typically provides that your spouse shall "indemnify and hold [you] harmless from liability" on the debt.

If you and your spouse have a joint debt and your spouse fails to pay, even though the court has ordered him or her to do so, the creditor may nevertheless attempt to collect from you. This is because a judge is without the power to change the creditor's rights and can only enter orders affecting you and your spouse.

In the event your spouse fails to pay a court-ordered debt and the creditor attempts collection from you, the *hold-harmless* provision in your divorce degree can be used in an effort to insist that payment be made by your former spouse with the help of the judge.

You should also consider language that makes the duty to pay a *domestic support order* that is consistent with the bankruptcy code, so that if your spouse files for bankruptcy after the divorce, you may have protection from the discharge of the debt.

13.9 Why do my former spouse's doctors say they have a legal right to collect from me when my former spouse was ordered to pay her own medical bills?

Under New Hampshire law, you may be held liable for the "necessities of life" of your spouse, including health care. Your divorce decree does not take away the legal rights of creditors to collect debts.

Contact your attorney about your right to enforce the court order that your spouse pays his or her own medical bills.

13.10 My spouse and I have agreed that I will keep our home. Why must I refinance the mortgage?

There may be a number of reasons why your spouse is asking you to refinance the mortgage. First, the mortgage company cannot be forced to take your spouse's name off of the mortgage note. This means that if you did not make the house payments, the lender could pursue collection against your spouse, which could affect your spouse's credit negatively.

Second, your spouse may want to receive their share of the home equity. It may be possible for you to borrow additional money at the time of refinancing to pay your spouse his or her share of the equity in the home.

Third, the mortgage on your family home may prevent your spouse from buying a different home in the future. Because there remains a risk that your spouse could be pursued for the debt to the mortgage company, it is unlikely that a second lender will want to take the risk of extending further credit to your spouse.

13.11 Can I file for bankruptcy while my divorce is pending?

Yes. Consult with your attorney if you are considering filing for bankruptcy while your divorce is still pending. It will be important for you to ask yourself a number of questions, including:

- Should I file for bankruptcy on my own or with my spouse?
- How will filing for bankruptcy affect my ability to purchase a home in the future?

- Which debts can be discharged in bankruptcy, and which cannot?

- How will a bankruptcy affect the division of property and debts in the divorce?

- How might a delay in the divorce proceeding due to a bankruptcy impact my case?

- What form of bankruptcy is best for my situation?

If you use a different attorney for your bankruptcy than you do for your divorce, be sure that each attorney is kept fully informed about any developments in both cases.

13.12 What happens if my spouse files for bankruptcy during our divorce?

Contact your divorce attorney right away, but you may need to contact a lawyer who specializes in bankruptcy, as well. The filing of a bankruptcy while a divorce is pending can have a significant impact on the proceedings.

Once a bankruptcy petition is filed, an *automatic stay* is entered under federal law against all creditors, which includes you and your spouse. If a creditor violates the automatic stay by trying to take assets or income without the permission of the bankruptcy court, this may be considered a contempt of court, and sanctions like attorney fees or a fine can be imposed.

Of first concern, bankruptcy is subject to a federal law, which means that the bankruptcy court now has jurisdiction or authority over any income, assets, and debts in a state court divorce proceeding. To proceed with a divorce, you will need a *relief from stay,* which is the express permission of the bankruptcy court for you to ask the divorce court to complete your divorce case.

You may have to request permission from the bankruptcy court judge to use rental income, to pay child or spousal support owed under a court order, or to obtain an order from the state divorce court that the federal bankruptcy court will respect and enforce. In most cases, parenting rights and responsibilities are not stayed by a bankruptcy filing.

An attorney can advise you as to whether certain debts are likely to be discharged in bankruptcy, the delay a bankruptcy may cause to your divorce, and whether bankruptcy is an appropriate option for you, as well, if you are not the spouse who originally filed.

13.13   Can I file for divorce while I am in bankruptcy?

Yes, but you must receive the bankruptcy court's permission to proceed with the divorce. Although in bankruptcy your property is protected from debt collection by an automatic stay, the stay can also prevent the divorce court from dividing property or awarding support from income until you obtain the bankruptcy court's permission.

13.14   What should I do if my former spouse files for bankruptcy after our divorce?

Contact your attorney immediately. If you learn that your former spouse has filed for bankruptcy, you may have certain rights to object to the discharge of any debts your spouse was ordered to pay under your divorce decree.

It is important to obtain immediate advice concerning whether any debts are dischargeable or non-dischargeable as a matter of federal law. If you fail to take action, it is possible that you will be held responsible for debts your spouse was ordered to pay.

13.15   If I am awarded child support or alimony in my divorce decree, can these obligations be eliminated if my former spouse files for bankruptcy?

No. Support obligations in the past or future such as child support and alimony are not eliminated, or "dischargeable," in bankruptcy. This means that these specific debts, as a matter of federal law, cannot be eliminated in a bankruptcy proceeding.

This can get very complicated if your spouse is paying your mortgage, a car payment, or health insurance premiums to a third party, so do not delay in getting legal advice.

13.16   What will happen if my former spouse does not pay his court-ordered obligations under the decree?

If your former spouse does not pay the debts assigned to him in the decree, you may be able to pursue contempt or enforcement by court action. A party is in contempt of court if they willfully disobey or disregard a court order.

Division of Debts

Talk with your attorney to determine whether a contempt of court action may be filed in your case to enforce your rights under the decree in your case. You may even have the right to recover interest and attorney fees if a spouse is found in contempt of court.

14

Income and Other Taxes

Nobody likes a surprise letter from the Internal Revenue Service or state tax authority saying that he or she owes more taxes or that a tax return from three years ago is subject to an audit. When your divorce is finalized, you want to be sure that you won't later discover you owe taxes you weren't expecting to pay.

A number of tax issues may arise in your divorce. Your attorney may not be able to answer all of your tax questions, so consulting your accountant or a qualified tax adviser for additional advice might be prudent and necessary.

Taxes are important considerations in both settlement negotiations and trial preparation. They should not be overlooked. Taxes can impact many of your decisions, including those regarding child-care tax credits, tax exemptions, alimony, division of property, the receipt of retirement benefits, or the allocation of a business.

You should not settle your divorce or proceed to trial without knowing all the reasonably foreseeable tax consequences of your divorce decree. These are not surprises you want to hear about years later.

14.1 Will either my spouse or I have to pay income tax when we transfer property or pay a property settlement to one another according to our divorce decree?

No. However, it is important that you know the future tax consequences of a subsequent withdrawal, sale, or transfer of any assets you receive in your divorce.

It is important to ask your attorney to take tax consequences or potential penalties into consideration when looking
at the division of your assets.

14.2 Is the amount of child support I pay tax-deductible, or is the amount I receive in child support taxable to me as income?

No. Under the Internal Revenue Code (IRC), child support
is neither taxable to the person receiving it nor deductible by
the person paying it.

14.3 What does the IRS consider *alimony?*

According to IRS rules, the amounts paid under your
divorce decree, or according to a written agreement entered
into by you and your spouse, will be considered alimony if:

- You and your spouse or former spouse do not file a
joint return with each other.
- The payment is made in cash (including checks or
money orders).
- The payment is received by or on behalf of your
spouse or former spouse.
- You and your former spouse are not members of the
same household when you make the payment.
- You have no liability to make the payment (in cash
or property) after the death of your spouse or former
spouse.
- Your payment is not treated as child support or a
property settlement.

Not all payments made according to a divorce or separation
decree are considered alimony. Alimony does not include:

- Child support
- Noncash property settlements
- Payments to maintain a spouse's property (though
payment for a mortgage may be considered alimony if
made through the proper channels)
- Use of the other spouse's property

14.4 Is the amount of alimony I am ordered to pay tax deductible or income that is taxable for me or my spouse?

Following the changes to the tax code in the *Tax Code and Jobs Act,* if your divorce decree is signed after December 31, 2018, alimony is no longer a tax-deductible expense, nor is it taxable to the recipient.

If you have questions about a pre-2019 alimony award's tax treatment, or wish to modify a pre-2019 alimony award, you should consult with a tax professional and/or attorney on this topic.

14.5 Will our tax filing status be affected during the divorce proceedings?

It can be. You are considered unmarried or divorced if your decree is final by December 31 of the calendar tax year. Under New Hampshire law, your decree becomes final for tax purposes on the date the decree is signed by the judge if done by agreement.

If you are considered unmarried or divorced, your filing status will either be "single" or, under certain circumstances, "head of household." If your decree is not final as of December 31, your filing status will be either "married filing a joint return" or "married filing a separate return," unless you live apart from your spouse and meet the exception for "head of household."

While your divorce is in progress, talk to your tax adviser and your attorney about your filing status. It may be beneficial to figure your taxes on both a joint return and a separate return to see which gives you the better outcome. IRS Publication 504, Divorced or Separated Individuals, provides more detail on tax issues while you are going through a divorce.

14.6 Should I file a joint income tax return with my spouse while our divorce is still pending in court?

Consult your tax adviser and lawyer to determine the risks and benefits of filing a joint return with your spouse. Compare this with the consequences of filing your tax return separately. Often the overall tax liability will be less with the filing of a joint return, but other factors are also important to consider.

Income and Other Taxes

When deciding whether to file a joint return with your spouse, consider any concerns you may have about the accuracy and truthfulness of the information your spouse lists on the tax return. If you have any doubts, consult both your attorney and your tax adviser before agreeing to sign a joint tax return with your spouse.

Just because your spouse will agree to an indemnity provision does not mean the IRS will not lien or attach your assets if there is an audit of a joint tax return or a tax deficiency/debt. Prior to filing a return with your spouse, try to reach an agreement about how any tax owed or refund expected will be shared, and ask your lawyer to assist you in getting this in writing.

14.7 My spouse will not cooperate in providing the necessary documents to prepare or file our taxes jointly. What options do I have?

Talk with your attorney about requesting that your spouse cooperate in the preparation and filing of your joint tax return. Although a judge cannot order your spouse to sign a joint return, he or she can determine who is awarded any tax refunds received prior to a divorce or who owes any tax debts incurred during the divorce.

The judge can also order tax refunds to be held in escrow pending resolution of these issues. In some cases this can be considered *economic fault* or *waste of marital assets* if a spouse acts unreasonably in these situations.

14.8 For tax purposes, is one time of year better to divorce than another?

It depends upon your tax situation. If you and your spouse agree that it would be beneficial to file joint tax returns for the year in which you are divorcing, you may wish to not have your divorce finalized before the end of the year.

Your marital status for filing income taxes is determined by your status on December 31. Consequently, if you both want to preserve your right to file a joint return, your divorce decree should not be effective before January 1 of the following year.

14.9 What tax consequences should I consider regarding the sale of our home?

If you are getting the home by agreement in the divorce or by an order from a judge after a trial, make sure you check first with a qualified and licensed accountant in the state where you own the real estate. You want to find out if any of your profit from the sale might be taxed. Sometimes, with some planning before the sale, you can reduce or even eliminate any federal or state tax.

Do not wait until after your divorce to find out about tax liabilities on your home. You may not be able to fix that later no matter how unfair the taxes may seem.

14.10 When might *capital gains* taxes be a problem for me after the divorce?

Future *capital gains* taxes on the sale of property (such as rental, commercial, or business property) should be discussed with your attorney during the negotiation and trial preparation stages of your case. This is especially important if the sale of the property is imminent. Failure to do so may result in an unfair outcome or cause you to pay taxes you did not anticipate and may not be able to afford.

For example, suppose you agree that your spouse will be awarded the proceeds from the sale of your home valued at $200,000, after the real estate commission, and you will take the stock portfolio also valued at $200,000.

Suppose that after the divorce, you decide to sell the stock. It is still valued at $200,000, but you learn that its original price was $120,000 and that you must pay capital gains tax of 15 percent on the $80,000 gain. You pay a tax of $12,000, leaving you with only $188,000.

Meanwhile, your former spouse sells the marital home but pays no capital gains tax because he qualifies for an exemption. He is left with the full $200,000.

All tax implications of your property division should be discussed with both your attorney and your tax adviser.

14.11 During and after the divorce, who gets to claim the children as dependents?

This issue should be addressed in settlement negotiations or during the trial, if settlement is not reached. Changes to the 2019 federal tax code may require you to ask an accountant for advice in order to maximize the tax benefits and to comply with New Hampshire's Child Support Guidelines. You may find more information at the IRS website. *See* Topic No. 602, Child and Dependent Care Credit at www.irs.gov/taxtopics/tc602.

For children of divorced or separated parents or parents living apart, a noncustodial parent who is claiming a child as a dependent should review the rules in IRS Publication 503, under the topic Child of Divorced or Separated Parents or Parents Living Apart at www.irs.gov/publications/p503. A child may be treated as the qualifying individual of the custodial parent for the child and dependent care credit, even if the noncustodial parent is entitled to claim the child as a dependent.

The judge has the discretion to determine which parent will be entitled to claim the children as exemptions for income tax purposes. Given the change in the tax laws in 2018, unless you and your spouse have equal parenting time, there is a presumption that the parent who has the children most of the time will receive the dependent exemptions.

Judges will order that the exemptions be shared or alternated if there is good reason to. For example, if you share parenting time equally, or if exemptions benefit one spouse much more and thereby increase the amount of money available for your family. However, most judges will order that the payer of child support and uninsured expenses be current on his or her child support obligation to be eligible to claim the dependent exemption for each tax year, so this should be made an explicit part of your order.

Be cautious, however, because the Internal Revenue Code may link the tax exemption to child-care tax credits or other tax benefits or credits, such as reduced health insurance premiums under your state health insurance exchange. This can become complex, so get professional advice before agreeing to trade or sign over tax exemptions.

14.12 My decree says I have to sign IRS Form 8332 so that my former spouse can claim our child as a dependent, because I have "custody." Should I sign it once for all future years?

No. Both parenting time and child support may be modified at some point in the future. If there is a future modification of parenting or support, which parent is entitled to claim the child as an exemption could change.

The best practice is to provide your former spouse with a timely copy of Form 8332 signed by you for the appropriate tax year only—and only when all support obligations have been met. If there is a dispute, you may need to return to court.

14.13 Must I pay taxes or penalties on the portion of my spouse's retirement plan that was awarded to me in the divorce?

If you have been awarded a portion of your former spouse's IRA, 401(k), or 403(b), or any qualified retirement plan, any distribution of these funds to you will be subject to regular income tax and early penalty withdrawals. You may elect to keep the funds in a qualified plan so as to avoid immediate taxes when the funds are transferred to you.

However, it may be possible for you to elect to receive all or a portion of these assets without incurring the 10 percent early withdrawal penalty (applicable if you are under age fifty-nine and a half), if you decide to take the money rather than keep an account in your name or roll over the assets to an IRA or other qualified account.

Talk with your attorney and your tax adviser to determine your options and consider your needs. You do not want to find out later that you are receiving less because of an improper transfer of the funds or because you made an unintended withdrawal.

14.14 Is the cost of getting a divorce, including my attorney fees, tax deductible under any circumstances?

Your legal fees for getting a divorce are not ordinarily deductible. However, a portion of your attorney fees may be deductible if they are for:

- Expenses related to your business and its valuation
- The collection of sums included in your gross income, such as alimony or interest income
- Advice regarding the determination of taxes or tax due
- Attorney fees may be *miscellaneous* deductions

More details can be found in IRS Publication 529, Miscellaneous Deductions, at irs.gov. You may also be able to deduct fees you pay to appraisers or accountants who help you during this time.

Talk to your tax adviser and attorney about whether any portion of your attorney fees or other expenses from your divorce is deductible.

14.15 Must I complete a new Form W-4 for my employer because of a divorce?

Completing a new Form W-4, an Employee's Withholding Certificate, will help you to claim the proper withholding allowances based upon your marital status and exemptions. Also, if you are receiving alimony that is taxable, you may need to make quarterly estimated tax payments. Consult with your tax adviser and lawyer to ensure you are making the most beneficial tax-planning decisions.

14.16 What is *innocent spouse relief* and how can it help me?

Innocent spouse relief refers to a method of obtaining relief from the Internal Revenue Service for taxes owed as a result of a joint income tax return filed during your marriage. Numerous factors affect your eligibility for innocent spouse tax relief, such as:

- You would suffer a financial hardship if you were required to pay the tax.
- You did not significantly benefit from the unpaid taxes.
- Your suffered abuse during your marriage.
- You thought your spouse would pay the taxes on the original return.

Talk with your attorney or your tax adviser if you are concerned about liability for taxes arising from joint tax returns filed during your marriage. You may benefit from a referral to an attorney who specializes in tax law.

15

Going to Court

For many of us, our images of going to court are created by movie scenes and our favorite television shows. We picture the witness breaking down after a grueling cross-examination. We see lawyers strutting around the courtroom, waving their arms as they plead their case to the jury. But divorce trials are not jury trials. Hollywood drama is a far cry from reality. Trials and the trial process can actually be very boring. Going to court for your divorce can mean many things, ranging from sitting in a hallway while waiting for the lawyers and judges to conclude a conference, to being on the witness stand giving mundane answers to questions about your monthly living expenses or your personal life from years ago.

Regardless of the nature of your court proceeding, the idea of going to court often promotes intense anxiety. Perhaps your divorce might be the first time that you have even been in a courtroom. Be assured that these feelings of nervousness and uncertainty are normal.

Understanding what will occur in court and being well prepared for any court hearings will relieve much of your stress. Knowing the order of events, the role of the people in the courtroom, proper etiquette in the courtroom, and what is expected of you will make the entire experience easier.

Your lawyer will be with you at all times to support you any time you go to court. Remember, every court appearance moves you one step closer to completing your divorce so that you can move forward with your life.

15.1 What do I need to know about appearing in court, and court dates in general?

Court dates are important. As soon as you receive a notice from your attorney about a court date in your case, confirm whether your attendance will be required and immediately put it on your calendar. Read all of the paperwork and notices from the court your lawyer sends to you.

Ask your attorney about the nature of the hearing, including whether the judge will be listening to testimony by witnesses, reviewing evidence, or merely listening to the arguments of the lawyers.

Ask whether it is necessary for you to meet with your attorney or take any other action to prepare for the hearing, such as providing additional information or documents.

Find out how long the hearing is expected to last. It may be as short as a few minutes or as long as a day or more.

If you plan to attend the hearing, determine where and when to meet your attorney. Dress properly, because image and respect matter. Depending upon the type of hearing, your lawyer may want you to arrive in advance of the scheduled hearing time in order to prepare.

Make sure you know the location of the courthouse, where to park, and the floor and room number of the courtroom. Planning for such simple matters as having the correct change for a parking meter can eliminate unnecessary stress. If you want someone to go to court with you to provide you with emotional support, check with your attorney first.

In today's modern world, more hearings are occurring either by telephone or video conference. If a hearing occurs by one of these methods and you are new or uncomfortable with the procedure, reduce stress by getting comfortable with the new method ahead of time. Speak with your lawyer about practicing and learning the technology to ensure your technology functions effectively.

15.2 When and how often will I need to go to court?

Whether and how often you will need to go to court depend upon a number of factors. Depending upon the complexity of your case, you may have only one hearing or numerous court hearings throughout the course of your divorce.

Some hearings, usually those on procedural matters, may be attended only by the attorneys. These could include requests for the other side to provide information or for the setting of certain deadlines. These hearings are often brief and held in the judge's chambers rather than in the courtroom. Most hearings, such as temporary hearings for parenting or support, review hearings, contempt hearings, or final hearings, require attendance by both parties and their attorneys.

If you and your spouse settle all issues in your case, you can waive the necessity of a final hearing and you may not have to appear at court at all.

If your case proceeds to trial, your appearance will be required for the duration of the trial. In New Hampshire, divorce matters are heard before a judge (or referee) only; juries do not hear divorces trials in New Hampshire—ever.

15.3 How much notice will I receive about appearing in court?

The amount of notice you will receive for any court hearing can vary from a few days to several weeks or months. This is often what frustrates clients the most. But please understand that your lawyer may have no control over the court calendar, so if you ask for a trial and a judge is available, the notice given may be short or the time or date may be inconvenient. Moving hearings can mean even longer delays, so keep this in mind when considering scheduling.

Ask your attorney whether and when it will be necessary for you to appear in court for your case so that you can have ease in preparing and planning. If you receive a notice of a hearing, contact your attorney immediately. He or she can tell you whether your appearance is required and what other steps may be needed to prepare.

15.4 I am afraid to be alone in the same room with my spouse. When I go to court, is this going to happen if the lawyers go into the judge's office to discuss the case?

Talk to your lawyer about this issue. Prior to any court hearing, you and your spouse may be asked to wait while your attorneys meet with the judge to discuss preliminary matters.

A number of options are likely to be available to ensure that you feel safe at such times. These might include having you and your spouse wait in different locations or having a friend or family member present. There also may be a bailiff or court security officer present if you remain in the courtroom.

Your lawyer wants to support you in feeling secure throughout all court proceedings. Just let him or her know your concerns.

15.5 Must I go to court every time there is a court hearing on any motion?

Not necessarily. Some matters will be decided by the judge after listening to only the arguments of the lawyers. Ask your lawyer about options for your presence to be excused if you do not wish to participate in a particular hearing.

15.6 My spouse's lawyer keeps asking for a *continuance of court dates*. Is there anything I can do to stop this?

Continuances of court dates, the need for a court hearing to be rescheduled, are not unusual in divorces. A court date might be postponed for many reasons, including a conflict on the calendar of one of the attorneys or the judge, the lack of availability of one of the parties or an important witness, or the need for more time to prepare.

In New Hampshire there is no centralized court scheduling system; the result is that different courts may schedule a lawyer to be in two places at the same time on two different cases. This is the most frequent type of request for a continuance. Discuss with your attorney your desire to move your case forward without further delay so that repeated requests for continuances can be resisted. A judge will respect scheduling conflicts, family emergencies, or vacations a few times, but that can be brought to an end if that strategy is abused by a spouse or his or her lawyer.

15.7 If I have to go to court, will I be put on the witness stand?

Whether you will be put on the witness stand under oath and subject to direct and cross-examinations will depend upon the nature of the issues in dispute, the judge assigned to your case, and your attorney's strategy for your case. Often this will not happen until the final divorce hearing.

15.8 My lawyer said I need to be in court for our *temporary hearing* next week. What's going to happen?

A *temporary hearing* is held to determine such matters as who remains in the house while your divorce is pending, temporary parenting schedules, temporary support, and other financial matters. The procedure for your temporary hearing can vary depending on the issues, but customarily they proceed by *offers of proof*—your lawyer offering testimony to the judge on your behalf while you are under oath. You have an obligation in that scenario to ensure what your lawyer says is accurate.

Your presence at the temporary hearing is still crucial, despite the fact that you may not be doing any speaking. Your attorney may need additional information from you during the hearing, and last-minute negotiations to resolve temporary issues are not uncommon.

In some counties, your hearing will be one of numerous other hearings on the judge's calendar scheduled at the same time or later that day. You may find yourself in a courtroom with many other lawyers and their clients, all having matters to be heard before the court that day. Even though you are present in the courtroom, your attorney may make your argument to the judge so you will not be required to provide formal testimony.

On the other hand, if important issues are disputed, you and other witnesses might be required to give brief testimony at your temporary hearing. However, this is unusual given most temporary hearings are scheduled for thirty minutes to an hour. If you will need to testify at a temporary hearing, meeting with your attorney in advance to fully prepare is very important.

15.9 Must I go to court if all of the issues in my case are settled?

No. In New Hampshire you may waive a final hearing by agreement if all issues are settled.

15.10 Are there any rules about courtroom etiquette that I need to know?

Knowing the following few tips about proper behavior in the courtroom will make your experience easier.

- Dress appropriately. Avoid overly casual dress, lots of jewelry, revealing clothing, and extreme hairstyles.

- Don't bring beverages into the courtroom. Most courts have rules that do not allow food and drink in courtrooms. If you need water, ask your lawyer.

- Dispose of chewing gum before giving your testimony.

- Don't talk aloud in the courtroom unless you're on the witness stand or being questioned by the judge.

- Do not enter the judge's office or move toward the judge's bench without invitation or direction.

- Stand up whenever the judge is entering or leaving the courtroom.

- Be sure to turn off (not merely silence) your electronic devices.

- Be mindful that the judge may be observing you and those you bring to the hearing at all times. Avoid inappropriate facial expressions such as laughing during serious testimony, smirking, eye rolling, or frowning. Your facial expressions may affect the judge's rulings.

Although you may feel anxious initially, you'll likely feel more relaxed about the courtroom setting once your hearing gets under way.

15.11 What is the role of the *bailiff* or *court security officer*?

The *bailiff* or *court security officer* provides support for the judge and lawyers in the management of the court calendar or docket and the courtroom. He or she assists in the calling of court hearings and the management of legal documents given to the judge for review, such as temporary proposed orders, exhibits, and divorce decrees. They also provide security in the courtroom for the judge, the parties, and lawyers.

15.12 Will there be a *court reporter,* and what will he or she do?

A *court reporter* is a professional trained to create an accurate record of the words spoken and documents offered into evidence during court proceedings. Most counties today use digital recording devices to create an audio recording rather than actual court reporters, though there may be a clerk assisting the judge in the courtroom with running the recording software and managing the judge's calendar.

A copy of the recorded hearing may be purchased from the court. You may then have the record professionally transcribed. If your case is appealed, the transcript is prepared by the court to be used as the official record by the appeals court to review the facts and laws pertaining to your case.

Some hearings are held *off the record,* which means that there is no official recording taken of what is being said. Ordinarily these are matters for which no appeal can be made.

15.13 Will I be able to talk to my attorney while we are in court?

During court proceedings, it is important that your attorney give his or her full attention to anything being said by the judge, witnesses, or your spouse's lawyer. For this reason, your attorney will avoid talking with you when anyone else in the courtroom is speaking.

It is critical that your attorney hear each question asked by the other lawyer and all answers given by each witness. If not, opportunities for making objections to inappropriate evidence may be lost. You can support your attorney in doing an effective job for you by avoiding talking to him or her while a court hearing is in progress.

Plan to have pen and paper with you when you go to court. If your court proceeding is under way and your lawyer is listening to what is being said by others in the courtroom, write a note concerning your questions or comments.

If your court hearing is lengthy, breaks will be taken. You can use this time to discuss with your attorney any questions or observations you have about the proceeding. Remember that once you are on the witness stand, however, your lawyer cannot interrupt your testimony to help you, and you may not be able to ask for a break to check in with your attorney.

15.14 What questions might my lawyer ask me about the problems in our marriage and why I want the divorce?

Because New Hampshire has a "no-fault" option and most divorces end on the basis of irreconcilable differences, your lawyer may ask questions to show the court that the marriage is irretrievably broken, without going into detail about the specific difficulties in your marriage.

The questions could be similar to these:

Attorney: Have differences arisen during the course of your marriage?

You: Yes.

Attorney: Have you and your spouse made efforts to reconcile those differences?

You: Yes.

Attorney: Have your efforts at reconciliation been successful?

You: No.

Attorney: Do you believe further efforts at reconciliation would be beneficial?

You: No.

Attorney: In your opinion, is your marriage irretrievably broken?

You: Yes.

If your spouse disagrees, he or she may give the opinion that the marriage can be saved. However, New Hampshire Supreme Court has recognized that it takes two willing partners for a marriage to be reconciled, and they interpret irreconcilable differences as existing if one party believes they exist. Judges will therefore routinely grant a divorce on those grounds.

If a fault ground is involved, such as adultery, imprisonment, abandonment, or treatment that endanger one's health or reason, both you and your spouse will likely be asked detailed questions about the nature of the marital problems that led to the divorce.

15.15 My lawyer said that the judge has issued a *pretrial order* having to do with my upcoming trial and that we'll have to comply with it. What does this mean?

Ask your lawyer for a copy of the *pretrial order.* Some judges will order that certain information be provided either to the opposing party or to the judge in advance of trial. This might include:

- A list of issues that have already been settled
- A list of issues that are still disputed
- Agreements, referred to as *stipulations,* as to the truth of certain facts or admissibility of evidence
- The names of witnesses
- Exhibits to be offered or admitted by agreement at trial
- A summary of how you want the judge to decide the case

Deadlines will be given by the judge for providing the information.

15.16 What is a *pretrial conference?*

A *pretrial conference* is a meeting held with the lawyers and the judge to review information related to an upcoming trial, such as:

- How long the trial is expected to last
- The issues still in dispute
- The law surrounding the disputed issues
- The identification of witnesses
- Any trial exhibits
- The status of negotiations
- Deadlines for exchange of information
- Updated financial affidavits are exchanged
- Proposed final decrees, parenting plans, and associated documents are exchanged

The trial date may be set at or shortly after the pretrial conference. If a pretrial conference is held in your case, ask your attorney whether you should attend. Your attorney may request that you be present for the conference or be available by phone, but this is not always necessary.

15.17 Besides meeting with my lawyer, is there anything else I should do to prepare for my upcoming trial?

Yes. Be sure to review your deposition and any information you provided in your discovery, such as answers to interrogatories. Also be sure to review any affidavits previously submitted to the judge, such as prior financial affidavits that were prepared previously in your case.

At trial, it is possible that you will be asked some of the same questions. If you think you might give different answers at trial, discuss this with your lawyer. It is important that your attorney know in advance of trial whether any information you provided during the discovery process has changed. Surprises can make you look less than truthful or candid. It is always better to let your lawyer know and prepare an explanation that is logical and honest.

15.18 I'm meeting with my lawyer to prepare for trial. How do I make the most of these meetings?

Meeting with your lawyer to prepare for your trial is important to achieving a good outcome. Come to the meeting prepared to discuss the following:

- The issues in your case
- Your desired outcome on each of the issues
- The questions you might be asked at trial by both lawyers
- The exhibits that will be offered into evidence during the trial
- The witnesses for your trial
- The status of negotiations

The meeting with your lawyer will help you better understand what to expect at your trial and make the trial experience easier.

15.19 My lawyer says that the law firm is busy with trial preparation. What exactly is my lawyer doing to prepare for my trial?

Countless tasks are necessary to complete in order to prepare your case for trial. These are just a few:

- Developing factual themes and legal arguments for contested issues
- Researching and reviewing the relevant laws in your case
- Reviewing the facts of your case to determine which witnesses are best suited to testify
- Reviewing, selecting, numbering, and preparing exhibits and making requisite copies
- Preparing questions for all witnesses
- Preparing legal argument
- Reviewing rules on evidence to prepare for any objections to be made or opposed at trial
- Determining the order of witnesses and all exhibits
- Preparing your file for the day in court, including preparing a trial notebook with all essential information
- Updating financial documents ahead of trial, such as your financial affidavit
- Reviewing opposing counsel's financials, exhibits, and proposals
- Updating your proposals

Your lawyer is committed to a good outcome for you in your divorce. He or she will be engaged in many important actions to fully prepare your case for trial.

15.20 How do I know who my witnesses will be at trial?

Well in advance of your trial date, your lawyer will discuss with you whether other witnesses, besides you and your spouse, will be necessary. Witnesses can include family members, friends, child-care providers, clergy members.

When thinking of potential witnesses, consider your relationship with the witness, whether that witness has had an opportunity to observe relevant facts, and whether the witness has knowledge different from that of other witnesses. For more information on identifying potential witnesses, please *see* question 8.22 in chapter 8.

You may also have expert witnesses testify on your behalf. An expert witness will provide opinion testimony based upon their specialized knowledge, training, or experience. For example, a psychologist, real estate appraiser, or accountant may provide expert testimony on your behalf.

In addition, your spouse will be required to disclose his or her witnesses before trial so that both parties and their lawyers should have no surprises concerning the identity of witnesses. What each witness actually testifies to under oath is much less predictable in a trial.

15.21 My divorce is scheduled for trial. Does this mean there is no hope for a settlement?

Many cases are settled after a trial date is set. An actual trial date may cause you and your spouse to seriously think about the risks and costs of going to trial. This can help you and your spouse focus on what is most important and may lead you toward a negotiated settlement.

Because the costs of preparing for and proceeding to trial are substantial, it is best to engage in settlement negotiations well in advance of your trial date. However, it is not uncommon for cases to settle a few days before trial—or even at the courthouse just before your trial begins.

15.22 Can I prevent my spouse from being in the courtroom?

Probably not. Because your spouse has a legal interest in the outcome of your divorce, he or she has a right to be present. In addition, New Hampshire courtrooms are open to the public. Consequently, it is not uncommon for persons not involved in your divorce to pass through the courtroom at various times simply because they have other business with the court.

15.23 Can I take a friend or family member with me to court?

Yes. Let your attorney know in advance if you intend to bring anyone to court with you. Some people who are important to you may be very emotional about your divorce or matters concerning your spouse. Be sure to invite someone who is better able to focus attention on supporting you than simply on his or her own feelings. If someone you invite behaves badly or instigates trouble at the courthouse, this can hurt your case.

15.24 Can my friends and family be present in the courtroom during my trial?

This depends upon whether they will be witnesses in your case. In most cases where witnesses other than the husband and wife are testifying, the attorneys request that the court *sequester* the witnesses. The judge would then order all witnesses, except you and your spouse, to leave the courtroom until after they have testified. Once a witness has completed his or her testimony, however, he or she will ordinarily be allowed to remain in the courtroom for the remainder of the trial.

An exception in which a judge may order a closed hearing may occur when there is testimony to be given by a child or about a child, or when child abuse and neglect are an issue. This is intended to protect the privacy of children.

15.25 I want to do a great job testifying as a witness in my divorce trial. What are some tips?

Keep the following in mind to be a good witness on your own behalf:

- Tell the truth. Although this may not always be comfortable, it is critical if you want your testimony to be believed by the judge.

- Listen carefully to the complete question before thinking of your answer. Wait to consider your answer until the full question is asked.

- Slow down. It's easy to speed up our speech when we are anxious. Taking your time with your answers ensures that the judge hears you and that the court reporter can accurately record your testimony.

- If you don't understand a question or know the answer, be sure to say so.

- If the question calls for a "yes" or "no" answer, simply say so. Then wait for the attorney to ask you the next question. If there is more you want to explain, remember that you have already told your attorney all the important facts and he or she will make sure you are allowed to give any testimony significant in your case.

- Don't argue with the judge or the lawyers or be sarcastic.

- Take your time. Breathe. You may be asked some questions that call for a thoughtful response. If you need a moment to reflect on an answer before you give it, allow yourself that time.

- Stop speaking if an objection is made by one of the lawyers. Wait until the judge has decided whether to allow you to answer.

- If you begin to feel emotional, your lawyer can ask for a short break.

15.26 Should I be worried about being cross-examined at trial?

When you take the witness stand, your lawyer will conduct a direct examination of you. This is the process by which you and your lawyer tell your story to the judge in a coherent and organized way. You may testify from memory or use trial exhibits to describe events from the past. The key is being clear and precise about what you believe are the facts and what you want the judge to order for you or your children.

If your case goes to trial, prepare to also be asked some questions by your spouse's lawyer. Many of these questions will call for a simple "yes" or "no" answer.

If you are worried about particular questions, discuss your concerns with your attorney. He or she can support you in giving a truthful response. Focus on preparing well for questions asked by your spouse's lawyer. Try not to take the questions personally; remember that the lawyer is fulfilling a duty to advocate for your spouse's interests.

Remember that you are just doing your best to tell the truth about the facts. Telling the truth is not only the right thing to do, but it will also help a judge find the facts you provide more likely to be true. You should remember that if judges find that one small fact is untrue, they may then conclude that all of your testimony is suspect.

15.27   What will happen on the day of the trial?

Although no two trials are alike, the following steps will occur in some trials:

- The judge may order the lawyers to discuss a settlement again with you and your spouse because you now have some input from the judge assigned to your case.

- Attorneys can give opening statements, but this step is often waived.

- Petitioner's attorney calls petitioner's witnesses to testify. Respondent's attorney may cross-examine each of them.

- Respondent's attorney calls respondent's witness to testify. Petitioner's attorney may cross-examine each of them.

- Petitioner's lawyer calls any rebuttal witnesses, that is, witnesses whose testimony contradicts the testimony of the respondent's witnesses.

- Closing arguments are made first by the petitioner's attorney and then by the respondent's attorney.

15.28   What will happen if we decide to settle before we start the trial? Can I change my mind after I get home?

This often occurs after judges meet with the lawyers and discuss the facts and the pertaining laws before the start of a trial. This can be very challenging for you and the professionals because everyone has incurred the time and stresses of preparation and you have incurred the expense, as well.

But you should be careful not to reject this opportunity out-of-hand. Before the trial begins, you should have a clear discussion with your lawyer about your best outcome and what you may be willing to reasonably accept in a settlement. You do not want surprises, but you also want to be rational.

Sometimes you or your spouse may realize that a trial will not help you or that there is little chance of getting what you might seek from a judge. Just because this happens at the last minute does not make it a bad thing.

If you reach a settlement agreement, the judge will require you to write it up by hand and sign it before you leave the courthouse building. The lawyers may summarize the agreement for the judge. The judge will then often approve the agreement and mail it back to your attorney. Sometimes the court will request a "confirming copy" or a typed-up version of the handwritten agreement.

If you change your mind after you get home, the judge will likely enforce the terms of the written agreement even if you want out of the deal. An opposing lawyer can file a motion to enforce the agreement, and in all likelihood, the judge will enforce the agreement in the absence of mutual mistake, fraud, or duress of a party.

The point is to be prepared and understand that any settlement is a compromise and will prevent a longer delay for a decree or a potential delay from expenses and appeals.

15.29   Will the judge decide my case the day of trial?

Probably not. Often there is so much information and evidence from the trial for the judge to consider that it is not possible for the judge to give an immediate ruling.

After the trial, the judge may require the lawyers (or the lawyers may request) to submit briefs setting forth the facts and legal arguments for the court to review (these are called *findings of fact* and *rulings of law*). This may mean a delay in filing for a few weeks from the trial date.

The judge may then want to review documents, review the law, perform calculations, review his or her notes, and give thoughtful consideration to the issues to be decided. For this reason, it may be days, weeks, or in some cases even longer before a ruling is made.

When a judge does not make a ruling immediately upon the conclusion of a trial, it is said that the case has been *taken under advisement.*

15.30   What if the divorce decree signed by the judge has factual errors, does not explain the judge's reasoning, or makes an error in the interpretation of law?

There may be unintentional errors in your divorce such as a wrong birth date or the omission of an order for a name change. These items can be corrected by a simple motion usually agreed to by both lawyers.

If there are more serious differences about facts or the laws applied by a judge, your lawyer may file a motion to reconsider or clarify, in part or in its entirety.

There are very short windows of time—ten days from the date on the clerk's notice (the date the clerk mails the order)—to file these specific motions. If you and your lawyer miss these deadlines, unfortunately, you may lose the opportunity to request reconsideration or clarification of this order except in certain circumstances, such as illness or if a court order is lost in the mail.

If you are thinking about filing an appeal, you must first ask the judge to reconsider or clarify. Do not delay this discussion with your lawyer.

16

The Appeal Process

You may find that despite your best efforts to settle your case, your divorce went to trial and the judge made major decisions that have a serious impact on your future. You may be gravely disappointed or even shocked by the judge's ruling.

The judge might have seen your case differently than you and your attorney did. Perhaps the judge made mistakes. Or it may be that New Hampshire law simply does not allow for the outcome for which you were hoping.

Whatever the reasons for the court's rulings, you may feel that the judge's decisions are not ones with which you can live. If this is the case, talk to your lawyer immediately about your right to appeal. Together you can decide whether an appeal is in your best interest, or whether it is better to accept the court's ruling and invest your energy in moving forward with your future without an appeal.

16.1 How much time after my divorce do I have to file an appeal?

You must file a notice of appeal within thirty days of the date of the final order that you wish to appeal. Most often, the deadline becomes thirty days after the judge's ruling on the post-decree motion (likely the motion to reconsider or clarify). Because your attorney may also recommend filing certain motions following your trial, discuss your appeal rights with your lawyer as soon as you have received the judge's ruling.

A timely discussion with your attorney about your right to appeal is essential so that important deadlines are not missed.

16.2   When should an appeal be filed?

You must file a notice of appeal within thirty days of the date of the final order that you wish to appeal. An appeal should be filed only after careful consultation with your lawyer when you believe that the judge has made a serious error under the law or regarding the facts of your case. Among the factors you and your attorney should discuss are:

- Whether the judge had the authority under the law to make the decisions set forth in your decree
- The likelihood of the success of your appeal
- The risk that an appeal made by you will encourage a further appeal by your former spouse
- The cost of the appeal
- The length of time an appeal can be expected to take
- The impact of a delay in the case during the appeals process

16.3   Can I appeal a temporary order?

Yes. Under New Hampshire law, you may file what is referred to as an *order that is not final* or an *interlocutory appeal*. The acceptance of an interlocutory appeal is completely discretionary to the Supreme Court. Appeals in general are extremely expensive and given the likelihood that the New Hampshire Supreme Court may decline to hear the case and the temporary nature of the order in question, consider carefully whether an interlocutory appeal is worthwhile in your case.

16.4   What parts of the decree can be appealed?

If you or your spouse is unhappy with any final decisions made by the judge in your case, either of you can file an appeal. Decisions that can be appealed include those related to parenting time, child support, spousal support, division of property, and attorney fees, as well as decisions made about the admissibility of evidence or other issues in your case.

16.5 Will my attorney recommend I appeal specific aspects of the decree, or will I have to request for him or her to do so?

Your attorney may counsel you to file an appeal with regard to certain issues of your case; you may also ask your lawyer whether there is a legitimate basis for an appeal of any decision you believe is wrong. Talk to your attorney regarding the decisions most dissatisfying to you. Your lawyer can advise you as to which issues have the greatest likelihood of success on appeal, in light of the facts of your case and New Hampshire law.

16.6 Are there any disadvantages to filing an appeal?

There can be several disadvantages to filing an appeal, including:

- Uncertainty as to the outcome
- Increased attorney fees and costs
- The risks of a worse outcome on appeal than you received at trial
- Delay of finalizing your case and division of assets
- Prolonged conflict between you and your former spouse
- The risk of a second trial occurring after the appeal if your case is sent back down from the Supreme Court to the trial court
- Difficulty in obtaining closure and moving forward with your life

16.7 Is an attorney necessary to appeal?

The appeals process is very detailed and specific, with set deadlines and specific court rules. Given the complex nature of the appeals process, you should use an attorney if you intend to file an appeal, though it is not required.

16.8 How long does the appeals process usually take?

The answer to this question depends on many different factors. An appeal can take anywhere from several months to well over a year. An appeal may also result in the appellate court requiring further proceedings by the trial court, resulting in further delays.

16.9   What are the steps in the appeals process?

There are many steps that your lawyer will take on your behalf in the appeals process, including:

- Identifying the specific issues to be appealed.
- Filing a motion to reconsider.
- Filing a notice of appeal.
- Obtaining the necessary court documents and trial exhibits to send to the appellate court.
- Obtaining a transcript of the trial, as well as a written copy of any testimony by witnesses and statements by the judge and the lawyers made in the presence of the court (this may be several hundred dollars if your trial is lengthy).
- Performing legal research to support your arguments on appeal.
- Preparing an appendix after consultation with the other party or lawyer. An *appendix* is a binder that contains the transcripts and exhibits for the trial along with parts of the record required by the appellate rules.
- If the court lays out a briefing schedule, preparing and filing a formal document known as a *brief,* which sets forth the facts of the case and relevant law, complete with accurate citations to the court transcript, court documents, and prior cases.
- If your spouse is the appealing party, preparing a responsive brief according to the schedule.
- If the court determines it appropriate or necessary, making an oral argument before the judges of the appellate court.

16.10   Is filing and pursuing an appeal expensive?

Yes. In addition to filing costs and lawyer fees, there is likely to be a substantial cost for the preparation of the transcript of the trial testimony. Legal fees and costs alone often total more than $10,000 for an appeal.

16.11 If I do not file an appeal, can I ever go back to court to change my decree?

Certain aspects of a decree are not modifiable, such as the division of property and debts or an award of attorney fees. Other parts of your decree, such as alimony or child support or matters regarding the children, may be modified later if there has been a "substantial change in circumstances" as specifically allowed by the law.

A modification of parenting time for minor children will also require you to show that the change would be in their best interest.

If your decree did not provide for alimony or it is within five years of your original order, it is unlikely that you will have any basis for a modification later without a substantial and unforeseen change in circumstances. However, if you believe that you have a basis for a modification of your divorce decree, consult with your attorney.

In Closing

Now, pause and breathe slowly and calmly. Acknowledge the courage you have shown in examining your unique situation, needs, and goals. Now you are facing your future—recasting yourself into a new life. You are looking more closely at your living situation, the needs of your children, your financial security, and your personal growth and healing. You are seeing your situation for what it is and acknowledging the truth about what you now need. You are taking action to propel yourself into new possibilities.

From here, it is time to take inventory of the lessons learned, goals met, and actions yet to take. Celebrate each of these steps forward, and be gentle with yourself during the occasional missteps backward. You have transitioned through this time when everything has been reduced to your core.

Gone are the familiar habits of your marriage. But with every day moving you closer to the completion of your divorce, your grief will begin to subside and your energy will improve as you move toward a fresh start. All the best to you as you progress forward on this life journey!

Appendix

Sample Petition for Divorce

THE STATE OF NEW HAMPSHIRE
JUDICIAL BRANCH
http://www.courts.state.nh.us

Court Name:_____

Case Name:_____

Case Number:_____

(If known)

PETITION FOR DIVORCE

1. Petitioner Name_____
   Date of Birth_____E-mail Address_____
   Residence Address_____
   Mailing Address (if different) _____
   Telephone (Cell)_____(Home)_____(Work)_____
2. Respondent Name_____
   Date of Birth_____E-mail Address_____
   Residence Address_____
   Mailing Address (if different) _____
   Telephone (Cell)_____(Home)_____(Work)_____
3. City and State where parties were married_____
   Date of Marriage_____
4. Length of time petitioner has been a resident of New Hampshire:_____
5. List minor children born to or adopted by the parties either before or during the marriage:

Name	Date of Birth	Current Address

Sample Petition for Divorce

(Continued)

If there are minor children born to or adopted by the parties either before or during the marriage, complete questions 6 – 10. This information is required under RSA 458-A, the Uniform Child Custody Jurisdiction and Enforcement Act (UCCJEA).
It is important that you answer these questions with as much detail and accuracy as possible. Lack of adequate information could significantly delay orders being issued in your case.

There are several situations that might result in New Hampshire exercising jurisdiction over child/ren. The continuous presence of the child/ren in New Hampshire for six (6) months is not the only basis for jurisdiction. In some emergency situations, the court may be able to exercise jurisdiction on a temporary basis.

6. List the places where the minor child/ren of the parties has/have lived in the last **five (5) years** and the names of the people they lived with at that time, if you know. Start with where the child lives now and work backward in time.

Dates From/To	Town/City, State	Parent(s)/Caretaker	Current Address/Contact Address of Parent/ Caretaker	Which Child/ren

If more space is needed, attach Extra Page (Form NHJB-2656-FP)
☐ I have attached Form NHJB-2656-FP)

7. Are there any person(s), not a party to this proceeding, who have physical custody of the child/ren or who claim to have custody, physical custody or parenting time rights? ☐Yes ☐No
If yes, list name(s) and address(es) of person(s):

_____
_____
_____

8. Check one of the following:
☐ I **have not** participated in any court case(s) concerning the custody, visitation, parenting time or placement of the child/ren in this or any other state.

OR

☐ I **have** participated in court case(s) concerning the custody, visitation, parenting time or placement of the child/ren in this or any other state. I have participated in the following:

Name of Court	State	Case No.	Date of Court Order

9. Are there any actions for enforcement, or proceedings relating to domestic violence, domestic relations, protective orders, marriage dissolution, paternity, legitimation, custody, parental rights and responsibilities, termination of parental rights, adoption, juvenile, or other proceedings in any court in any state affecting any children named in this petition or parents of those children? ☐ Yes ☐ No If yes, complete the following:

Sample Petition for Divorce   (Continued)

Name of Court	State	Case No.	Date of Court Order

10. Optional: ☐   I am alleging, under oath, that my or my child/ren's health, safety, or liberty would be jeopardized by the disclosure of identifying information set forth in this Petition. To support my allegation, I state as follows:

_____

_____

_____

11. Please check one of the following regarding public assistance.

☐   No public assistance (TANF) is now being or has within the last 6 months been provided, nor is medical assistance (Medicaid) presently being provided, for any minor child of the parties.

☐   The N. H. Department of Health and Human Services is providing or has provided within the last 6 months public assistance (TANF) and/or medical assistance (Medicaid) for a minor child or children of the parties. If you check this box, you must mail copies of this petition and the Personal Data Sheet **(NHJB-2077-F)** to DHHS at:

New Hampshire Department of Health and Human Services
Bureau of Child Support Services - Legal Unit
129 Pleasant Street
Concord, NH 03301

12. To the knowledge of the parties, is either party pregnant?   ☐ Yes   ☐ No
13. Do the parties own real estate jointly?   ☐ Yes   ☐ No
  Does the petitioner own real estate individually?   ☐ Yes   ☐ No
  Does the respondent own real estate individually?   ☐ Yes   ☐ No
14. The cause for divorce is: **(Check one or both)**

☐   Irreconcilable differences have developed that have caused the irremediable breakdown of the marriage.
☐   Other:

15. Requests for court orders:

A.   TEMPORARY. The Petitioner respectfully requests that the Court issue temporary orders on any of the following issues. **(check all that apply)**. A temporary order is in effect until the divorce is granted.

☐ Child support   ☐ Parenting Plan   ☐ Use of personal property and payment of debt
☐ Alimony   ☐ Use of family home
☐ Other:_____

B.   FINAL. The Petitioner respectfully requests that the Court grant a divorce, equitably divide personal property, real estate, debts and obligations of the parties, and issue a final order approving or establishing the following **(check all that apply):**

☐ A parenting plan which describes the parties' parental rights and responsibilities relating to minor children;
☐ Child support obligations for any minor children;
☐ Alimony;
☐ Any other relief which may be appropriate;
☐ Other:_____

Sample Petition for Divorce (Continued)

I acknowledge that I have a continuing duty to inform the court of any court action in this or any other state that could affect the child/ren in this case.

I swear or affirm that the foregoing information is true and correct to the best of my knowledge.

_____   _____
Date   Signature of Petitioner

State of_____, County of_____

This instrument was acknowledged before me on_____by_____

My Commission Expires_____   _____
Affix Seal, if any   Signature of Notarial Officer / Title

_____
Signature of Attorney for Petitioner

_____
Printed Name, Address and Phone Number of Attorney   Bar #

Appendix

Sample Joint Petition for Divorce

THE STATE OF NEW HAMPSHIRE
JUDICIAL BRANCH
http://www.courts.state.nh.us

Court Name:_____

Case Name:_____

Case Number:_____
(If known)

JOINT PETITION FOR DIVORCE

1. Petitioner Name_____
   Date of Birth_____E-mail Address_____
   Residence Address_____
   Mailing Address (if different) _____
   Telephone (Cell)_____(Home)_____(Work)_____
2. Respondent Name_____
   Date of Birth_____E-mail Address_____
   Residence Address_____
   Mailing Address (if different) _____
   Telephone (Cell)_____(Home)_____(Work)_____
3. City and state where parties were married_____
   Date of Marriage_____
4. Length of time parties have been a residents of New Hampshire: (P)_____(R)_____
5. List minor children born to or adopted by the parties either before or during the marriage:

Name	Date of Birth	Current Address

If there are minor children born to or adopted by the parties either before or during the marriage, complete questions 6 – 9. This information is required under RSA 458-A, the Uniform Child Custody Jurisdiction and Enforcement Act (UCCJEA).

It is important that you answer these questions with as much detail and accuracy as possible. Lack of adequate information could significantly delay orders being issued in your case.

There are several situations that might result in New Hampshire exercising jurisdiction over child/ren. The continuous presence of the child/ren in New Hampshire for six (6) months is not the only basis for jurisdiction. In some emergency situations, the court may be able to exercise jurisdiction on a temporary basis.

Sample Joint Petition for Divorce (Continued)

6. List the places where the minor child/ren of the parties has/have lived in the last **five (5) years** and the names of the people they lived with at that time, if you know. Start with where the child lives now and work backward in time.

Dates From/To	Town/City, State	Parent(s)/Caretaker	Current Address/Contact Address of Parent/ Caretaker	Which Child/ren

If more space is needed, attach Extra Page (Form NHJB-2656-FP)
☐   **I have attached Form NHJB-2656-FP)**

7. Are there any person(s), not a party to this proceeding, who have physical custody of the child/ren or who claim to have custody, physical custody or parenting time rights?   ☐Yes   ☐No
If yes, list name(s) and address(es) of person(s):

_____
_____
_____

8. Check one of the following:
    ☐   I **have not** participated in any court case(s) concerning the custody, visitation, parenting time or placement of the child/ren in this or any other state.
OR
    ☐   I **have** participated in court case(s) concerning the custody, visitation, parenting time or placement of the child/ren in this or any other state. I have participated in the following:

Name of Court	State	Case No.	Date of Court Order

9. Are there any actions for enforcement, or proceedings relating to domestic violence, domestic relations, protective orders, marriage dissolution, paternity, legitimation, custody, parental rights and responsibilities, termination of parental rights, adoption, juvenile, or other proceedings in any court in any state affecting any children named in this petition or parents of those children? ☐   Yes ☐   No If yes, complete the following:

Name of Court	State	Case No.	Date of Court Order

Sample Joint Petition for Divorce (Continued)

10. Please check one of the following regarding public assistance.

☐ No public assistance (TANF) is now being or has within the last 6 months been provided, nor is medical assistance (Medicaid) presently being provided, for any minor child of the parties.

☐ The N. H. Department of Health and Human Services is providing or has provided within the last 6 months public assistance (TANF) and/or medical assistance (Medicaid) for a minor child or children of the parties. If you check this box, you must mail copies of this petition and the Personal Data Sheet (NHJB-2077-F) to DHHS at:

New Hampshire Department of Health and Human Services
Bureau of Child Support Services-Legal Unit
129 Pleasant Street
Concord, NH 03301

11. To the knowledge of the parties, is either party pregnant?   ☐ Yes   ☐ No
12. Do the parties own real estate jointly?   ☐ Yes   ☐ No
    Does the petitioner own real estate individually?   ☐ Yes   ☐ No
    Does the respondent own real estate individually?   ☐ Yes   ☐ No
13. The cause for divorce is: (Check one or both)

☐ Irreconcilable differences have developed that have caused the irremediable breakdown of the marriage.
☐ Other:

14. Requests for court orders:

A. TEMPORARY. The Petitioner respectfully requests that the Court issue temporary orders on any of the following issues. (check all that apply). A temporary order is in effect until the divorce is granted.

☐ Child support   ☐ Parenting Plan   ☐ Use of personal property and payment of debt
☐ Alimony   ☐ Use of family home
☐ Other:_____

B. FINAL. The Petitioner respectfully requests that the Court grant a divorce, equitably divide personal property, real estate, debts and obligations of the parties, and issue a final order approving or establishing the following (check all that apply):

☐ A parenting plan which describes the parties' parental rights and responsibilities relating to minor children;
☐ Child support obligations for any minor children;
☐ Alimony;
☐ Any other relief which may be appropriate;
☐ Other:_____

I acknowledge that I have a continuing duty to inform the court of any court action in this or any other state that could affect the child/ren in this case.

I swear or affirm that the foregoing information is true and correct to the best of my knowledge.

_____   _____
Date   Signature of Petitioner

State of_____, County of_____

Sample Joint Petition for Divorce

This instrument was acknowledged before me on_____ by_____

My Commission Expires_____

Affix Seal, if any

Signature of Notarial Officer / Title

_____

Signature of Attorney for Petitioner

_____

Printed Name, Address and Phone Number of Attorney   Bar #

Appendix

Sample of Acceptance of Service

THE STATE OF NEW HAMPSHIRE
JUDICIAL BRANCH
http://www.courts.state.nh.us

Court Name:_____

Case Name:_____

Case Number:_____
(If known)
For:

AFFIDAVIT OF RECEIPT OF SERVICE

For:
- ☐ Petition for Divorce
- ☐ Petition for Legal Separation
- ☐ Petition for Civil Union Dissolution Parenting Petition
- ☐ Other:_____

I,_____, do hereby state under oath that I received the petition specified above and the:
- ☐ Notice to Spouse
- ☐ Notice to Co Respondent
- ☐ Notice of Post-Decree Action
- ☐ Child Impact Program Notice
- ☐ Have you considered Mediation?
- ☐ Notice_____
  (Fill in type of notice)

- ☐ Notice to Parties
- ☐ Appearance
- ☐ Checklist for Rule 1.25-A
- ☐ UCCJEA Affidavit
- ☐ Motion

_____
Date

Phone Number:_____

_____
Signature

Address:_____
_____
_____

State of_____, County of_____

This instrument was acknowledged before me on_____by_____

My Commission Expires_____
Affix Seal, if any

_____
Signature of Notarial Officer / Title

271

Resources

American Academy of Matrimonial Lawyers
150 North Michigan Avenue, Suite 1420
Chicago, IL 60601
Phone: (312) 263-6477
Fax: (312) 263-7682
www.aaml.org

Bureau of Child Support Services (BCSS)
129 Pleasant Street
Concord, NH 03301-3852
Phone: (603) 271-4427
www.dhhs.nh.gov/dcss

Child Impact Seminar
New Hampshire Community Behavioral Health Association
1 Pillsbury Street, Suite 200
Concord, NH 03301-3570
Phone: (603) 225-6633
https://cip.nhcbha.org/ChildrenFirst.cfm

Domestic Violence Advocates
Haven
20 International Drive, Suite 300
Portsmouth, NH 03801
24-Hour Support Line
1-603-994-SAFE (7233)

Free Annual Credit Report
Annual Credit Report Request Service
P.O. Box 105281
Atlanta, GA 30348-5281
AnnualCreditReport.com

Modest Means Legal Program
2 Pillsbury Street, Suite 300
Concord, NH 03301
Phone: (603) 715-3290
www.nhbar.org/lawyer-referral-service/modest-means-legal-program

New Hampshire Bar Association
2 Pillsbury Street, Suite 300
Concord, NH 03301
Phone: (603) 224-6942
Fax: (603) 224-2910
www.nhbar.org

New Hampshire Coalition Against Domestic and Sexual Violence
PO Box 353
Concord, NH 03302
Phone: (603) 224-8893
https://www.nhcadsv.org/

New Hampshire Collaborative Law Alliance
P.O. Box 803
Londonderry, NH 03053
www.collaborativelawnh.org

New Hampshire Department of Health and Human Resources
129 Pleasant Street
Concord, NH 03301-3852
Phone: (844) 275-3447
www.dhhs.nh.gov

NH Lawyer Referral Service
2 Pillsbury Street, Suite 300
Concord, NH 03301
Phone: (603) 229-0002
www.nhbar.org/lawyer-referral-service

Resources

The Pro Bono Program of the New Hampshire Bar Association
2 Pillsbury Street, Suite 300
Concord, NH 03301
Phone: (603) 224-5387
https://nhlegalaid.org/about/pro-bono

Family Division Rule 1.25-A
www.courts.state.nh.us/fdpp/mandatory-disclosure.htm

Resources for Divorcing Parents in New Hampshire
https://cip.nhcbha.org/resourcelinks_resourcesforparents.cfm
Support Groups
Mental Health: www.naminh.org/find-support/support-groups
Divorce: www.psychologytoday.com/us/groups/divorce/new-hampshire
Catholic: www.catholicnh.org/family2/family/support/separated

Crisis Hotlines
https://www.naminh.org/resources-2/crisis-lines/#

How to Find a Counselor
www.nhmhca.org/content.aspx?page_id=154&club_id=46276

NH Certified Guardian *ad Litem*
www.oplc.nh.gov/guardian-*ad-litem*-board

Glossary

A

affidavit: A written statement of facts made under oath and signed before a notary public. Affidavits are used primarily when there will not be a hearing in open court with live testimony. The attorney will instead prepare an affidavit to present relevant facts. Affidavits may be signed by the parties or in some cases by witnesses. The person signing the affidavit may be referred to as the *affiant.*

alimony: Court-ordered support payments from one party to another, often to enable the recipient spouse to become economically independent. Also know as *spousal support.*

allegation: A statement that one party claims is true.

answer: A written response to the petition for divorce. It serves to admit to or deny the allegations in the petition and may also make claims against the opposing party. This is sometimes called a *responsive pleading.* An answer should be filed within thirty days of either the petition being served by the sheriff, or the respondent's voluntary appearance being filed with the court.

appeal: The process by which a higher court reviews a decision of a lower court. In New Hampshire family law cases, a person will first file an appeal with the New Hampshire Supreme Court.

C

child support: Financial support for a child paid by the parent to the custodial parent.

contempt of court: The willful and intentional failure of a party to comply with a court order or judgment. Contempt may be punishable by a fine or jail.

contested case: Any case in which the parties cannot reach an agreement. A contested case will result in a trial to have the judge decide on disputed issues.

court order: A court-issued document setting forth the judge's orders. An order can be issued based upon the parties' agreement or the judge's decision. An order may require the parties to perform certain acts or set forth their rights and responsibilities. An order is put in writing, signed by the judge, and filed with the court.

court order acceptable for processing (COAP): A type of court order that provides for payment of civil service retirement to a former spouse.

cross-examination: The questioning of a witness by the opposing counsel during trial or at a deposition, in response to questions asked by the other lawyer.

custody: See parenting time.

D

deposition: A witness's testimony taken out of court, under oath, and in the presence of lawyers and a court reporter. If a person gives a different testimony at the time of trial, he or she can be impeached with the deposition testimony; that is, statements made at a deposition can be used to show untruthfulness if a different answer is given at trial.

direct examination: The initial questioning of a witness in court by the lawyer who called him or her to the stand.

discovery: A process used by attorneys to discover information from the opposing party for the purpose of fully assessing a case for settlement or trial. Types of discovery include depositions, interrogatories, requests for production of documents, and requests for admissions.

dissolution: The act of terminating or dissolving a marriage.

divorce decree: A final court order dissolving the marriage, dividing property and debts, ordering support, and entering other orders regarding the finances and minor children.

E

equitable distribution of property: The method by which real and personal property and debts are divided in a divorce. Given all economic circumstances of the parties, New Hampshire law requires that marital property and debts be divided in a fair and reasonable manner.

Glossary

ex parte: Usually in reference to a motion, the term used to describe an appearance of only one party before the judge, without the other party being present. For example, an *ex parte* restraining order may be granted immediately after the filing of a divorce complaint.

G

guardian *ad litem* (GAL): A person, often a lawyer or mental health professional, appointed by the court to conduct an investigation regarding the children's best interest.

H

hearing: Any proceeding before the court for the purpose of resolving disputed issues between the parties through the presentation of testimony, affidavits, exhibits, or arguments.

hold-harmless clause: A term in a court order that requires one party to assume responsibility for a debt and to protect the other spouse from any loss or expense in connection with it, as in to hold harmless from liability.

I

interrogatories: Written questions sent from one party to the other that are used to obtain facts or opinions related to the divorce.

M

mediation: A process by which a neutral third party facilitates negotiations between the parties on a wide range of issues.

motion: A written application to the court for relief, such as temporary child support, custody, or restraining orders.

N

no-fault divorce: A type of divorce which does not require evidence of marital misconduct. This means that abandonment, cruelty, or adultery are neither relevant nor required to be proven for the purposes of granting the divorce. In New Hampshire there are opportunities to persue a fault-based divorce.

notice of hearing: A written statement sent to all parties listing the date and place of a hearing and the nature of the matters that will be heard by the court.

P

parenting time: The legal right and responsibility awarded by a court for the possession of, care of, and decision making for a minor child.

party: The person in a legal action whose rights or interests will be affected by the divorce. Both spouses are included in the divorce process.

pending: During the term of the case. For example, the judge may award you temporary support while your case is pending.

petition: The first document filed with the clerk of the court in an action for divorce, separation, or paternity. The petition sets forth the facts on which the requested relief is based.

petitioner: The person who files the petition initiating a divorce.

pleadings: Documents filed with the court seeking a court order.

Q

qualified domestic relations order (QDRO): A type of court order that provides for direct payment from a retirement account to a former spouse.

qualified medical support order (QMSO): A type of court order that provides a former spouse with certain rights regarding medical insurance and medical information.

R

respondent: The responding party to a divorce; the party who did not file the complaint initiating the divorce.

request for production of documents: A written request for documents sent from one party to the other during the discovery process.

S

sequester: To order prospective witnesses out of the courtroom until they have concluded giving their testimony.

settlement: The agreed-upon resolution of disputed issues.

shared decision-making responsibility: The shared right and responsibility of both parents awarded by the court for the possession, care, and decisionmaking for minor children.

show cause: Written application to the court to hold another person in contempt of court for violating or failing to comply with a current court order.

spousal support: *See* alimony.

stipulation: An agreement reached between parties or an agreement reached by their attorneys and submitted to the judge as binding on both parties.

subpoena: A document delivered to a person or witness that requires him or her to appear in court, appear for a deposition, or produce documents. Failure to comply could result in punishment by the court. A subpoena requesting documents is called a subpoena *duces tecum.*

T

temporary restraining order (TRO): An order of the court prohibiting a party from certain behavior. For example, a temporary restraining order may order a person not to transfer any funds during a pending divorce action.

trial: A formal court hearing in which the judge decides disputed issues raised by the parties' pleadings.

U

under advisement: A term used to describe the status of a case, usually after a court hearing on a motion or a trial, when the judge has not yet made a decision.

Index

Index

Index

Index

Index

About the Authors

Jessica L. Ecker, Esq., is a partner in the law firm Weibrecht & Ecker, PLLC, in Dover and Portsmouth, New Hampshire. Her focus is on family law, mediation, and collaborative law in New Hampshire and in Maine.

Ecker graduated from the University of New Hampshire in Durham and attended Albany Law School in Albany, New York. She is a long-serving board member of the New Hampshire Conflict Resolution Association, a member of the Rockingham and Strafford County Bar Associations, and was past president of the Rockingham County Bar Association.

Ecker has presented at numerous continuing legal education seminars for the National Business Institute, as well as the New Hampshire Association of Justice. She received the *"Pro Bono* Rising Star" award from the New Hampshire Bar Association in 2012, for her consistent *pro bono* contributions. She has been a Super Lawyers Rising Star for multiple years. Ecker resides in the seacoast of New Hampshire with her husband and two daughters. She may be reached through her website: www.weibrechtecker.com.

Dana E. Prescott, J.D., M.S.W., Ph.D., , is a partner in the law firm of Prescott Jamieson Murphy Law Group, LLC and has been in private practice as a family law attorney in Maine and Massachusetts since 1983. He is a fellow of the International Academy of Family Lawyers and the American Academy of Matrimonial Lawyers and has served as president of the New England Bar Association and the Maine State Bar Association.

He is a rostered guardian *ad litem* in Maine and the co-author of *Divorce in Maine: The Legal Process, Your Rights, and What to Expect.* Prescott also holds a master's of social work degree and a Ph.D. degree in social work. He presents and publishes frequently on topics related to family law, child custody, professional ethics, and forensics. He is also adjunct faculty in social work at the Boston College School of Social Work. Additional information and his curriculum vitae are available at Prescott Jamieson Murphy Law Group, LLC at **www.southernmainelaw.com** and at Raven Consulting and Community Services at **www.ravenconsultingeducation.com.**

Divorce Titles from Addicus Books

Visit our online catalog at www.AddicusBooks.com

Divorce in Alabama: The Legal Process, Your Rights, and What to Expect $21.95

Divorce in Arizona: The Legal Process, Your Rights, and What to Expect—2nd Edition $21.95

Divorce in California: The Legal Process, Your Rights, and What to Expect $21.95

Divorce in Connecticut: The Legal Process, Your Rights, and What to Expect $21.95

Divorce in Florida: The Legal Process, Your Rights, and What to Expect $21.95

Divorce in Georgia: Simple Answers to Your Legal Questions $21.95

Divorce in Idaho: The Legal Process, Your Rights, and What to Expect. $21.95

Divorce in Illinois: The Legal Process, Your Rights, and What to Expect—2nd Edition. $21.95

Divorce in Kansas: The Legal Process, Your Rights, and What to Expect $21.95

Divorce in Louisiana: The Legal Process, Your Rights, and What to Expect $21.95

Divorce in Maine: The Legal Process, Your Rights, and What to Expect $21.95

Divorce in Maryland: The Legal Process, Your Rights, and What to Expect $21.95

Divorce in Michigan: The Legal Process, Your Rights, and What to Expect. $21.95

Divorce in Mississippi: The Legal Process, Your Rights, and What to Expect. $21.95

A Guide to Divorce in Missouri: Simple Answers to Complex Questions $21.95

Divorce in Nebraska: The Legal Process, Your Rights, and What to Expect—2nd Edition $21.95

Divorce in Nevada: The Legal Process, Your Rights, and What to Expect. $21.95

Divorce in New York: The Legal Process, Your Rights, and What to Expect $21.95

Divorce in North Carolina: Answers to Your Legal Questions. $21.95

Divorce in Oklahoma: The Legal Process, Your Rights, and What to Expect $21.95

Divorce in Pennsylvania: The Legal Process, Your Rights, and What to Expect $21.95

Divorce in South Carolina: The Legal Process, Your Rights, and What to Expect $21.95

Divorce in Tennessee: The Legal Process, Your Rights, and What to Expect $21.95

Divorce in Texas: The Legal Process, Your Rights, and What to Expect. $21.95

Divorce in Virginia: The Legal Process, Your Rights, and What to Expect $21.95

Divorce in Washington: The Legal Process, Your Rights, and What to Expect $21.95

Divorce in West Virginia: The Legal Process, Your Rights, and What to Expect $21.95

Divorce in Wisconsin: The Legal Process, Your Rights, and What to Expect $21.95

Daily Meditations for Healing from Divorce: Discovering the New You. $21.95

.